MATERIAL TRACES OF WAR

MATERIAL TRACES OF WAR

Stories of Canadian Women and Conflict, 1914–1945

STACEY J. BARKER
Canadian War Museum

KRISTA COOKE
Parks Canada

MOLLY MCCULLOUGH
Ingenium—Canada's Museums of Science and Innovation

Mercury Series
History Paper 62

CANADIAN MUSEUM OF HISTORY &
UNIVERSITY OF OTTAWA PRESS
2021

Co-published by the **Canadian Museum of History** *and the* **University of Ottawa Press.**

The University of Ottawa Press gratefully acknowledges the support extended to its publishing list by the Government of Canada, the Canada Council for the Arts, the Ontario Council for the Arts, the Federation for the Humanities and Social Sciences through the Awards to Scholarly Publications Program, and the University of Ottawa.

Copy editing — Tanina Drvar
Proofreading — James Warren
Typesetting — John van der Woude, JVDW Designs
Indexing — Tere Mullin
Cover design — Steve Kress
Cover image — Molly Lamb Bobak, *Canadian Women's Army Corps Parade Through the Town*, CWM 19710261-1582, Beaverbrook Collection of War Art, Canadian War Museum

Legal Deposit: Fourth Quarter 2021
Library and Archives Canada
Printed in Canada

Library and Archives Canada Cataloguing in Publication

Title: Material traces of war : stories of Canadian women and conflict, 1914-1945 / Stacey Barker, Krista Cooke, Molly McCullough.

Names: Barker, Stacey, 1973- author. | Cooke, Krista, author. | McCullough, Molly, author.

Series: Mercury series. History paper ; 62.

Description: Series statement: Mercury series. History paper ; 62 | Includes bibliographical references and index.

Identifiers: Canadiana (print) 20210203943 | Canadiana (ebook) 20210204672 | ISBN 9780776629209 (softcover) | ISBN 9780776629216 (PDF)

Subjects: LCSH: World War, 1914-1918—Women—Canada—Biography. | LCSH: World War, 1939-1945—Women—Canada—Biography. | LCSH: Women and war—Canada—History—20th century. | LCSH: Material culture—Canada—History—20th century. | LCGFT: Biographies.

Classification: LCC D639.W7 B37 2021 | DDC 940.3092/520971—dc23

The Mercury Series

Strikingly Canadian and highly specialized, the *Mercury Series* is proudly published by the Canadian Museum of History and the University of Ottawa Press. Created in 1972, the series consists of peer-reviewed academic research and includes numerous landmark contributions in the disciplines of Canadian history, archaeology, culture, and ethnology.

La Collection Mercure

Remarquablement canadienne et hautement spécialisée, la *collection Mercure* est publiée avec fierté par le Musée canadien de l'histoire et les Presses de l'Université d'Ottawa. Fondée en 1972, elle propose des recherches scientifiques évaluées par les pairs et regroupe de nombreuses contributions majeures à l'histoire, à l'archéologie, à la culture et à l'ethnologie canadiennes.

Series editor/Direction de la collection: Pierre M. Desrosiers

Editorial committee/Comité éditorial: Laura Sanchini, Janet Young, John Willis

How to Order

All trade orders must be directed to the University of Ottawa Press:
  Web: www.press.uottawa.ca
  Email: puo-uop@uottawa.ca
  Phone: 613-562-5246

All other orders may be directed to either the University of Ottawa Press (as above) or to the Canadian Museum of History:
  Web: www.historymuseum.ca/shop
  Email: publications@historymuseum.ca
  Phone: 1-800-555-5621 (toll-free) or
      819-776-8387 (National Capital Region)
  Mail: Mail Order Services
      Canadian Museum of History
      100 Laurier Street
      Gatineau, QC, K1A 0M8

Pour commander

Les libraires et autres détaillants doivent adresser leurs commandes aux Presses de l'Université d'Ottawa :
  Web : www.presses.uottawa.ca
  Courriel : puo-uop@uottawa.ca
  Téléphone : 613-562-5246

Les particuliers doivent adresser leurs commandes soit aux Presses de l'Université d'Ottawa (voir plus haut) soit au Musée canadien de l'histoire :
  Web : www.museedelhistoire.ca/magasiner
  Courriel : publications@museedelhistoire.ca
  Téléphone : 1-800-555-5621 (numéro sans frais) ou
      819-776-8387 (région de la capitale nationale)
  Poste : Service des commandes postales
      Musée canadien de l'histoire
      100, rue Laurier
      Gatineau (Québec) K1A 0M8

u Ottawa

ABSTRACT/RÉSUMÉ

Material Traces of War: Stories of Canadian Women and Conflict, 1914–1945, looks at how Canadian women experienced the world wars through objects, images, and archival documents. The book puts individual women and their related material culture at its heart. Thematically organized vignettes tell stories of women who served in the military, volunteered their time, worked as civilians, and grieved lost loved ones. The authors place these personal narratives in the larger context of the world wars, while demonstrating that the experience of living through global conflict was as individual as a woman's particular circumstances. Drawing from the collections of the Canadian War Museum, the Canadian Museum of History, and other public and private collections in Canada, *Material Traces of War* brings lesser-known stories into view.

L'ouvrage *Material Traces of War: Stories of Canadian Women and Conflict, 1914–1945* se penche, au moyen d'objets, d'images et de documents d'archives, sur les façons dont les Canadiennes ont vécu les deux guerres mondiales. Les femmes et leur culture matérielle sont donc au cœur de cet ouvrage. Des chroniques thématiques relatent l'histoire de femmes qui ont servi dans l'armée, qui ont donné de leur temps, qui ont travaillé comme civiles et qui ont pleuré des êtres chers. Les auteurs intègrent ces récits individuels dans des contextes plus larges de guerres mondiales, tout en démontrant que la vie en temps de conflit international était une expérience tout aussi personnelle que pouvait l'être la situation particulière de chaque femme. En puisant dans les collections du Musée canadien de la guerre, du Musée canadien de l'histoire et d'autres collections publiques et privées du Canada, *Material Traces of War* met en lumière des histoires peu connues.

CONTENTS

LIST OF FIGURES

FOREWORD
by CHARLOTTE GRAY

"Girls, you are needed now as never before... Swing into action today!" This 1943 government appeal captures the tangled message directed at Canadian women during two world wars. Be part of the war effort, it urges, but don't forget that you are still "girls" in a man's world.

Throughout history, wars have devastated families; the conflicts of both 1914–1918 and 1939–1945 were no different. Sons, husbands, and fathers left, and either never returned, or limped home, wounded in body and mind. Women's roles were seen through the prism of men's lives; their primary contribution was "noble sacrifice."

Yet the move towards total war in the twentieth century blurred the line between battle front and home front. Canada did not suffer within its borders the horrific damage that nations elsewhere incurred, but these global conflicts penetrated more deeply into civil society. They offered women opportunities that had hitherto been unthinkable.

Traditional gendered expectations were upended when the war machine—the munitions factories, the battle-front hospitals, the shipyards—ran short of labour.

With skilled hands in short supply, it no longer mattered if they were male or female fingers that filled the shell casings or tightened the bolts on aircraft assembly lines. Women flocked into these jobs for many reasons—patriotism, good wages, and the camaraderie of shared lunchrooms and dormitories. Letters and diaries from those years resonate with pride in the writers' accomplishments, as well as excitement and a new sense of independence. Women who grasped the chance to enlist, serve as nurses at the front, or organize volunteers were actively part of the war effort. Many were also escaping dreary domestic lives at a time when there were limited opportunities for women's paid participation in the peacetime workforce.

As the need for recruits accelerated, so more barriers evaporated. A handful of individuals who belonged to racialized minorities or the LGBTQ2S+ community managed to take part, but the public space for women had widened.

In their choice of artifacts and their lively commentary, Stacey Barker, Krista Cooke, and Molly McCullough have given us unique starting points for an original history. We are taken from the individual to the general, from the particular to the political. There are so many personalities and achievements to linger on here.

One of my favourites is Private Minnie Eleanor Gray, a Nova Scotian with a Black father, who had grown up in a Nova Scotia orphanage and who worked as a domestic servant until she joined the Canadian Women's Army Corps. In 1945, Minnie was assigned to the coveted position of medical attendant and chaperone to the Canadian Women's Army Corps Pipe Band. Look at the smile on her face, as recorded in her photo album! She and the band completed a seven-month tour of European cities. But then the time came for Minnie and her musicians to disband. "I really don't want to go home," she wrote in her diary. I'm not surprised.

ACKNOWLEDGEMENTS

Our first acknowledgements must be extended to colleagues who worked on and contributed to the *World War Women* exhibitions. It takes a whole museum to develop an exhibition. Ashlee Beattie, Britt Braaten, Caroline Dromaguet, Patricia Grimshaw, Sandra O'Quinn, and Kirby Sayant, thank you for ensuring that the exhibitions made it to the museum floor and that visitors connected with the stories we told. Thank you to Fiona Anthes, Maggie Arbour, Nancy Bacon, Kenn Bingley, Arlene Doucette, Paul Durand, Eric Fernberg, Anneh Fletcher, Shannyn Johnson, Sylvie Laflamme, Anne Macdonnell, Meredith MacLean, Carol Reid, Susan Ross, Alain Simard, Christina Parsons, and Lindsay Towle, our colleagues in Collections, for providing crucial assistance and expertise. Thanks also to historians Christina Bates, Laura Brown, Andrew Burtch, Nic Clarke, Tim Cook, Tim Foran, Xavier Gélinas, Rhonda Hinther, Mélanie Morin-Pelletier, John Maker, Peter MacLeod, Jeff Noakes, James Trepanier, and John Willis.

The exhibitions and this book would have been impossible without Laura Brandon and Amber Lloydlangston's years of research into women and war. Our Can Car connections depended on Kelly Saxberg's help. John Willis kick-started the book project and we never would have kept going without his words of encouragement and belief in the importance of these stories. Ingenium— Canada's Museums of Science and Innovation gave us time and space to write and discuss, thank you Anna Adamek and Will Knight. Alan McCullough leant us his great experience and knowledge, catching mistakes to which we were blind. To our families, we are grateful for your support. Many thanks to Charlotte Gray for writing a foreword to the book. Special thanks are due to our editor, Pierre Desrosiers, for his guidance, and to Pascal Laplante, Pascal Scallon-Chouinard, and Lee Wyndham, for answering all our questions. The manuscript was reviewed by anonymous readers; thank you for your astute feedback. Finally, and most importantly, we would like to acknowledge the individuals and institutions whose objects, images, family stories, and experiences are at the heart of *Material Traces of War*.

WORLD AT WAR, WOMEN AT WAR

THE WORLD WARS (1914–1918 AND 1939–1945) WERE TRANSFOR-
mative events for Canadians. Their effects were intrusive and wide-ranging,
and fighting them required involvement from society as a whole. As a result,
the body of literature on these conflicts is vast. Academic histories on various
aspects of the two war efforts claim considerable shelf space along with popular
works emphasizing the heroism of everyday folk. If these disparate books have anything in common other than war, it is the gender of those at the centre of these stories. Men strategized and fought, and their war stories—as soldiers, planners, and
leaders—dominate the discourse. But they were not the only ones who experienced
the brutal world wars of the twentieth century. The wars also shaped women's lives
in myriad ways, presenting challenges and forcing changes. Few women who lived
through these conflicts remained untouched. Their stories are as much a part of
Canada's war record as the stories of the men who marched off and the battles they
fought. Using artifacts and archival collections as a starting point, this book seeks
to uncover women's experiences and to shift the usual focus away from the battlefields to encompass a wider range of wartime stories: those of world war women.

In 1914, Canada went into the First World War as a Dominion of the British Empire. After four years of bitter fighting, Canada emerged as a country with increased stature on the world stage but deeply divided at home. In 1939, Canada again took up arms. By 1945, Canadians were tired of war and more than ready for peace. The wars had placed many "ordinary" individuals into extraordinary situations. For men, this often meant armed service with all its potentially harrowing results. For women, barred from combat, the wars had different, but still disruptive and often traumatic, impacts. These impacts were shaped by circumstances, gender, context, time, and place. Some women experienced the wars primarily as mothers or wives of serving soldiers, spending years worrying or grieving the deaths of their loved ones in uniform. Other women lived the world wars as an adventure, particularly during the Second World War, when options for military service and paid work expanded rapidly. Class and race also shaped women's wartime circumstances. Upper-class white women played prominent public roles during both wars, while marginalized and racialized women struggled against racism and prejudice in their desire to serve in the military or voluntary associations. Highlighting the variety of women's experiences is essential to gaining a better understanding of the war's impact on Canadians, and in providing a more nuanced global portrait of Canada's world wars.

Material Traces of War grew out of several projects developed at the Canadian War Museum (CWM) in Ottawa. In 2015, the CWM opened a special exhibition entitled *World War Women*. Public popularity and interest in the original prompted the museum to develop three further *World War Women* exhibitions. The first, adapted to focus solely on the Second World War, was presented at the Canadian Warplane Heritage Museum in Hamilton in 2017. Another reduced scale version began travelling to museums across Canada in 2018. The third, retitled *Grandes Femmes dans La Guerre 1939-1945 (Great Women During the War, 1939–1945)*, was developed in partnership with the Juno Beach Centre in Normandy, France, to commemorate the 75th anniversary of D-Day and opened in March 2019. Focusing entirely on the Second World War, this exhibition combined some *World War Women* stories with a number of European ones. All of the exhibitions focused on the lives of individual women in the world wars, as told through artifacts, documents, and images related to their wartime experiences. This book, written by three members of the teams that developed these exhibitions, expands on these stories.

The exhibitions that formed the basis for this publication represented a different museological approach to wartime history at the CWM. The museum's permanent galleries, and some of its special exhibitions, use individuals and artifacts to support overarching chronological histories. With *World War Women*, the artifacts and individual stories came first and dictated the exhibition narrative. In most cases, the teams only included artifacts in the exhibitions if they had a specific woman's story associated with them. The reverse was also true: individual women's stories only made it into the exhibitions if there was an associated object or strong archival collection that helped to tell her story. Rather than tell an exhaustive, chronological history of women and the world wars, the exhibitions presented the women's stories as entry points for larger historical themes and events. The women of *World War Women* were presented as historical agents who made history through their actions and reactions to war. The women's stories were grouped thematically, into four main sections: Serving, Volunteering, Working, and Worry and Loss.

In the exhibitions, these larger themes were a way of situating individual women's experiences within a larger collective narrative. The groupings reflect major themes related to women's wartime lives. To a certain extent, these are false categories. In some cases, women's full biographical stories overlapped the boundaries of these themes. For example, Betty Butcher mourned the loss of both her brother and fiancé during the Second World War but was an active wartime volunteer who also worked in her father's law office, filling the job once reserved for her brother. She had hopes of joining the Canadian Red Cross overseas, but her application, coming in the later years of the war, was not accepted. Her story was featured in the Worry and Loss section because the artifacts and archival material associated with her story—which she chose to donate—best reflected that theme. However, her experiences, like those of all women, defy easy categorization. In other cases, a woman's story technically belonged in one theme but made more sense in another from the point of view of a visitor. Saskatchewan's Joan Bamford Fletcher, for example, was technically a volunteer with Britain's First Aid Nursing Yeomanry (FANY), but her service with the FANY had her performing military tasks. As a result, she appears in the military service sections in the exhibitions and in this book.

Artifacts and photographs provide an intriguing way into the history of wartime Canada. Objects have the power "to tell, or at least ask, historians things that the written word alone cannot."[1] Women left traces of their wartime experiences behind in material ways and the collections at the CWM and Canadian Museum

---

1 Arnold, "Museums and the Making of Medical History," 145.

of History (CMH) are replete with personal stories of wartime Canada. Often, these stories bring a different dimension to familiar histories of war. Take the pair of white leather gloves (figure 4.4), for example, that Mary Hall wore to receive her son's Victoria Cross. Her son, Frederick Hall, was immortalized in Historica Canada's *Valour Road* Heritage Minute and is relatively well known: a story of bravery, sacrifice, and premature death on the battlefields of the Western Front during the First World War. Mary Hall, however, remains in the shadows. Objects like these gloves exist in the collections of museums and archives but are often seen as secondary to the primary story. For those interested in women's perspectives, however, these hidden objects reveal stories that give us a more comprehensive understanding of war's impact.

Many of the objects and related stories in the *World War Women* exhibitions came from research that CWM and CMH staff conducted over the course of many years. Research performed by historians Laura Brandon, Amber Lloydlangston, and one of the authors of this book, Krista Cooke, was vital. Their work on women and war began in 2005 shortly after the opening of the new CWM building. As Laura Brandon later explained, like many military history museums, the CWM had "historically positioned the conduct of war as a primarily masculine activity."[2] The team conducted collections assessments at the CMH and CWM, revealing previously unexhibited objects, untold stories, and exciting opportunities for new research. A series of targeted research projects, including a gendered assessment of the CWM's war art collection, a borrowed art exhibition about war brides, a literature review, and oral history projects focusing on women war workers and women in the modern Canadian Forces, broadened the museums' knowledge base and brought new material into the collections. The Canadian Car and Foundry (Can Car) oral history project, for example, included 20 individuals who provided eight oral history interviews and 17 photograph and artifact collections to the CMH, filling an important collections gap. Of these new collections, eight were featured in the *World War Women* exhibitions, contextualized by academic research conducted by Helen Smith, Pamela Wakewich, Suzanne Klausen, Pamela Sugiman, and others.[3]

---

2   Brandon, "Looking for the 'Total' Woman," 105.
3   Wakewich and Smith, "The Politics of 'Selective' Memory"; Klausen, "The Plywood Girls"; Sugiman, *Labour's Dilemma.*

The teams that worked on the *World War Women* exhibitions, including the other two authors of this book, historian Stacey Barker and creative development specialist Molly McCullough, built upon this foundation and unearthed other women's stories through deeper analysis and exploration of artifacts and documents already in the museums' collections. We comprehensively reviewed the museums' databases, finding dozens of untold stories from across the country. Sometimes this involved studying artifacts not typically considered military history objects, such as Connie Laidlaw's ventriloquist figure "Charlotte" (figure 2.21). At other times, we uncovered women's stories by "turning collections on their heads" to find the women hidden behind men's stories. For example, a collection acquired to tell the wartime experiences of William Robert Boucher, a soldier killed during the First World War, became the story of his mother Jeannie Cassels Boucher (figures 4.1 and 4.2). Her experiences had always been present but had not been recorded or interpreted in any great detail. By looking closely at objects and documents such as those of the Bouchers, material originally acquired and catalogued in relation to men's stories, researchers discovered buried connections to women's wartime experiences.

The team for the initial *World War Women* exhibition had decided early on to draw, with a few exceptions, exclusively from the collections of the CWM and the CMH. The team's decision to use only artifacts with strong provenance linked to identifiable women further complicated the goal of including a wide range of stories and themes. If we wanted to exhibit stories that reflected larger social history topics such as wartime labour unrest, family dissolution, or racism, we had to find an object and a particular woman's experience that allowed us to tell that story. Sometimes we succeeded, as in the case of Nora Gibson's lunchbox (figure 3.12), which we used to tell the story of wartime workplace sexual harassment.

Other times, we were less successful. For the purposes of this book, we have chosen to feature objects held in other institutions or archival materials, allowing us to tell a greater diversity of stories. Years of sifting through museum collections across Canada paid off, and we have been able to include numerous viewpoints; the book features rural and urban women of various ages and socioeconomic backgrounds from across the country. In a further expansion of our original exhibition parameters, we also include artifact spotlights that focus on material for which we do not provide extensive information about a related individual but that reveal a key aspect of women's collective wartime experience.

Even with the addition of artifact spotlights, archival materials, and collections from other institutions, we had trouble finding material suitable to tell certain stories. Stories of overt wartime dissent, for instance, are less often present in museum collections and are difficult to illustrate via this method. The patriotic fervour of the two world wars and their aftermath likely contributed to better documentation of war supporters than of those who questioned war. Many stories of dissent, such as those belonging to Lady Henriette Pope (figure 4.9) are buried deep in archival collections as personal reflections or passing moments of self-doubt as opposed to the visually compelling objects of wartime support included elsewhere, making women's resistance to the two world wars doubly difficult to include in this project. Other subjects that often remain buried but that were, nevertheless, an important aspect of wartime Canada include things like sexuality, divorce, religion, domestic violence, and prostitution. Volumes remain to be written about these topics.

Women marginalized because of their race, socioeconomic status, or sexual orientation were also more difficult to include than white, middle-class, heterosexual Canadian women, whose stories are amply represented in *Material Traces of War*. Museum and archival collections have tended to privilege the stories of the privileged, and this book's focus on objects, images, archival material, and biography made it challenging to include as many diverse voices as would be truly representative of Canadian society during the two world wars. By working with descendants whose private collections contain family treasures, searching widely in the literature and in other museums, and using newly acquired collections, we found new voices to include here. Conversations with the descendants of Indigenous woman Edith Anderson Monture, Japanese Canadians Tsune Yatabe and Michiko (Ishii) Ayukawa, and Black Canadian Verda Sharp, were essential to building these stories. Without their assistance, we could not have developed these sections of the book. Many more women's experiences remain hidden, waiting to be acknowledged. New research by scholars studying Jewish women's wartime participation and work by the Chinese Canadian Military Museum, to name some recent initiatives, are bringing new stories to the fore.[4]

Material Traces of War, and the work upon which it is partly based, owes much to past scholars who adopted new perspectives on Canada's war experiences.

---

4   Chinese Canadian Military Museum, "Chinese Canadian Women in the War;" Lander, "Thanking the Jewish Ladies;" Lipton, "She Also Served."

Beginning in the 1980s, Ruth Roach Pierson, Rosamond Greer, Jean Bruce, and Carolyn Gossage, inspired by the first generation of academic women's historians, published studies of military women in Canada.[5] Books written in the 1980s, 1990s, and into the twenty-first century by authors such as Veronica Strong Boag, Pierson and Beth Light, Alison Prentice, Joan Sangster, and Andrée Levesque shed light on women's experience of the twentieth century including their wartime lives.[6] Influenced by new historiographical trends, a few military historians such as Desmond Morton began to widen their perspectives, increasingly treating subjects that went beyond traditional battlefield histories and touched on the home front.[7] Other authors (Calvin Ruck, Roy Ito, Timothy Winegard, and Marjorie Wong included) have delved into the military histories of racialized minorities, bringing new voices and a multitude of previously unpublished experiences to light.[8]

By 2020, key social histories of wartime Canada written by Jonathan Vance and Jeff Keshen were joined by dozens of more narrowly focused books on wartime topics ranging from female pilots (Shirley Render), Nursing Sisters (Cynthia Toman), mourning culture (Suzanne Evans), wartime consumers (Graham Broad), food (Ian Mosby), war and memory (Tim Cook), as well as a variety of local wartime histories (Serge Durflinger, Jim Blanchard, Adriana Davies, Bryan Tennyson) and personal memoirs.[9] Sarah Glassford and Amy Shaw edited two volumes on women's experiences in the world wars which are especially noteworthy.[10] The last decade has also seen new histories related to Indigenous wartime experiences (Timothy Winegard, P. Whitney Lackenbauer, Janice Summerby,

5   Pierson, *They're Still Women*; Greer, *Girls of the King's Navy*; Bruce, *Back the Attack!*; Gossage, *Greatcoats*.

6   Strong-Boag, *New Day*; Light and Pierson, *No Easy Road*; Prentice, *Canadian Women*; Sangster, *Earning Respect*; Lévesque and Klein, *Making and Breaking*.

7   Morton, *Fight or Pay*.

8   Ruck, *Canada's Black Battalion*; Ito, *We Went to War*; Gaffen, *Forgotten Soldiers*; Wong, *Dragon and the Maple Leaf*.

9   Vance, *Death So Noble*; Keshen, *Saints*; Render, *No Place for a Lady*; Toman, *Sister Soldiers*; Toman, *An Officer and a Lady*; Evans, *Mothers of Heroes*; Broad, *A Small Price*; Mosby, *Food Will Win*; Cook, *Fight for History*; Durflinger, *Fighting from Home*; Blanchard, *Winnipeg's Great War*; Davies and Keshen, *Frontier of Patriotism*; Tennyson, *Nova Scotia at War*; Peate, *Girl in a Sloppy Joe Sweater*; Department of National Defence, *Equal to the Challenge*; Lambton, *Sun in Winter*; Kitagawa and Miki, *This Is My Own*; Day, Spence, and Ladouceur, *Women Overseas*.

10 Glassford and Shaw, *Sisterhood of Suffering* and *Making the Best of It*.

and Robert Talbot among others) including some studies of Indigenous women's wartime contributions (Grace Poulin, Alison Norman).[11] All of these resources have combined to create a generous ecosystem of Canadian wartime histories on which to base the exhibition and book projects.

The museological literature has followed a similar trajectory. The drive to include histories of class, race, and gender in museums and public history sites has had a significant impact on how many Canadian museums structure their exhibitions and study or classify their collections. British, Australian, Scandinavian, and American authors (for instance, Gaby Porter, Margaret Anderson, and Gail Dubrow) began what was to become a vibrant international dialogue about the inclusion/exclusion of women's history in museums.[12] Begun in the mid-1980s, this movement saw hundreds of books, articles, and special edition journals published. As curators questioned how they could better represent ethnicity and class through their collections, programs, and exhibitions, they also spent time pondering questions of gender representation. Canadian authors (Christina Bates, Alan McCullough, Helen Knibb, Sharon Reilly, Phaedra Livingston, and Laura Brandon, among others) contributed to the discussion and worked at their respective institutions to increase the inclusion of women's stories in museum exhibitions and collections.[13] In Canada, people continue to debate the best means to represent racial diversity, including Indigenous stories, in museums. Authors, such as Caitlin Gordon-Walker, Rachelle Dickenson, Susan Ashley, and Michael Maranda, question Canadian museums' ongoing commitment to inclusion in a cultural landscape that many still consider to be narrowly focused on Canada's elite male Anglo-Canadian majority.[14] Alongside the academic literature on women and wartime in Canada, these museology and material culture publications informed our approach to the exhibitions and the book. As a result, this

11   Winegard, *For King and Kanata*; Lackenbauer et al., *Aboriginal Peoples*; Summerby, *Native Soldiers*; Talbot, "It Would Be Best"; Poulin, *Invisible Women*; Norman, "In Defense of the Empire."

12   Porter, "Seeing through Solidity"; Anderson and Winkworth, "Museums and Gender"; Dubrow and Goodman, *Restoring Women's History*.

13   Bates and Knibb, "Museum as a Teaching Resource"; McCullough, "Parks Canada"; Knibb, "Present but Not Visible"; Reilly, "Material History"; Livingstone, "Reading the Science Centre"; Brandon, "Looking for the 'Total' Woman."

14   Gordon-Walker, *Exhibiting Nation*; Dickenson, "The Stories Told"; Ashley, *Museum in Public*; Maranda, "Hard Numbers."

publication sits squarely in the middle of trends of ongoing evolution in two distinct fields: museum research and military history research.

Inspired by the exhibitions, this study is divided into chapters that reflect some of the common ways women responded to war: military service, wartime volunteering, paid civilian work, and worry and loss. As in *World War Women*, these categories are fluid and are intended as an organizing principle rather than a statement that women only fit into one specific category. Each chapter is divided into sections featuring the stories of individual women and their related objects, images, and archival material. Biographical sections vary in length and approach—with content dictated by what we have been able to learn about each woman. Subthemes consider the personal and social motives that compelled many women to contribute to the war efforts; the crucial role that women played in the wars; the extent to which women's participation formed a meaningful part of their lives; and how wartime women were granted new opportunities while at the same time were limited by gender-based norms.

A brief note about our chosen naming convention. For clarity, we refer to women by the name they used during "their" war. Many of our subjects were unmarried young women, and we refer to them by their maiden names. We deviate from this approach in the case of women who became more widely known under their postwar married names, such as Molly Lamb Bobak or Edith Anderson Monture. For women whose later-in-life reminiscences are an important part of their story, as in the case of Dorothy Cannon (née Effemy) whose story is told through the voice of a child as well as that of a senior citizen, we have used both names to draw attention to the period.

Material Traces of War serves a number of functions. It brings lesser-known objects, images, and archival material to public view, draws attention to untold stories, and provides a comparative study of individual women's experiences against the broader narrative of wartime Canada. It blends social, academic, military, and material culture history, taking a different approach to the subject of war. Scholars seeking new perspectives on the two world wars will find it a useful addition to the existing historiography of the First and Second World Wars in Canada. Readers of biographies and those interested in visual or material culture will benefit from the dozens of women profiled and the multitude of museum artifacts featured. We hope that this book inspires readers to dig further into public collections across the country, uncovering and sharing more women's stories.

1

THAT MEN MAY FIGHT

Women and Military Service during the World Wars

"I can't do this for the rest of my life, I'll go nuts!" The year was 1943, and 20-year-old Lorna Stanger was bored stiff with her civil service job in Ottawa. One afternoon, Stanger left her offices at the Dominion Bureau of Statistics and applied to enlist in the army, the air force, and the navy. She had no great preference for any one of these branches, and she joined the first to accept her: the Women's Royal Canadian Naval Service (WRCNS). Stanger was in the navy until the end of the war, serving overseas as a naval photographer. Later in life, she recalled her time in the military with pride. It had changed her for the better, she noted, and while she greeted the end of the war with elation, she saw her discharge from the service as "a big let-down."[1] After the excitement of war, the prospect of returning to a dreary peacetime job was not appealing. There were thousands of Canadian women in uniform like Lorna Stanger.

OPPOSITE: FIGURE I.I. *Nursing Sister,* ca. 1916, Richard George Mathews.
Source: Beaverbrook Collection of War Art, Canadian War Museum 19710261-6070.

---

1   Cooney, "Lorna Cooney."

Stanger was fortunate that this path had been open to her at all. Until 1941, general military service was an option for men only. War, as the gender norms of the day dictated, was a man's business. During the First World War, women who wanted to join the forces could only do so as nurses, and even then, the military wanted applicants for its medical corps to be professionally trained, graduate nurses. Women were thus admitted only as medical caregivers, a role that conformed to prevailing stereotypical views of the fairer sex. The Second World War did not erase those rigid gender lines entirely, but it did cause them to shift. By 1942, women such as Lorna Stanger could serve in one of three women's service branches: the Canadian Women's Army Corps (CWAC), the Royal Canadian Air Force Women's Division (RCAF-WD), and the Women's Royal Canadian Naval Service (WRCNS). All were non-combatant, but for the first time, women had the option to serve in uniforms other than that of a nurse.

This chapter describes what some Canadian women did in the military along with how they pushed and lobbied for expanded roles. From military nurses in both wars, to paramilitary auxiliary corps, to the establishment of the women's service branches in 1941–1942, the stories in this chapter follow the evolution of these roles from 1914 to 1945. It also highlights the challenges and opportunities facing women who opted for military service, as they moved into an area previously closed to them. New skills and adventures had to be balanced against public opinion that was not always in favour of women in uniform. Their varied, yet shared, experiences—vital to winning the world wars—form the core of this chapter.

LT./NURSING SISTER BLANCHE LAVALLÉE, CANADIAN ARMY MEDICAL CORPS

Depending on the viewer, the woman depicted in the pastel sketch in figure 1.1 could seem tired, sad, or even dreamy.[2] Based on other clues in the portrait, fatigue may be the reason for her heavy-lidded expression. Her clothing—the veil, apron, and blue dress—identifies her as a Canadian First World War nurse. Nicknamed "bluebirds" because of their uniforms, these women served on the home front as well as in England, France, Belgium, Egypt, Turkey, and Greece. They treated men whose injuries were at times devastating, and they faced a scale of death that

2   Mathews, *Nursing Sister*.

was completely unknown to them. Among other tasks, they changed dressings, cleaned suppurating wounds, watched for gangrene, assisted with surgeries, and administered drugs. Those closer to the action often lived and worked in harsh conditions. They encountered injury, illness, and death themselves. While not posted directly on the front lines, they were still frequently within range of enemy fire. It is understandable, then, that this nurse might appear exhausted.

In the First World War, nursing was the only way women could serve in the Canadian military. Though entire societies mobilized to support the war effort, this mobilization adhered strongly to prevailing gender norms. Men fought, but women—while expected to be supportive—were to remain firmly behind the lines. Women shouldering weapons, fighting, killing, was unthinkable for most Canadians. Indeed, the military's acceptance of nurses as formal members was a relatively recent phenomenon.[3] Following the American Civil War and Crimean War, during which American and British women took on increasingly important medical roles alongside military doctors, a handful of Canadian women accompanied troops sent to fight the Northwest Resistance in 1885.[4] Fourteen years later, nurses officially made up part of the contingent Canada sent to fight the South African War. By 1914, nurses were an established—if small—part of the Canadian military. The approximately 3,000 women who joined the Canadian Army Medical Corps over the course of the First World War were not civilians but formal members of the military, drawing pay and subject to the rules and regulations of army life.[5]

The sketch that opens this section is titled *Nursing Sister* and depicts Canadian nurse Blanche Lavallée, a Montrealer who enlisted with the Canadian Army Medical Corps (CAMC) in March 1915.[6] The title does not include her name, but the portrait so closely resembles Lavallée as she appears in photographs from the time, as seen in figure 1.2, that there is little doubt that it is her.[7] The artist Richard George Mathews served as an honorary officer attached to the CAMC and likely encountered Lavallée as she went about her duties.[8]

3   Dundas, *History of Women*, 17–26.
4   Domm, "From the Streets of Toronto."
5   Toman, *Sister Soldiers*, 39; Mann, "Where Have All the Bluebirds Gone?"
6   Blanche Lavallée, CEF Personnel Record.
7   The portrait is widely believed to be Lavallée and is identified as such in Dundas, 14. A similar portrait by Mathews, also of Lavallée, is held by Library and Archives Canada.
8   Richard George Mathews, CEF Personnel Record.

Lavallée was typical of Canadian military nurses in that she was a graduate nurse, the term used for those who had undergone a prescribed course of professional nursing training and education at a teaching hospital. The military generally recruited women who had already practised nursing for several years. Lavallée was unusual in that she had only recently finished her training at Montréal's Hôtel-Dieu hospital when she enlisted.[9] The military had no difficulty finding candidates as many women had nursing qualifications; there were 70 schools of nursing operating in Canada by 1909.[10] At the time, women had a limited choice of professions and nursing was one of only a few options for those who wanted a career. Qualified women clamoured to enlist, and there were regularly more nurses who wanted to serve than there were available positions with the CAMC.

Lavallée was also atypical in that she was Francophone. Though historians have not firmly identified the number of CAMC nurses who were Francophone, French-speaking nurses, like French-speaking soldiers, were a minority in the Canadian Expeditionary Force (CEF).[11] Lavallée would not have stood out in the unit she joined, the No. 4 Stationary Hospital (French Canadian). Lieutenant-Colonel Arthur Mignault organized the No. 4 in Montréal in March 1915.[12] A Montréal physician and militia officer, Mignault had already helped found the French-Canadian Royal 22nd Regiment, also known as the Van Doos.[13] The No. 4 was primarily staffed with personnel drawn from Quebec, including 34 nurses, one of whom was Blanche Lavallée.[14] Lavallée and her colleagues ran a 520-bed hospital located at the Saint-Cloud racecourse in Paris, on a street now called Rue du Camp Canadien.[15]

The portrait of Lavallée also captures some of the military and society's views and expectations of nurses during the First World War. Nurses were respected and granted a certain amount of authority. This authority is present in the form

---

9   Toman, *Sister Soldiers*, 66.

10 McPherson, "The Nightingale Influence," 80.

11 Toman, *Sister Soldiers*, 47, 233. A recent study based on the analysis of recently digitized CEF files show that upwards of 70,000 enlisted men were francophone or approximately 11 percent of the total CEF. See Jean Martin, "Francophone Enlistment."

12 Morin-Pelletier, "Des oiseaux bleus," 59.

13 Litalien, "MIGNAULT, ARTHUR."

14 Toman, *Sister Soldiers*, 47, citing Michel Litalien's detailed study of the two Quebec medical units, *Dans la tourmente*.

15 Kalbfleisch, "War, Love and Women's Rights," A18.

of two bronze stars visible on Lavallée's shoulder. These are military rank stars, also known as pips, and they indicate that Lavallée held the relative rank of lieutenant (Lt./Nursing Sister), the lowest and most common rank assigned to military nurses. The rank was "relative" because while being a lieutenant nursing sister or a matron (one rank higher) conferred an officer's status, nurses' authority was limited to the medical sphere in which they worked, which was not the case for male officers.[16] Nonetheless, having even limited authority was useful for nurses operating in an overwhelmingly male world where women were expected to defer to men. As officers, nurses could enforce discipline among patients, some of whom may have been reluctant to obey a woman. As the *Instructions for Members of Canadian Army Medical Corps Nursing Service* stated: "The matrons and sisters are to be regarded as having authority in and about Military Hospitals next after the officers of the C.A.M. Corps and are at all times to be obeyed accordingly, and to receive the respect due to their position."[17] The Canadian military's decision to grant the nurses officer status was noteworthy, and sometimes caused tension between the different allied nursing service personnel, whose statuses varied according to nation.[18]

Their officer status also caused a dispute over medals. While eight Canadian nurses were awarded the Military Medal during the war, the British authorities, who then controlled the granting of medals to the Canadian military, did not deem them eligible for the Military Cross, an officers' medal.[19] Canadian military authorities pushed back against the British decision, but to no avail. British nurses did not enjoy the same status as did Canadians; the British nursing corps (Queen Alexandra's Imperial Military Nursing Service) had not been officially incorporated into the military hierarchy.[20] It was through this lens that the British military authorities viewed the Canadian nurses. So while the Canadian nurses were respected and their service appreciated by the men who surrounded them, their gender still took precedence as far as the British military was concerned. They were women first, nurses second.

---

16   Mann, *War Diary*, xxiv; McKenzie, *War-Torn Exchanges*, 5.
17   Army Medical Services, *Instructions*, 1.
18   Toman, *Sister Soldiers*, 191–192; McKenzie, *War-Torn Exchanges*, 5. Members of the Australian Army Nursing Service were given honorary ranks in 1916.
19   Fowler, "The Canadian Nursing Service."
20   McKenzie, "'Our Common Colonial Voices,'" 95.

Some of Richard Mathews's stylistic choices reflect conflicted attitudes towards military nurses. The portrait is soft and clean, an effect that downplays the determination and strength of character nurses would have needed to do their work. At the hospital at Saint Cloud, Lavallée and the other medical staff treated wounded soldiers in unsanitary, rainy, and vermin-infested conditions.[21] Lavallée faced pressure from home as well as at the hospital, which must have added to her burden. To keep her family afloat (she had seven siblings), Lavallée assigned a portion of her salary to her ailing father. While Mathews has perhaps acknowledged Lavallée's fatigue, he has glossed over the grittiness of her work, making her image ethereal. Her veil is more transparent than it would have been in reality, and her clothing is free of grime and stains. Compare the painted portrait to the photograph of Lavallée. Taken in 1915 before her departure to Europe, the photo shows a sharply dressed woman looking directly into the camera. She appears resolute and professional in her uniform coat, gloves, and hat, with a military kit bag at her feet. Here, Lavallée looks every inch the soldier, as opposed to the soft and romantic portrait completed just a year later.

The title given to military nurses, that of Nursing Sister, also emphasizes an expected role. During this era, the term would have been familiar to Canadians, harkening back to the days when women in holy orders provided nursing care. The use of Nursing Sister and the image conferred by the veil helped preserve an aura of virtue for the nurses who, secular or not, were expected to have "high moral character and dignified deportment."[22]

The military required nurses to be unmarried and could immediately dismiss them if they became pregnant.[23] They were also expected to keep their relationships with soldiers strictly chaste and professional. Here, their officers' rank might have helped deter relationships, as fraternization with other (lower) ranks was discouraged. In spite of official policies dissuading relationships between soldiers and nurses, romances occurred frequently. Blanche Lavallée met her future husband while stationed at the hospital in Paris. Lieutenant Georges-Alexandre-Henri

OPPOSITE: FIGURE I.2. Lt./Nursing Sister Blanche Lavallée, 1915.
Source: Library and Archives Canada/Department of National Defence fonds/e011162549.

21   Kalbfleisch, "War, Love and Women's Rights," A18.
22   Toman, *Sister Soldiers*, 39.
23   A tiny percentage of CAMC nurses—1.7 percent—were married. Toman, *Sister Soldiers*, 51.

Trudeau was a fellow Canadian officer. The Mathews portrait was likely painted the summer Lavallée met Trudeau, in 1916. Trudeau's visits to the hospital to see Lavallée cemented their relationship and the couple married in 1924.[24]

Lavallée's European war service was cut short due to illness. Exhausted, malnourished, and beset with appendicitis and a chronic cough, she was invalided back to Canada at the end of 1917.[25] Following an appendectomy and several months of convalescence, Lavallée returned to duty, though not as a battlefield nurse. Instead, she travelled to Washington, DC, where, before being discharged in the spring of 1919, Lavallée lobbied the U.S. Congress on behalf of American nurses who were fighting for greater formal recognition. Their efforts focused in particular on securing officers' ranks similar to those enjoyed by Canadian nurses in the CEF, a fight they won in 1920 with the passage of the *Army Reorganization Act*.[26] For Blanche Lavallée, the war years were a time to not only do her duty to her country, but also to her professional colleagues.

NURSE EDITH ANDERSON MONTURE, AMERICAN EXPEDITIONARY FORCE

Men who fought during the First World War came home with a variety of souvenirs of service: everything from bits of enemy kit, to postcards and photos, to pieces of shrapnel dug out of their own bodies. The women who served as nurses also accumulated material related to their military service, each piece connected in some way to their own experience of war. While some of these items lend themselves to easy interpretation, others are more inscrutable. Unless the importance of the object is recorded in some way, once the veteran is gone, the treasured item loses much of its personal significance.

One item many men and women brought back home was trench art, objects crafted from the detritus of war by soldiers or those close to the battlefields, for

OPPOSITE: FIGURE 1.3. Edith Anderson Monture's shell casing vases.
Source: Private collection of John Moses, Photograph by Canadian War Museum.

24   Morin-Pelletier, "Des oiseaux bleus," 62.
25   Blanche Lavallée, CEF Personnel Record.
26   American nurses won relative rank but not equal pay. See Feller and Cox, *Highlights in the History*, 11.

themselves or for others. Figure 1.3 shows two pieces of trench art. We see two brass tubes—discarded shell casings—open at the top and closed at the bottom. The top and bottom portions of each shell are smooth and shiny, while the middle portions are textured, with the stylized letters "AEF" and the year "1918." The shells have an art deco feel, and were clearly made by a craftsperson with considerable skill. While some trench art was made by individual soldiers with varying degrees of talent, there were also trench art workshops where artists turned out souvenir items for sale, and it is possible that these two casings were a product of this industry.[27]

The casings belonged to Edith Anderson Monture, a woman from the Six Nations of the Grand River reserve near Brantford, Ontario, and now they belong to her family.[28] But why would a woman from Ontario bring back American Expeditionary Force trench art? The answer reflects the racism prevalent in Canada at the time. Monture, who was born in 1890, wanted to train as a nurse, but discrimination made this impossible. Canadian teaching hospitals at that time rarely, if ever, admitted Black, Asian, or, as in Monture's case, Indigenous women.[29]

Unable to train in Canada, Monture went to the United States, after seeing an advertisement in the *Brantford Expositor*. She later recalled that she "had nothing to lose" in applying and was surprised to be accepted.[30] Monture studied at the New Rochelle Nursing School just outside of New York City, graduating as a registered nurse in 1914. For several years, she worked as a private school nurse, hearing from home that many of her male friends and relatives from Six Nations had joined the Canadian Expeditionary Force. In the summer of 1917, only a few months after the United States' entry into the war, Monture filled in a mobilization questionnaire that led to her recruitment as a member of the Army Nurse Corps. Figure 1.4 shows her in uniform. Both Canada and the United States enlisted

OPPOSITE: FIGURE 1.4. Nurse Edith Anderson Monture, 1917.
Source: Courtesy of Helen Monture Moses.

---

27 Saunders, "Bodies of Metal."

28 The trench art and photographs were loaned to the CWM for the purposes of exhibition by Monture's family. John Moses, Monture's grandson, graciously contributed to the research and revision of this story.
29 McPherson, "The Nightingale Influence," 83.
30 Monture, "Introduction," 2.

Indigenous soldiers in their expeditionary forces, 4,000 and 10,000, respectively.[31] In both countries, women were confined to nursing roles. According to her family, she was the only Six Nations woman to have served the war effort in a military capacity.[32] Monture may have enlisted in the American forces because she was already living and working in the United States and had built a life for herself in New Rochelle, forming close friendships with several nurses from her graduating class. Westchester County Unit B, the local unit Monture joined, had 20 nurses; of those, 15 were Canadian.[33] Her training lasted three months before she left the United States. Shipped overseas, she worked at Buffalo Base Hospital 23 in Vittel, France, where, like other nurses in the AEF and CEF, she cared for wounded and ill soldiers.

Monture's decorated artillery shell casings reflect many participants' wartime experiences. Shells were an integral part of First World War warfare, fired en masse at opposing lines during attempts to break the entrenched stalemate that had settled over the Western Front. This storm of steel and the physical and psychological toll taken on combatants gave rise to the term shell shock, a type of post-traumatic stress disorder that was common among front-line troops. The sheer number of shells fired during the conflict—one source estimates 1.5 billion—resulted in an abundance of disused casings.[34] Soldiers and local artisans used these casings as canvasses for art.[35] In a newspaper interview, Monture recalled the devastating effects of mortar shells like the ones she later brought home as souvenirs. "We would walk right over where there had been fighting. It was an awful sight—buildings in rubble, trees burnt, spent shells all over the place, whole towns blown up."[36]

Throughout her time with the AEF, Monture kept a diary, later published as *Diary of a War Nurse: Army Nurse Corps, American Expeditionary Force 1918*. Like the memoirs of many First World War nurses, it records a rich social life squeezed into moments of respite from hospital duties. Public lectures, shared dinners, excursions into local villages, French lessons, and even dance parties are recounted in Monture's diary along with glimpses of her duties in the hospital. Her notations

31   Winegard, *For King and Kanata*, 6; Davis, *Native America*, 341.
32   Monture, "Foreword," 1.
33   Norman, "Race, Gender, and Colonialism," 219–220.
34   Doel, *Geographies of Violence*, chap. 11, Kindle.
35   See Saunders, *Trench Art*.
36   Summerby, *Native Soldiers*, 17.

often suggest long hours at work. Occasionally she included details about her patients or workload. In one entry, she describes a night shift spent caring for 57 patients and three German prisoners. In another, she writes: "Operated all day. No time off."[37] One of her patients, who had adopted her as a big sister, died suddenly one night and she recorded her grief in her diary, writing, "The poor boy lost consciousness immediately. My heart was broken. Cried most of the day and could not sleep."[38] The life of a war nurse was not easy, mentally or physically.

Monture returned to the Six Nations of the Grand River after her time with the Army Nurse Corps came to an end in 1919. She married Claybran Monture shortly after, and together they raised four children and many grandchildren. She continued nursing, delivering babies and caring for the sick at the Lady Willingdon Hospital in Ohsweken until her retirement.[39] Monture's military history remained important to her and her family. When she died, in 1996, just days before her 106th birthday, she was the last surviving AEF nurse and the last First World War veteran from Six Nations.[40] She was buried with a full military funeral, where a carefully folded American flag was passed to her daughter Helen, namesake of one of Monture's lifelong friends, Helen Krueger, whom she had met during nursing training in New Rochelle.

LT./NURSING SISTER MURNEY PUGH AND LT./NURSING SISTER ELLANORE PARKER, CANADIAN ARMY MEDICAL CORPS

While military service inevitably involved hardship and sadness, for many women it was also an experience that remained significant throughout their lifetime, both for the work they did, and the relationships they formed. A gravestone (figure 1.5) at St. Luke's Anglican Cemetery in Victoria, British Columbia, demonstrates just how lasting women's wartime experience could be. Two names share the stone: Murney M. Pugh and Ellanore Parker. Their grave offers clues as to their relationship. Their upright headstone sits atop a large rectangular grave plot outlined in

---

37   Monture, *Diary*, June 6 and July 26, 1918.
38   Monture, *Diary*, June 16, 1918.
39   Monture, *Diary*, 4; Poulin, *Invisible Women*, 8.
40   Monture, *Diary*, 1.

FIGURE 1.5. Murney Pugh and Ellanore Parker's shared gravestone.
Source: Courtesy of Ken Campbell, Victoria.

stone blocks, similar to other graves surrounding it. According to one scholar of cemetery symbolism, borders like these are important markers of a family relationship.[41] That they strongly identified as Canadian military nurses and war veterans is clear from the headstone, and the format of the words is instructive as well. While many of the shared gravestones in St. Luke's churchyard conform to the nineteenth-century tradition of placing the male head of household at the top of the stone and subordinate wife at the bottom, the more modern placement of Pugh and Parker's names side-by-side and the mirrored, near identical text suggests that the women were more equal partners.[42] Parker and Pugh met during the First World War and stayed together for the rest of their lives.

While some might read their life together as a tale of a lifelong friendship, it is far more likely that theirs was a love story. Same-sex relationships have always existed, but social stigma has, until relatively recently, forced them into the shadows, keeping them hidden from history. Of late, historians have been increasingly interested in uncovering those relationships, using new sources and interpretive

41 Nutty, "Cemetery Symbolism," 8.
42 Gaudio and Ellison, *Gone but Not Forgotten*, 34–35; Ritter, "Grave Exclamations," 40.

techniques. This extends to same-sex relationships in the military, though much of the historiography relates to the Second World War, is from outside of Canada, and more often than not, examines relationships between men.[43] One exception is Andrea McKenzie's study of the strong bond between Canadian First World War military nurses Laura Holland and Mildred Forbes.[44] Kathryn McPherson argued that in the context of military nursing, "bonds between women were accepted and encouraged. Yet when nurses forged intimate relationships with other women, the norms of compulsory heterosexuality [...] served to marginalize or to make invisible homoerotic relations."[45] Certainly, the two world wars provided an unparalleled opportunity for LGBTQ2S+ individuals to form relationships, providing years of sex-segregated friendships and housing, as well as a break from the pressure to marry. According to some scholars, the world wars were followed by a type of gay renaissance in many larger urban centres.[46]

Much of what we know about Pugh and Parker's time together is drawn from service and census records, as well as photo albums and documents held in the collection at the Royal BC Museum.[47] These types of sources provide a lot of information while at the same time leaving many questions. For instance, when and how did Pugh and Parker meet? The two enlisted on the same day but in different cities (Parker in Winnipeg, Pugh in Québec City), and after that, their military careers generally overlap. They may have crossed paths on the voyage to England, as both left Canada on September 29, 1914, and arrived on October 16. Possibly, they met while amassing at Salisbury Plain in England before sailing to France, which is what their catalogue record at the Royal British Columbia Museum and Archives seems to indicate. They both had their first posting at the No. 2 Canadian General Hospital.[48] We also know that as of March 1915, they were both stationed in Le Treport. Service records indicate that they stayed at each other's side as

43 Bérubé, *Coming Out Under Fire*; Jackson, *One of the Boys*; Kinsman and Gentile, *Canadian War on Queers*; Vickers, *Queen and Country*, 167–194.

44 McKenzie, *War-Torn Exchanges*.

45 McPherson, *Bedside Matters*, 16.

46 Doan, *Disturbing Practice*, vii; Duder, *Awfully Devoted Women*, 105; Bérubé, *Coming Out Under Fire*, 271.

47 Ellanore Parker and Murney Pugh, Personal Papers.

48 Nursing Sister Murney May Pugh, CEF Personnel Record; Nursing Sister Ellanore Parker, CEF Personnel Record.

FIGURE 1.6. Lt./Nursing Sister Murney Pugh and Lt./Nursing Sister Ellanore Parker, as denoted in pen, at Le Treport, near Dieppe, 1915.
Source: Royal BC Museum and Archives, Ellanore Parker fonds, J-00779.

much as possible during the war. Both left on leave on October 15, 1915. The couple shared a second leave from Le Treport in June and July 1916 but were separated early in 1917 when Parker was hospitalized and sent to England for recuperation. She returned to her nursing duties in France in the spring of 1918, but was soon hospitalized again in Rouen.[49]

Parker's photo album, constructed by hand with cardboard, string, and surgical tape, records her experiences at the hospital in Le Treport. The photographs inside the album show a close, intimate friendship. The two are frequently seated close together, as seen in figure 1.6, and are often touching. This was not unusual in photographs of servicemen or nursing sisters from the time, but their long association certainly suggests a deeply felt emotional connection.

According to her service file, Parker suffered from repeated bouts of respiratory illness. She may have inhaled gas while treating soldiers wounded in gas attacks near the French front.[50] As we saw in Blanche Lavallée's story, exhaustion, poor living conditions, and incredible mental and physical stress were part of the

49   Ellanore Parker, CEF Personnel Record.
50   Gas inhalation from wounded soldiers' clothing was not unusual. Toman, *Sister Soldiers*, 102.

war experience for soldiers and front-line medical staff alike. Many nurses contracted serious illnesses, and it was not unusual for them to require treatment in hospitals and rest homes.

The two returned to Canada separately (Parker as a patient aboard a hospital ship), though their ships departed England on the same day, and quickly reunited, spending the rest of their lives together. After their return, they promptly immigrated to the United States. The 1920 United States census records them as "trained nurses" and their industry as "war nurses."[51] Census data from the 1920s through the 1940s shows them living together in California. Parker is consistently registered as the "head" of the household, with Pugh sometimes recorded as her "partner" or "sister." The couple returned to Canada in 1948, settling in Victoria, British Columbia. These two women, brought together by their participation in the First World War, stayed side-by-side for the rest of their lives.

Their shared tombstone suggests that the war not only gave them a meaningful, long-lasting relationship but also provided them with cherished experiences and an identity that remained significant for decades; their military titles and years of service occupy half of the tombstone inscription. Ellanore Parker and Murney Pugh remained engaged with their military pasts, even going so far as to name their California home "Vimy Ridge" after the well-known battle.[52] Parker, a writer in her postwar life, based two books of fiction, *The Flower of the Land* and *The Land Lay Waiting*, on their wartime experiences. Nursing history scholar Cynthia Toman argues that *The Flower of the Land*, whose main character Parker referred to as her "alter ego," was in fact autobiographical, with the postings of the character following Parker's own trajectory with the CAMC.[53] Parker was a part of veterans' groups such as the Red Chevron Association and the Overseas Nursing Sisters' Association of Canada, both of which allowed them to maintain their ties to other nursing sisters.

Ellanore Parker died at the age of 86 in 1965. Murney Pugh sent their military nursing uniforms, as well as all of Parker's writings and photograph albums, to the Royal BC Museum. Pugh died nine years later at the age of 91.

---

51   1920 United States Federal Census.

52   Parker's CEF personnel record gives their address as "Vimy Ridge, Arroyo Drive, San Gabriel California."

53   Toman, *Sister Soldiers*, 57.

DR. MARGARET ELLEN DOUGLASS, WINNIPEG WOMEN'S VOLUNTEER RESERVE

This photograph (figure 1.7) depicts a group of almost 100 women standing at attention. Their clothing, including jackets with belts and epaulettes, resembles a military uniform. They stand upright, their heels together, eyes forward, and their arms are at their sides. Their expressions are serious. Though their stance and clothing suggest they belong to the military, they do not.

As we have seen, aside from nursing, women's military contributions to the First World War were rare. Deterred by rules barring women from non-medical service, they remained far outside the formal military structure. Some women, however, pushed at these boundaries and turned their hands to civil defence and paramilitary training. This photograph shows the Winnipeg Women's Volunteer Reserve (WWVR), a uniformed group led by Dr. Margaret Ellen Douglass. Born in New Brunswick in 1878, Douglass had attended the University of Toronto and became a physician at a time when there were few women doctors. Like many others in the first decade of the twentieth century, she went west, moving to Winnipeg to practise medicine.[54] Douglass is in the foreground of this WWVR photograph, the only woman wearing an insignia or badge on her chest, as well as what appear to be rank stars on her shoulders.

Douglass was very active in the home front war effort. She took a lead role in the nursing division of Winnipeg's St. John Ambulance Association, which was responsible for training local Voluntary Aid Detachment (VAD) volunteers for deployment as nursing aides.[55] In 1915, Douglass founded a group for patriotically minded women, the WWVR. Douglass's aim was to train a cohort of women who could "handle the work back of the firing line." She believed that women had just as much of a duty as men to guard their communities and be ready for combat should the need arise. To that end, she ensured that the members of the WWVR learned various military skills, such as marching, shooting, riding, driving, and signals. While Douglass likely knew the WWVR would never see front-line duty, she believed the organization was worthwhile. "Even should the Militia never require the W.W.V.R. for active service," she wrote in 1916, "the benefit acquired

---

54   Kinnear, *In Subordination*, 57.
55   Quiney, *This Small Army*, 26–27, 202; Blanchard, *Winnipeg's Great War*, 56.

AT THE KINALMEAKY FARMS, HEADINGLY. OCT, 16, 1915.

FIGURE 1.7. Dr. Margaret Ellen Douglass (*foreground*) with
the Winnipeg Women's Volunteer Reserve, 1915.
Source: Archives of Manitoba, Foote Collection 2306.

mentally, physically and morally, will equip these girls to fill important places in
the future of their country."[56]

For Winnipeg residents, the sight of women marching around in quasi-military
uniforms may have been a novelty, but the 200 or so members of the WWVR were
serious about their training. In August 1916, under Douglass's watchful eye, the
group travelled to Gimli, Manitoba, where they set up Camp Preparedness. For two
weeks, they engaged in such activities as route marches, target shooting, even bridge
building. The women were reportedly loath to return to civilian life after the two
weeks were up. "No battalion of khaki-clad soldiers," wrote the *Winnipeg Tribune*,
"ever looked so disconsolate at the prospect of leaving camp as the W.W.V.R. did on
the day of departure, when after tents had been struck, and every sign of the recent

56   Douglass, "Winnipeg Women's Volunteer Reserve," 256.

FIGURE 1.8. Dr. Margaret
Ellen Douglass, ca. 1918.
Source: Winnipeg Tribune,
December 15, 1919, p. 8.

occupation of the open lot of the lake-front at Gimli was obliterated."[57] Over the next two years, the WWVR became a regular feature of life in Winnipeg, as did other, similar groups in cities and towns across Canada.

Of all the women's paramilitary auxiliaries created throughout the country, the Winnipeg group was one of the most prominent. Montréal, Edmonton, and Toronto also boasted noteworthy women's reserves. As the war dragged on, with increasing numbers of men killed or injured, and as recruiting levels dropped, the prospect of Canadian women joining the military in non-nursing roles began to seem less outlandish. Other countries, including Britain, had created women's divisions, but Canada remained reluctant. For her part, Douglass was not content to wait. In January 1918, she went overseas with St. John Ambulance, as officer in charge of a group of VAD nursing aides.[58] Douglass then enlisted with the Imperial forces, joining the Royal Army Medical Corps. She was attached to the Women's Auxiliary Army Corps (WAAC) as a physician and sent to France, where she spent the next two years. Douglass later received the Victory Medal and the British War Medal for her service.[59]

Most of the women Douglass led in the WWVR never found their way overseas. Had the war lasted longer, they may have had the chance. In May 1918, Canada's

57   "Women Reserves Sorry," 5.
58   "Women Physician to Take Nurses," 2; "Winnipeg Farewells First Detachment," 1; Blanchard, *Winnipeg's Great War,* 56; Quiney, *This Small Army,* 27.
59   "Women Given Service Medals," 3.

Militia Council finally discussed the possibility of accepting women in non-nursing roles, and considered creating a Canadian equivalent of Britain's WAAC. The council sent the issue to a subcommittee that, in September 1918, proposed an organization called the Canadian Women's Corps. The Militia Council agreed with the plan in principle, with the next step being the Prime Minister's approval. But the government took no further action, likely because the war soon came to an end in November 1918.[60] When the Second World War started, nursing was still the only place for women in the Canadian military, and pioneers like Douglass once again fought for greater opportunities to serve with Canada's armed services.

DISPOSABLE SANITARY NAPKINS

After the First World War, the makers of Kotex touted Nursing Sisters as innovators of disposable sanitary napkins. Military nurses, with access to plenty of gauze, may indeed have used surgical dressings similar to those in figure 1.10 as menstrual pads.[61] In this newspaper ad (figure 1.9), one of the earliest examples from that advertising campaign, the company promoted the connection between Nursing Sisters and Kotex pads, stating, "Made from Cellucotton and fine

FIGURE 1.9. Advertisement for Kotex Sanitary Napkins, 1921. *Source: Sheboygan Press* [Wisconsin], June 21, 1921.

gauze, Nurses in France started the Kotex Idea, and now it's adopted everywhere." Without the nurses' direct testimony about this very private topic, it is a difficult claim to substantiate. However, Kotex ran with

---

60   Department of National Defence, "The Canadian Women's Army Corps," 2–3.
61   Field Dressing, CWM 19800543-004.

FIGURE 1.10. First World War field dressings, sometimes
used by nursing sisters as sanitary napkins.
Source: Canadian War Museum 19800543-004.

it, placing their advertisements in newspapers and women's magazines
read across North America, including the popular *Ladies Home Journal.*[62]

Because of the early twentieth century's codes of modesty, few
women commented directly on menstruation, sex, pregnancy, or birth
control. Women's diaries and letters occasionally reveal details about
private bodily functions, but more frequently researchers are forced to
extrapolate from veiled language.[63] Nurse Edith Anderson Monture's
private diary referenced her laundry arrangements and included a nota-
tion that she had spent time washing what she termed "toilet articles."[64]
Nurses' letters home from the First World War frequently mention the
lack of laundry facilities among the harsh living conditions encountered
overseas. Female relatives would have recognized that this laundry
included washable sanitary cloths.

---

62   Heinrich and Batchelor, *Kotex,* 39.

63   Millar, *Unmentionable History of the West,* 12–16; Light and Pierson, *No Easy Road,* 170.

64   Monture, *Diary,* April 22, 1918.

By the Second World War, there was less secrecy around the topic of menstruation.[65] With health and sexual education beginning to be introduced in classrooms across Canada, birth control advocates like Margaret Sanger and Dorothea Palmer featured in newspapers, and 20 years of sanitary napkin advertisements in the public consciousness, discussions of women's hygiene had become more open. Disposable menstrual pads were expensive but commonplace. So commonplace, in fact, that military women during the Second World War were issued a ration of disposable sanitary napkins and did not have to make their own from field dressings. Former servicewomen recalled the "Blue Box Day Parade," when they lined up to get their monthly ration of sanitary napkins.[66]

LT./NURSING SISTER MARY ADELAIDE COONEY, ROYAL CANADIAN ARMY MEDICAL CORPS

At first glance, the Canadian Second World War battle dress uniform shown in figure 1.11 might look as though it belonged to a man.[67] However, details such as the Royal Canadian Army Medical Corps (RCAMC) insignia and the uniform's diminutive size open up the possibility that it belonged to a Canadian military nurse. Battle dress uniforms like this one represent a shift in the perception of military nurses and are indicative of the changing nature of women's integration into the Canadian military. While the blue dress, white apron, and veil remained, during the Second World War the Canadian military also issued battle dress to those posted to areas of combat.[68]

FOLLOWING PAGE (LEFT): FIGURE 1.11. Lt./Nursing Sister Mary Adelaide Cooney's battle dress uniform.
Source: Canadian War Museum 20130046-005, 006, 007.
FOLLOWING PAGE (RIGHT): FIGURE 1.12. Lt./Nursing Sister Mary Adelaide Cooney, ca. 1944.
Source: George Metcalf Archival Collection, Canadian War Museum 20130046-025.

---

65   Light and Pierson, *No Easy Road*, 82–86.
66   Greer, *Girls of the King's Navy*, 85.
67   Lt./NS Mary Adelaide Cooney's Battle Dress Uniform, CWM 20130046-005, CWM 20130046-006, CWM 2013046-007.
68   Toman, *An Officer and a Lady*, 105.

This included the Canadian nurses sent to Italy in 1943, among them Lt./Nursing Sister Mary Adelaide Cooney, the owner of this uniform.

Figure 1.12 shows Cooney in her nursing blues, with lacy handkerchief and a voluminous, white veil, similar to that worn by Lt./Nursing Sister Blanche Lavallée in figure 1.2. The addition of battle dress to the nurses' very feminine wardrobe acknowledged that medical care in the field required clothing that placed practicality above airy notions of womanhood. The traditional skirted working dress for the Canadian military nurses uniform both concealed and revealed the feminine shape. In contrast, the baggy battle dress jackets and trousers had an unmistakably androgynous appearance. Trousers protected the legs better than skirts, and were warmer and easier to move about in. Bandanas were often used instead of the traditional white veils. The new battle dress uniform's drab wool serge was tough and likely easier to keep looking clean in field conditions.

Mary Adelaide Cooney had first-hand experience of the dangerous nature of nursing and the importance of practical clothing. Along with the other nurses who were part of the No. 14 Canadian General Hospital, Cooney was aboard ss *Santa Elena* when it was torpedoed in the Mediterranean. The practical uniform may have helped to save the nurses' lives, allowing them freedom of movement while evacuating their sinking ship.

ss *Santa Elena* was part of a large convoy moving troops, equipment, and supplies from England to Italy, where Allied forces were fighting.[69] Sailing through the Mediterranean at this stage of the war was a perilous undertaking. On the night of November 6, 1943, Luftwaffe airplanes attacked the convoy. As klaxons sounded, the nurses moved to the corridors and prepared to evacuate. Cooney recounts that they had only been there a few minutes when "suddenly, the ship jarred and shook from a terrific blow. It was a German torpedo, fired by an attacking plane which a moment later crashed into the sea."[70] Hit in the stern, *Santa Elena* listed and the nurses scrambled to their boat stations. When the order came to abandon ship, they climbed into lifeboats, which were then lowered to the sea. Eventually, two American vessels, the troopship ss *Monterey* and uss *Tillman*, a destroyer, picked up the nurses. Cooney and those rescued by *Monterey* climbed a 60-foot scramble net over the side of the ship. Lt./Nursing Sister Ethel Rowell

69 Nicholson, *Official History of the Canadian Army*, 351–352.
70 Lebel, "Torpedoed!"

remembered that "with each swell of the ocean, we were told when the boat goes up, grab a hold of the scramble net... So that's what we did. The lifeboat came up high and we grabbed onto that scramble net and I hung onto that scramble net as tight as a spider could hang onto his web."[71] According to Lt./Nursing Sister Betty Jamieson, their climb up the netting would have been "impossible, except for battledress. They could not have done it in skirts."[72]

NO. 14 CANADIAN GENERAL HOSPITAL PLATE

An illustration on the bottom side of this plate (figure 1.13) depicts the attack on SS *Santa Elena*.[73] Here, the ill-fated ship lists noticeably, a German plane flies overhead, and a lifeless body floats in the sea. In the distance, SS *Monterey* appears. The plate belonged to Lt./Nursing Sister Margaret Mowat, another nurse who served with the No. 14 Canadian General Hospital.[74] Large and colourful, the plate illustrates the wartime journeys and experiences of the hospital unit. Lines of red, yellow, and blue circle the top of the rim.

FIGURE 1.13. Commemorative plate for the No. 14 Canadian General Hospital, Royal Canadian Army Medical Corps. *Source:* Canadian War Museum 19940080-001.

Each vignette symbolizes a key place or event in the history of the No. 14. Depictions include the recruiting of personnel in Westmount, Quebec, and the ship *Stirling Castle* steaming overseas with the No. 14 aboard. A

71   Rowell, "Veteran's Stories."

72   Clark, "99."

73   Commemorative Plate, No. 14 Canadian General Hospital, CWM 19940080-001.

74   Along with this plate, a collection of Lt./NS Margaret Mowat's wartime photos and documents is also held by the Canadian War Museum.

series of postings in England follow (including a training exercise named "Tiger'" represented by a rather out-of-place jungle cat). Caserta, Italy, where the No. 14 set up in December 1943, is represented by anthropomorphized clouds blowing winds overhead, signifying the cold, wet, windy conditions the nurses experienced. At Cancello, Italy, puffs around tents represent the eruption of Mount Vesuvius, which covered everything in several inches of ash. Finally, a tobacco leaf stands in for the time the No. 14 spent stationed in a former tobacco factory in Perugia. The RCAMC's insignia appears in the well of the plate, surrounded by the names of the major battles whose casualties the No. 14 treated: Dieppe, Ortona, Cassino, and Rimini, as well as the modes of transportation by which the wounded arrived at the hospital.[75]

Major Jules Gosselin, a radiologist with the No. 14, reportedly designed the plate and they were produced by a pottery factory in Perugia in 1944. The first set of plates contained a spelling error, and so a second set was made, selling for 1,000 lira (the error plates were sold for 500 lira). We do not know where or when Mowat acquired her plate, but we know that several members of the No. 14 owned copies, and that Henry Morgan's department store in Montréal also sold some of the plates in the late 1940s. According to Anita Gibson, the owner of another No. 14 General Hospital plate that is now part of the CWM collection, a Morgan's buyer on a trip to Italy saw the plate and ordered some for the store, since he was aware that the No. 14 had been raised in Montréal.[76] A visually striking artifact, it is a distinctive way of telling the history of a military unit.

LANCE CORPORAL MARY WEAVER, WENTWORTH WOMEN'S AUXILIARY CORPS

For those familiar with women's Second World War service branches, the details of this dark green cotton dress (figure 1.14) clearly indicate that it is not an official military uniform. It is not a nurse's uniform, nor does it belong to the army,

---

75   Gibson, "Plate."
76   Gibson, "Plate."

navy, or air force. It appears homemade, and the insignia do not belong to any official military units. In fact, this uniform was worn by a member of Hamilton's Wentworth Women's Auxiliary Corps (WWAC).[77] As Dr. Margaret Ellen Douglass and other women had done in the First World War, Canadian women signalled their willingness to serve in the Second World War through grassroots paramilitary organizations. Again, the keenest women formed groups to prepare themselves for service should the opportunity arise. As the *Ottawa Journal* reported, they included "physical training, learning first aid, army cookery, wireless telegraphy, motor mechanics, signalling and map reading."[78] The woman to whom this uniform belonged, Mary Constance Weaver, would have learned skills like these in the WWAC. Weaver was young, and her husband had enlisted and gone overseas—joining an auxiliary may have been a way for her to feel more involved in the war effort. This unofficial uniform, in its own simple way, testifies to women's clear and powerful drive to serve their country and communities in a time of crisis.

We know little about Mary Weaver's experience with the Wentworth Women's Auxiliary Corps. We do know, however, that the contours of Weaver's wartime life conformed in many ways to those of other Canadian women of the time. In 1941, she married Tom Fleetwood Weaver, a British Columbia mill worker and a soldier with the Rocky Mountain Rangers.[79] The couple was one of many young Canadians getting married—the marriage rate shot up at the very beginning of the war and stayed high throughout.[80] The uncertainty of war gave everything a sense of urgency, and quick marriages were one consequence. Birthrates also increased, an unsurprising result of the jump in marriage rates and post-Depression prosperity, beginning the steady climb towards the baby boom.

FOLLOWING PAGE (LEFT): FIGURE 1.14. Lance Corporal Mary Weaver's Wentworth Women's Auxiliary Corps uniform.
Source: Canadian War Museum 20110011-002.
FOLLOWING PAGE (RIGHT): FIGURE 1.15. Lance Corporal Mary Weaver in her Wentworth Women's Auxiliary Corps uniform, ca. 1941.
Source: Canadian War Museum 20110011 (AQN file).

77   Mary Weaver's Wentworth Women's Auxiliary Corps Uniform, CWM 20110011-002.
78   "Women Want to Help," 6.
79   Tom Fleetwood Weaver, Service Files of the Second World War – War Dead, 1939–1947.
80   Keshen, *Saints,* 121.

In 1942, the Weavers welcomed a daughter. When she was still an infant, Tom Weaver was shipped overseas.[81] At some point over the next year or so, Mary Weaver moved back to her hometown of Hamilton, perhaps to be closer to her family. There, she joined the WWAC. Figure 1.15 shows her in uniform. The group was aimed at women who were between the ages of 16 and 45, especially those who were either married to (or friends of) men serving in the military.[82] Members kept busy over the course of the war, training in basic military skills, organizing an array of patriotic activities, and fundraising for the war effort. We know Weaver served with the group for at least a year because of the service chevron that is stitched onto the right sleeve of her uniform (each chevron indicated one year of service), but we do not know if she continued her involvement with the WWAC after her husband was killed in action in 1944.

Weaver was one of thousands of women who enlisted with paramilitary organizations during the Second World War. They were led by women such as Joan B. Kennedy of the British Columbia Women's Service Corps (BCWSC), one of the earliest and most influential figures of this movement. Founded amid rising global tensions in the late 1930s, the BCWSC was a bellwether; over the next few years, dozens of similar organizations sprung up around Canada, training potential female recruits should the military ever seek their services.[83] Kennedy and others did not care to wait for the military to realize their potential; instead, they actively pressed officials to admit women. She and other leaders repeatedly presented their case to Ottawa, where officials were unreceptive, neither seeing a need, nor having a desire, to enroll women in uniformed service.[84]

Eventually, several factors converged to reverse the official stance on female military personnel. Joan Kennedy's campaign and the participation of thousands of women across Canada, like Mary Weaver, in paramilitary auxiliaries undoubtedly helped the cause. Another factor was military officials' growing recognition that there were many jobs in the military that women could take over from men, freeing more male personnel for combat.[85] The final event that likely pushed

---

81 Tom Fleetwood Weaver Service File.
82 "Airwoman Jeannett Touchette."
83 Gossage, *Greatcoats*, 31–32.
84 Pierson, *They're Still Women*, 100.
85 Pierson, *They're Still Women*, 100.

recalcitrant military officials into recruiting women was the appearance of members of Britain's Women's Auxiliary Air Force in Canada to work on the British Commonwealth Air Training Plan.[86] The presence of uniformed British women was awkward for officials who would still not let Canadian women serve. And so, on July 2, 1941, the RCAF authorized the creation of its own women's branch, the Canadian Women's Auxiliary Air Force or CWAAF (later renamed the Royal Canadian Air Force Women's Division). Shortly after, in August, the army formed the Canadian Women's Army Corps (CWAC). Finally, the navy established the Women's Royal Canadian Naval Service (WRCNS) in July 1942.

Recruiting women for the new branches was done with public opinion in mind. While necessity had dictated this change in policy, the idea of women serving in the military was not universally embraced, and in fact many Canadians were hostile to the idea. Rumours abounded that women who wanted to join had loose morals or were otherwise suspect.[87] For the RCAF, the women who would make up the first batch of recruits had to be beyond reproach. The recruits they picked would be pioneers—the first women to join the Canadian armed forces in a non-medical capacity, and as such, they would attract much attention. The *Montreal Gazette* reported on the scene at the local RCAF recruiting centre, where "photographers and newsmen buzzed around, flashing pictures and firing questions" as "14 determined-looking young Montreal women" joined up.[88] More serious, perhaps, was Princess Alice's speech at the graduation exercises for the first ever women RCAF officers and NCOs. Princess Alice, the honorary commander, reminded the women that they were "pioneers in a new field of action" and that "the eyes of Canada" were on them. As the vanguard of officers for the nascent CWAAF, she went on, the "success and good name" of the organization rested on their shoulders. And if that was not pressure enough, she pointed out that they were now "wearing the uniform of His Majesty's Service and will be performing tasks never before done by women."[89] Unlike male recruits, they bore a double burden: not only were they not to let their country down, they had the added pressure of proving that women were up to the task of military service.

---

86 Keshen, *Saints*, 176.
87 Pierson, *They're Still Women*, 170.
88 "Montreal Women Join Air Auxiliary," 13.
89 "Address Given by Princess Alice," 8.

Mary Weaver would not be one of those women. We do not know whether she was interested in joining the formal military, but being the mother of a young child likely would have kept her from serving. While women's paramilitary organizations played a key role in garnering official acceptance for women in uniform, actually serving in the women's branches was not for everyone, nor was it open to all. Joining the WWAC arguably provided Weaver with an outlet for patriotic energy while caring for her child. For other women, enlisting in the newly formed women's service branches was a viable and appealing option.

WING OFFICER WILLA WALKER, ROYAL CANADIAN AIR FORCE WOMEN'S DIVISION

This uniform (figure 1.16), in air force blue with "Canada" across the shoulder and three stripes on the sleeve of the service jacket, looks trim and professional. Certainly not homemade, the stripes indicate that it belonged to a wing officer in the Royal Canadian Air Force Women's Division, an elevated rank held by only a few.[90] The owner of this uniform, Wilhelmina "Willa" Walker, came from an affluent, well-connected family. By the age of 28, her life had been shaped by travel, a good education, and opportunities to meet influential people. Reaching the level of wing officer, however, required more than just an advantaged background. Walker was also intelligent, decisive, and devoted to supporting the war. In 1940, the Germans had captured her husband, Scotsman David Harry Walker, at Dunkirk. For three months, Willa Walker knew nothing of her husband's fate. Once she learned that he was a prisoner of war (POW), she tried to help him escape, even concealing maps in one of his POW parcels.[91] The escape attempts failed, but soon Walker had another way to fight the war. When the first women's services branches were announced in 1941, Walker was among the first to apply. Recruiting campaigns for women often claimed that by joining up, women were

OPPOSITE: FIGURE 1.16. Wing Officer Willa Walker's uniform.
Source: Canadian War Museum 19750344-012, 19750344-014, 19750344-250.

90 Wing Officer Willa Walker's RCAF-WD Service Dress Jacket, Service Dress Skirt, and Service Dress Cap, CWM 19750344-012, CWM 19750344-250, CWM 19750344-014.
91 Ryell, "Natural-Born Leader," S8.

"freeing men to fight."[92] Unsuccessful in her attempts to help free her soldier husband from captivity, it is tempting to think Walker was doing the next best thing by enlisting herself.

The air force was choosy in deciding who would fill the limited spots within the CWAAF ranks, aware, perhaps, that the first women in uniform would be scrutinized. As a first step, women were asked to indicate their interest in military service to the Department of National War Services. By the middle of August 1941, over 7,300 women from across Canada had done so, and application forms were sent out.[93] In September, CWAAF selection boards interviewed applicants in major Canadian cities.[94] During this process, 150 women were selected for the first training course to be held in Toronto in October; from this group the CWAAF chose its first officers and non-commissioned officers (NCOs). NCOs, such as sergeants, have less authority than commissioned officers, who generally hold the rank of lieutenant and above. Once the officer corps was in place, general recruiting and training of other trades would begin. Walker was undoubtedly viewed as an ideal candidate.

Walker started her military career in basic training, like any other recruit. In late October, she travelled to Toronto, to the CWAAF Manning Depot, situated on Toronto's Jarvis Street.[95] Officers on loan from the British Women's Auxiliary Air Force (WAAF) along with male RCAF personnel were brought in as instructors.[96] Initially, Walker was simply Airwoman, Second Class, like the others in her group. On a typical day, the recruits were awoken at 6:30 a.m. They paraded after breakfast, and then, for the next nine-and-a-half hours, took part in a varying assortment of lectures, drills, and other training, interrupted only for lunch. After supper in the evening, the lights went out at 10:30 p.m.[97] They did it all over again the next day, until the five-week course concluded. A series of examinations, including written and oral exams, and drills, followed the course.[98]

---

92 The Canadian government's promotional materials used variations of "That Men May Fly" or "We Serve That Men May Fight" to attract new recruits to the women's branches. For an example, see "...That Men May Fly," *Ottawa Citizen*, July 2, 1943, 6.

93 "7,319 Women Eager to Enlist," 8.

94 "Will Interview Women," 3.

95 "Toronto Girls Receive Training," 4.

96 Ziegler, *We Serve*, 8.

97 "Initial Drill is Enjoyed," 4.

98 "Princess Alice to Attend," 5.

After she had taken over as senior officer for the women's division, Walker said that during basic training she had been a "wide-eyed, green recruit" and had "skinned her knees shinnying into an upper bunk in the barracks block and who was spoken to severely on parade on occasion for not having her buttons bright enough."[99] Despite this, Walker took to military life. She won the Brookes Medal, named for Air Commodore George Brookes, as the top recruit in her class. In 1942, the Brookes Medal became the Brookes Trophy, and Walker's name was engraved on it as the first top graduate of the inaugural officer's training course.[100]

After training, Walker was posted to No. 1 training command, headquartered in Toronto. To her fell the difficult task of integrating the first CWAAF recruits into the 16 Service Flying Training Schools that formed a part of the British Commonwealth Air Training Plan (they would eventually be sent to other BCATP facilities, as well as overseas). This proved challenging as not all male RCAF personnel—including commanding officers—welcomed the arrival of women.[101] But Walker persisted in her duties as the liaison between the RCAF and CWAAF. Eventually, as she noted, "some of the stations which were the least enthusiastic are the most enthusiastic now."[102] Meanwhile, the CWAAF became the Royal Canadian Air Force Women's Division (RCAF-WD, or informally the WDs). More than just a name change, this meant that women in the air force no longer served as auxiliaries, but as full members of the RCAF.[103] In June 1942, Section Officer Walker was posted to the No. 7 Manning Deport at Rockcliffe, in Ottawa, as Officer Commanding.[104] Figure 1.17 shows Walker, now holding the rank of flight officer, standing with a group of airwomen at Rockcliffe. The women behind her stand "at ease," with their eyes ahead, feet apart, and arms clasped behind their backs. In front of them, Walker looks very much in command. In 1943, she continued her rise up the air force ladder, becoming the Senior Staff Officer for the RCAF-WDs in Canada.

Walker was not done yet. On May 12, 1943, a small article appeared on page 12 of the *Ottawa Journal* informing readers that Willa Walker had attained the rank of

---

99   Ecker, "Considers Service Training," 17.
100 "Top Graduate," 4.
101 Ziegler, *We Serve*, 30.
102 Ecker, "Considers Service Training," 17.
103 "R.C.A.F. (Women's Division)," 12.
104 "Willa Walker is Promoted," 22.

FIGURE 1.17. Flight Officer Willa Walker and airwomen, 1942.
Source: Library and Archives Canada/Willa Walker collection/e011162676.

wing officer—the first in the branch to do so, and one that matched her position as Senior Staff Officer.[105] Wing officer, the piece pointed out, was equivalent in rank to wing commander for men. In a war where so many women were accomplishing firsts, Walker's achievement was considered newsworthy, but it was still relegated to the "For and About Women" section of the paper. Women may have been doing great things in the war, but in the public eye, women they remained. While a handful of others would attain the rank of wing officer over the course of the war, this rank proved to be the limit as to how high women in the RCAF-WDs could climb.

Authority and obedience are fundamental to any military organization. Ranks are a basic element of military life, establishing a hierarchy that creates order and governs relationships within the force. When the women's service branches were

105   "Willa Walker Promoted," 10.

created, their rank structures generally mirrored those of the male forces, but with some important distinctions. In the RCAF, women were not referred to as airmen or aircraftmen, rather, the lowest ranks were aircraftwoman, 1st and 2nd class, and leading aircraftwoman. WDs were not allowed to fly planes, so they were not given the designation of pilot officer or flying officer; instead, they were section officers and assistant section officers.[106] Other air-related terms were deemed acceptable. Higher ranks included flight officers, squadron officers, and wing officers. While technically the top three ranks of group officer, air commandant, and air chief commandant existed on paper, no woman ever held those ranks.[107] Note too, that the highest ranks available all carried within them the term officer, while men got to be leaders, commanders, and captains. Officer, a more generic term, left just enough room for implied subordinate status.

But why were the highest air force ranks deemed off-limits to women? In the days before the first group of CWAAF recruits began training in October 1941, the RCAF stated that "the day is not in sight when any woman's cap will bear the golden oak leaves of those high ranks."[108] The reason given was that these ranks were reserved for those of outstanding ability who had also put in *many years' service*. With the Women's Division being so new and the war (it was assumed) a temporary event, authorities considered it unlikely that any woman would serve long enough to earn them. Women were serving for the duration only; admitting women into the permanent forces would require another significant shift in attitude on the part of military authorities, and it would not come until the post–Second World War years.

Throughout Willa Walker's time in the air force, David Walker remained in German hands. Then, in the summer of 1944, word came that he might soon be released. With that possibility in mind, Willa Walker asked for her retirement from the RCAF. That autumn, she was duly transferred to the RCAF (Reserve), General Section, and then went to Scotland, to be there if and when her husband was released.[109] He remained a POW until 1945, when American troops liberated

---

106 Wadge, *Women in Uniform*, 271.
107 "Wing Officer is Top Rank," 11.
108 "Wing Officer is Top Rank," 11.
109 Air Marshal Robert Leckie to Wing Officer Willa Walker, September 20, 1944, Willa Walker fonds.

Colditz prison. They were reunited, and eventually settled in Saint Andrews, New Brunswick, where they raised a family. Willa Walker became heavily involved in the community, opened a business, and wrote local history. She died in 2010 at age 97.[110]

PRIVATE MINNIE ELEANOR GRAY, CANADIAN WOMEN'S ARMY CORPS

In many cases, newly minted servicewomen found themselves restricted to the type of work they would have done in civilian life, though now they did it in uniform. Just as a woman from a privileged background such as Walker might find herself in a commanding role, a woman from a humble background could expect a relatively modest job in the military. Some new recruits might have imagined themselves single-handedly defeating Hitler, but as Joan Kennedy remarked, "Any woman who goes into this with the idea of finding glamour is entirely misled... Her job will probably be pounding a typewriter, scrubbing floors, cooking, or something equally commonplace but necessary."[111] The woman shown posing on porch steps in figure 1.18 appears to be deeply involved in unglamorous work. Holding a broom and bucket, she has rolled up the sleeves of her wrinkled coveralls. Her shoes are scuffed. The handwritten caption—"Sad Saq"—seems to joke about the inelegant nature of army life.[112] Sad Sack was military slang and also the name of a popular comic strip that poked fun at the life of a private. The woman in the photograph, Minnie Eleanor Gray, was a Canadian Women's Army Corps (CWAC) medical orderly, a position that assisted medical staff through first aid, cleaning, and administration. Gray's wartime story can be pieced together from a large group of documents, uniform pieces, and photographs that the CWM acquired after her death in 2005. Her experiences provide insight into how women could do unglamorous work similar to their civilian experiences, but still have new and exciting opportunities in the services.

OPPOSITE: FIGURE 1.18. Private Minnie Eleanor Gray, 1944.
Source: George Metcalf Archival Collection, Canadian War Museum 20110057-020_p4a.

---

110 Ryell, "Natural Born Leader," S8.

111 Allinson, "A Petticoat Army," D12.

112 Minnie Eleanor Gray, Snaps and Scraps – Photograph Album of Minnie Eleanor Gray, 1944–1945, CWM 20110057-020.

There were a number of reasons why Minnie (or Eleanor as she later became known) Gray may have wanted to join the military. Patriotism and the desire to help defeat fascism likely played no small role. There were other incentives as well. In the 1942 pamphlet *Women in Khaki*, which Minnie Gray kept in one of her scrapbooks, the military promised recruits a wide range of occupations, and that they could look forward to being paid two thirds of the salary awarded to male soldiers in corresponding ranks.[113] She may also have been attracted to the adventure and travel offered by the services. Whatever Gray's reasons, she was determined to enlist.

In February 1944, Gray began her basic training in Kitchener at #3 CWAC Training Centre. While women were not given weapons training, CWAC promotional materials promised that women's instruction was in other ways equal to that of male recruits. The work represented in Gray's first album of photographs, taken during her month-long basic training course, is mainly unspecialized tasks such as cooking, cleaning, and shovelling snow, the general "grunt work" required of new recruits. Towards the end of her training, the album also includes some hospital ward photos, foreshadowing her later occupation.[114]

Following basic training, the women pursued further education related to their assigned trade. Most CWAC trades closely mirrored the traditionally female jobs that would have been available to them before their military service, and women were often assigned work based on the skills they brought from civilian life. They were given jobs such as cooks, laundresses, clerks, typists, stenographers, or telephone operators. In 1941, there were 30 trades available, but by the end of the war the variety of trades had nearly doubled, as increasing numbers of men left their home front military assignments for duty overseas. Minnie Gray lacked the education to become an officer and her options for selecting a trade would have been limited without specialized mechanical or clerical skills. However her previous work as a domestic servant and childcare provider dovetailed nicely into

OPPOSITE: FIGURE 1.19. Private Minnie Eleanor Gray's photo album showing images of basic training.
Source: George Metcalf Archival Collection, Canadian War Museum 20110057-020_p4.

113   Canadian Women's Army Corps, *Women in Khaki*.
114   Gray, Snaps and Scraps.

the healthcare trades. In 1944, she joined the Orderly Course #4 at Chorley Park in Toronto and graduated in January 1945. As an orderly, Gray would have had to demonstrate "a fair knowledge of the anatomy and physiology of the human body and first aid procedure, [as well as]...a good practical knowledge of nursing procedures" including the ability to record temperatures, take a pulse, measure respiration, and sterilize instruments.[115] A formal group photograph of her graduating class and a note in her pay book record her successful completion of the course and her official designation as a Nursing Orderly, Group C #24.

While Gray was a typical recruit in many ways, in other respects her experiences differed from the average CWAC. Gray's personal story is less well documented than her military career, but we know that she had a difficult start in life. Born to a Black father and a white mother in Nova Scotia, Gray was orphaned at age five when her parents were killed in an accident.[116] By the age of eight, she was a ward of the Township of Horton Poor Farm in Greenwich, Nova Scotia.[117] At age 14, she found a permanent home with a foster family.[118] Gray and her new family had a close relationship—they provided for her and ensured she continued her schooling—but it is likely that Gray experienced racism growing up in a largely white community.[119]

During the First World War, Black Canadians, Japanese Canadians, and Indigenous people fought to make places for themselves within the ranks of the Canadian military, though very few (if any) women from these communities served officially during the First World War.[120] Again, during the Second World War, the military showed reluctance to enlist Black women, using unofficial

OPPOSITE: FIGURE 1.20. Private Minnie Eleanor Gray (*right*) with a member of the Canadian Women's Army Corps Pipe Band, ca. 1945.
Source: George Metcalf Archival Collection, Canadian War Museum 20110057-022_6716.

115   Minnie Eleanor Gray, "Trades Test for Medical Orderlies," Photograph Album of Minnie Eleanor Gray in Europe, 1945-46, CWM 20110057-021.

116   Obituary, Minnie Eleanor Gray, B17.

117   Minnie Gray, Birth Register; Canadian census, 1921; Quinn, *Greenwich Times*.

118   CWM Acquisition File 20110057.

119   William Pearly Oliver's memories of growing up as a Black Nova Scotian in Wolfville during the same time period are useful in understanding Gray's experience. Thomson, *Born with a Call*.

120   See work on race and the First World War by James Walker, Timothy Winegard, P. Whitney Lackenbauer, Calvin Ruck, Fred Gaffen, Richard Holt and Roy Ito to name just a few.

channels to deter prospective applicants even after official regulations had ceased to support overt racism.[121] Grace Fowler, a Black Canadian woman, later recounted her frustration at trying to enlist and of encountering numerous roadblocks. She recalled, "I told them, 'I'm not asking you for something, I'm offering it to you. And you're giving me a hard time trying to give it to you.' So I got over it [...] didn't give a damn whether I joined the army or not."[122] As the Second World War progressed, however, the military began to accept an increasingly diverse cross-section of Canadian women. Faced with a shortage of new recruits and mounting pressure from various cultural communities that wanted to help their young people to enlist, the military finally granted access to women like Minnie Gray who wanted to contribute by joining the women's service branches.

Because Minnie Gray did not mention race in the travel diary she kept nor leave any correspondence in a public collection, it is difficult to know if her mixed-race heritage ever affected her military life. While some women's stories of Second World War service do include incidents of bigotry, many veterans from minority communities reported that race never played a negative role in their military experience.[123] Of course, memory is mutable, and how these women's lived experiences compared to their wartime memories is a field of study unto itself.[124] Without Minnie Gray's own thoughts on the subject, we can only infer from other women's memories on the topic.

Minnie Gray's wartime experiences were atypical in that she travelled overseas with the CWAC. While the military overcame its reluctance to enlist women, it still hesitated to send women overseas. As the manpower needs of the Canadian military forces in England increased, however, the potential usefulness of service-women became clear.[125] In the fall of 1942, the first draft of CWACs embarked for Britain. Still, of the approximately 46,000 women who served in the RCAF-WD, the CWAC, and the WRCNS, only a small percentage went overseas. Gray was one of the lucky ones. After working in a hospital in Kitchener for half a year,

---

121 For further reading on exclusion of minorities during the Second World War, see Mathias Joost, Ellin Bessner, P. Whitney Lackenbauer, Jack Granatstein, Marjorie Wong, Carmela Patrias, Scott Sheffield, J. H. Thompson, Grace Poulin, and others.

122 Brand, *No Burden to Carry*, 183.

123 Russell, *Proudly She Marched*, 162; Poulin, *Invisible Women*, 37–39.

124 See Thomson, "Memory and Remembering," 77–95.

125 Department of National Defence, "The Canadian Women's Army Corps Overseas," 5.

she was sent overseas in July 1945 with 250 other women. She was assigned to a coveted post as medical attendant and chaperone to the Canadian Women's Army Corps Pipe Band. The excitement in Gray's diary is palpable: "At last it came. I was [...] informed I was going to the continent as M.O. [medical orderly] to the Pipe Band. What a day!—and what a break. I certainly never expected anything as perfect as that. The kids were as excited as I about my posting. They would have given anything to be in my shoes."[126] The pipe band toured England, France, the Netherlands, and Belgium, visiting dozens of cities in seven months. Gray's scrapbooks from the tour are full of photographs, ticket stubs, labels, and other souvenirs of their social gatherings. Her diaries record the fun she had with the members of the pipe band, whom she called "kids." She was sad to see the end of the band's time together, stating, "We certainly hated to see all the gang breaking up, but I guess it had to be... Wish we knew where we were going in Canada. I really don't want to go home."[127] Figure 1.20 depicts Gray walking with purpose and smiling at the camera, with a member of the pipe band. The group disbanded in February, and Gray returned to Halifax, where she was discharged from the military in March 1946.

Though Minnie Gray's work as a medical orderly was similar to the domestic and childcare jobs she had held in Nova Scotia before the war, military service gave her other, novel, experiences that changed her life's direction. Through Gray's travel diaries, scrapbooks, and captioned photographs, we can feel her delight in the communal living and camaraderie of the military experience. Gray's "Sad Saq" image is one of many on a page of photographs, most of which show smiling friends in uniform (figures 1.18 and 1.19). Although her days with the pipe band were filled with fairly mundane work such as first aid, laundry, rations, and mail, Gray nonetheless experienced the glamour and excitement of touring in Europe with a group of relative celebrities, as the pipe band was frequently profiled by the press and drew attention wherever they went. Like many women who joined the services, Gray's confidence grew.[128] Minnie Gray did not return to work as a housekeeper when the conflict was done. Gray used her military credentials (and possibly veteran's schooling funding) to enroll in a course at the Parker School for

---

126 Diary of Minnie Eleanor Gray, CWAC, August 7, 1945, CWM 20110057-018.
127 Diary of Minnie Eleanor Gray, January 1946.
128 Dundas and Durflinger, "The Canadian Women's Army Corps."

Trained Attendants in Montréal, graduating in December 1947.[129] She stayed in Montréal for the rest of her life, working as a health attendant with small children and the elderly until she retired.

PRIVATE ROY, CANADIAN WOMEN'S ARMY CORPS

Official military material rarely depicts Black men and women. One notable exception is official war artist Molly Lamb Bobak's portrait of Private (later Sergeant) Eva Roy (figure 1.21).[130] In the painting, Roy stands with her arms crossed, wearing uniform shirt sleeves. A waitress and canteen worker, Bobak captured her in a moment of rest, with food and drink sitting on the counter in front of her. Art historian and Canada Research Chair in Transatlantic Black Diasporic Art Charmaine Nelson interprets Private Roy's closed stance as a reflection of her feelings of detachment, writing that "Bobak captured an acute feeling of alienation, reinforced by Private Roy's crossed arms and the crowded counter that separates her body from the space of the viewer."[131] It is impossible to know what she experienced or was feeling at the time, but racism unquestionably existed within the armed services,

FIGURE 1.21. *Private Roy, Canadian Women's Army Corps*, 1946, Molly Lamb Bobak. *Source:* Beaverbrook Collection of War Art, Canadian War Museum 19710261-1626.

---

129   Minnie Eleanor Gray, Certificate from the Parker School for Trained Attendants, December 17, 1947, CWM 20110057-013.

130   Bobak, *Private Roy, Canadian Women's Army Corps*.

131   Nelson, *Representing the Black Female Subject*, 29.

as in Canadian society in general. Roy, a singer, applied to join The Army Show, an entertainment unit within the Canadian Army, but she was not accepted.[132]

As discussed above, the military admitted applicants from minority ethnic or religious backgrounds reluctantly, beginning with the army, then the air force in 1942, and finally the navy in 1943. The navy had been forced to admit service people of all races when the Privy Council ruled that, since the army and the air force were doing so, the navy must follow suit.[133] Despite the change, the persistence of racism in the services ensured that barriers to military service remained.[134] Though small numbers of volunteers from minority communities were able to enlist, these individuals remained exceptions rather than the rule. Whether Eva Roy's wartime experience was positive remains elusive, but she did attend the first postwar CWAC reunion held in Toronto in 1949 where she was, a news article pointed out, the only Black woman in attendance.[135] Four years later, Roy re-enlisted in the army.[136]

SERGEANT HELEN WALTER, CANADIAN WOMEN'S ARMY CORPS

Like the material Minnie Gray saved, Helen Walter's letters and scrapbooks reveal pride in her military service and show how the military offered women new opportunities even while they performed "women's work."[137] Like most women in the armed forces, Walter's work lacked glamour but was essential to the smooth functioning of the military. Formerly a Bell Telephone operator in North Bay, Ontario, she enlisted in January 1942 with the Canadian Women's Army Corps and worked as a switchboard operator in a Toronto military hospital. Walter found working at the switchboard "dull" and within the first few months after

132   Michelle Gewurtz, *Molly Lamb Bobak*.

133   Poulin, *Invisible Women*, 11.

134   Theobald, "A False Sense of Equality," 45–46.

135   "First Peacetime CWAC," 1.

136   Gewurtz, *Molly Lamb Bobak*.

137   Fonds of Helen Walter, CWAC, March 1942–February 1946, CWM 20030265-002 and Scrapbook of Helen Walter, CWAC, 1942–2001, CWM 20030265-001.

ABOVE: FIGURE 1.22. Letters Sergeant Helen Walter wrote to her mother.
Source: George Metcalf Archival Collection, Canadian War Museum 20030265-002_1.
OPPOSITE: FIGURE 1.23. Sergeant Helen Walter, ca. 1944.
Source: George Metcalf Archival Collection, Canadian War Museum 20030265-001.

basic training managed a transfer.[138] She later recalled that, "after a few months I visited the administrative offices to change my trade to that of a stenographer as I had completed a commercial course in High School. These appeared to be the magic words for the day. Apparently there was a demand for clerical people."[139] Stenography (taking dictation and notes in shorthand either by hand or on a machine) was more challenging than working a switchboard. Walter was proud of being a stenographer and liked the job, hoping to keep it after the war. In one of her letters to her mother, she wrote, "Thank god [*sic*] I'm a stenographer & not just a typist."[140] Walter was perfectly placed to be part of a clerical sector that was expanding thanks to the growing economy, an explosion of government regulation, and the resulting boom in civil service employment across the country.

138   Rochon, "*I Wouldn't Have Missed it*," Scrapbook of Helen Walter, 1942-2001, CWM 20030265-001, 1.
139   Rochon, "*I Wouldn't Have Missed it*," 1.
140   Helen Walter to Vera Walter, June 8, 1942, Fonds of Helen Walter.

To Mother
with Love
Helen

In addition to opening doors to possible future careers, Walter's military service allowed her the financial freedom to leave home. Some of her letters hint at family tension and financial problems. Walter frequently wrote to her mother, offering money to help her with expenses. "I often feel like a heel being away from it all," she wrote, "but for the first time in this past few years I can meet people & can stand on my own ground."[141] For some servicewomen, their time in the military offered opportunities for a new life and a way out of difficult circumstances, even if only temporarily.

Beyond helping women take their first steps away from home, the travel and adventure offered by military life were added bonuses. Pleased about the many new opportunities she was able to enjoy during her time with the CWAC, Helen Walter kept careful track, in her letters and scrapbook, of her travels in Canada, the United States, the United Kingdom, Germany, and France. Walter actively sought new postings and opportunities whenever she could, describing herself in one of her letters as having "itchy feet" and a desire to go overseas.[142] In her unpublished memoir, written a few years after the war, she recalled her time in the services with fondness and mused that her postwar civilian life felt "dull and monotonous" in comparison to her years with the CWAC.[143]

For Walter, the military experience built confidence and she later reflected that this newfound self-assurance was the true development for Canadian women as a result of the war: "I think it was the first major breakthrough because then these girls came back and became more independent. Because of their service and because they had now seen a bit of the world."[144]

Though women in the services often enjoyed their experience and looked back on it fondly, at the time, being in the military was not always seen as a positive development for women, regardless of their field of work. Even women with socially acceptable and traditional trades were susceptible to public scrutiny. Walter later recalled hearing from her male cousin, who was with the air force, that military women had a reputation for promiscuity among servicemen:

---

141 Helen Walter to Vera Walter, July 20, 1942, Fonds of Helen Walter.
142 Rochon, "*I Wouldn't Have Missed it*," 2; Helen Walter to Vera Walter, January 5, 1945, Fonds of Helen Walter.
143 Rochon, "*I Wouldn't Have Missed it*," 9.
144 Rochon, "Veteran's Stories."

There were still a lot of men that held to the old school, that the women shouldn't be in the services. I was quite astounded. A first cousin who was in the air force [...] kept saying to me, "Helen, get out of the services, no one will ever marry a girl who's been in the service." And on and on and on. And I finally said, "Arthur, are you talking from experience?" That was the end of that conversation.[145]

Beginning in 1942, rumours abounded that women who joined the military were sexually promiscuous, unfeminine, or lesbians. This whispering campaign created serious difficulties for recruiters trying to fill the ranks of the newly formed women's branches. One woman who had served with the RCAF-WD recalled being booed by the public while on parade.[146] A 1943 Elliott Haynes Ltd. survey captured a range of insulting opinions about servicewomen's loose morals, including beliefs that recruits were promiscuous, that huge numbers of women bore illegitimate babies in specially constructed birthing barracks, and that servicewomen were undesirable tenants because they all had syphilis.[147] These unfounded rumours threatened recruitment seriously enough that government organizations in Canada, the United States, and Great Britain countered them through targeted propaganda campaigns depicting military women as wholesome and their service essential to Allied military success. The feeling of being morally suspect stuck in the memories of some women who served. Even in 1952, Helen Walter continued to protest the innocence of servicewomen, asserting, "I still maintain that there were as many 'nice girls' in the service as there are in other walks of life. For my part [despite the controversy] I wouldn't have missed the opportunity for the world."[148]

SWEETHEART JEWELRY

Helen Walter's frequent letters home to North Bay reflected her affection for those left behind, particularly her mother. Letters, lockets, embroidered handkerchiefs, and other small gifts sent from training camps and European towns to wives and mothers in Canada, often called sweetheart

---

145 Rochon, "Veteran's Stories."
146 Fleming, interview.
147 Gossage, *Greatcoats*, 162.
148 Rochon, "*I Wouldn't Have Missed it,*" 1.

tokens, are evidence of the challenges long-distance relationships can bring. Sweetheart jewelry, such as this locket, pendant, and earrings (figure 1.24), reminded women of those serving away from home and was a tangible symbol of their loved one. Although men sometimes wore lapel pins, most sweetheart jewelry was intended for female relatives. The jewelry is often decorated with regimental crests or patriotic symbols like maple leaves or Union Jacks. They usually date from the First and Second World Wars, although earlier examples exist. Sometimes called "in service," "honour," or "mother" pins and brooches, servicemen easily purchased these small items at jewelry shops and department stores and mailed them home.[149]

FIGURE 1.24. Sweetheart jewelry.
Source: Canadian War Museum 20110109-004, 20110109-005, 20110109-006.

During the Second World War, metal rationing made tin, previously an important ingredient in costume jewelry, less available and manufacturers looked to new materials, including the plastic base used for this earring and pendant set.[150] Many of these items were treasured by recipients and have survived in museum collections, reminders of the emotional upheaval of war.

This particular collection of jewelry is somewhat unusual. In most cases, a man sent home the sweetheart jewelry, and the CWM collection

149 See Snider, *Sweetheart Jewelry.*
150 "Can't Sell Tin," 7.

is replete with bracelets, lockets, lapel pins, and earrings purchased by male soldiers for their female loved ones. During the Second World War, with women leaving home in greater numbers to join the services, some of these tokens came instead from servicewomen. Joyce Burgess, who served with the Royal Canadian Air Force Women's Division, sent this jewelry to her mother in 1944. Each of the pieces bears an RCAF emblem, the locket contains a photo of Burgess, and the pendant is inscribed with the word "Mother."[151]

LIEUTENANT MOLLY LAMB BOBAK, CANADIAN WOMEN'S ARMY CORPS

The work of official war artist Molly Lamb Bobak illustrates the lives of average Canadian servicewomen.[152] Scenes of women marching, cooking, sorting mail, and typing capture the essential if commonplace tasks the majority of Canadian servicewomen performed.[153] Figure 1.25, *Number 1 Static Base Laundry*, depicts women folding laundry. They stand, in coveralls and turbans, at rows of tables raised on blocks. These risers likely put their work surface at a height where they could work comfortably, for longer. The teacups that sit nearby also suggest the scale of their work; they have been folding laundry for some time. As Lamb Bobak reflected in a 2000 interview, "The girls in the CWAC [...] did all kinds of things like sort mail, give messages and all kinds of things for the troops. They were really very handy. They weren't over there having just fun... And so I sort of caught them at these jobs that were very mundane. But that's how it was."[154] While the subject matter of Lamb Bobak's paintings seem quotidian today, for women to even be portrayed in uniform, by an official war artist who was herself a woman, is note-worthy. Women's very presence in the services was a significant development for the military and for Canadian society. And yet, any expansion of women's roles within the military had been gradual and carefully considered. Many of Lamb

---

151 Sweetheart Jewelry, CWM 20110109-004, CWM 20110109-0005, CWM 20110109-006.
152 Though Molly Lamb Bobak went by her maiden name (Lamb) during the war, she is a well-known artist and is usually referred to by her married name.
153 Bobak, *Number 1 Static Base Laundry*.
154 Bobak, interview.

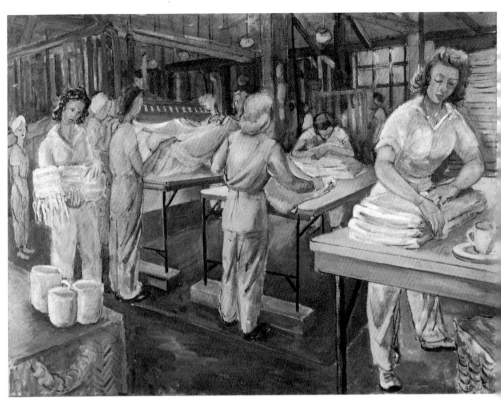

Bobak's paintings quietly show this growth. We see, for instance, the opening up of a wider variety of military trades to women, as they replaced servicemen in previously male domains. Lamb Bobak's paintings and sketches of Canadian servicewomen in Europe capture this development, featuring women serving as auto mechanics, wireless operators, and signallers in addition to more traditional tasks. In figure 1.26, CMHQ *Garage, Chelsea, London*, two CWACs, again wearing coveralls and turbans, clean the windows of a military car in London, England.[155]

Molly Lamb Bobak's own experience embodied the expansion of women's trades and experiences in the military. The government sponsored artists in a number of ways to produce Second World War artworks. Some were commissioned as civilians, while others served in uniform with the army, navy, and air force. Lamb Bobak was the only woman of 32 official artists. She is shown among her colleagues in figure 1.27. A trained artist, the 22-year-old had enlisted in the Canadian Women's Army Corps in 1942, initially as a draughtswoman. With her proven artistic skill, and a prize at the 1944 Canadian Army Art Exhibition, Lamb Bobak was appointed an official war artist in 1945.[156] She later remembered that being the first woman war artist was "a great thing" because "the Army didn't want women in it, in those days."[157] Lamb Bobak's appointment did not result in her immediate posting overseas. In fact, the military resisted sending her into a dangerous front-line situation, although her male colleagues had been working overseas throughout the conflict. She landed in England in June 1945, some weeks after VE Day.[158]

Once overseas, Lamb Bobak sketched and painted wartime scenes in the UK, the Netherlands, and Germany. A member of the CWACs for several years before her appointment as a war artist, Lamb Bobak's own experiences and observations informed her art. While in the UK, she was assigned to share a studio with

OPPOSITE TOP: FIGURE 1.25. *Number 1 Static Base Laundry*, 1945, Molly Lamb Bobak.
Source: Beaverbrook Collection of War Art, Canadian War Museum 19710261-1618.
OPPOSITE BOTTOM: FIGURE 1.26. CMHQ *Garage, Chelsea, London*, 1945, Molly Lamb Bobak.
Source: Beaverbrook Collection of War Art, Canadian War Museum 19710261-1566.

155 Bobak, CMHQ *Garage, Chelsea, London.*
156 Lloydlangston, "Molly Lamb Bobak," 119.
157 "Molly Lamb Bobak: Canada's First Female Official War Artist (Part 3 of 3)."
158 Gewurtz, *Molly Lamb Bobak.*

FIGURE 1.27. Canada's Official War Artists, including Molly Lamb Bobak, 1946.
Source: Canadian War Museum 19940072-004.

another official war artist, Bruno Bobak. According to A. Y. Jackson, who was well acquainted with both, Bruno Bobak was offended not only by having to share his studio space, but at having to share it with a woman.[159] He even built a wall of crates down the middle of their shared studio, a tale he laughingly told after they had married. Some male contemporaries may have viewed Molly Lamb Bobak with suspicion, but her training, skill, and connections made her a natural fit for the war artist program. Growing up in a home with a father who was a well-known art critic and attending the Vancouver School of Art, she had deep connections with many artistic luminaries of the day, including members of the Group of Seven. Indeed, she later credited A. Y. Jackson (an official war artist during the

159 Riordon and Beaverbrook Art Gallery, *Bruno Bobak*, citing A. Y. Jackson, *A Painter's Country*, 45.

First World War who was associated with the War Artists Selection Committee during the Second) for helping her get into the program.[160] Still, while her connections helped, Molly Lamb Bobak was appointed an official war artist because of her talent, and she left a body of war art that remains unparalleled.

SERVICEWOMEN, SEX, AND ENTERTAINMENT

Molly Lamb Bobak depicted these women, members of the Canadian Army Show, backstage in various stages of undress, contrasting their feminine undergarments and colourful costumes (hung around the room) with their regular drab serge uniforms.[161] Some of the women sit in front of a long wall mirror in white underwear, while others appear to be stepping back into their uniforms. Colourful costumes—a red-feathered

FIGURE 1.28. *Comedy Convoy Back Stage at the Tivoli Theatre Apeldoorn*, 1945, Molly Lamb Bobak.
Source: Beaverbrook Collection of War Art, Canadian War Museum 19710261-1567.

160 Bobak, *Wildflowers of Canada*, 44.
161 Bobak, *Comedy Convoy*.

hat, yellow, blue, and pink dresses—hang on the walls. The performers, who Molly Lamb Bobak identified as part of the Comedy Convoy, appear to be finishing an evening's performance at the busy Tivoli Theatre (which seated hundreds) and readying themselves to return to their barracks. With Canadian personnel in various parts of Europe in the latter half of the Second World War, each service branch established formal entertainment groups. Enlisted men and women, who often had regular military duties, distracted and entertained the troops with comedy, dancing, sing-a-longs, and musical acts. The Comedy Convoy was one of dozens of Army Show acts touring Europe at the time.[162]

Women frequently wore enticing, even revealing costumes as part of these shows. CWAC Eleanor Barlow, who performed in Ottawa with the Army Show recalled, "We had a magician [...] and I was his assistant in a short skirt."[163] For many female performers, the exuberant sexuality they displayed in these shows was merely part of the act. Their off-stage comportment had little to do with their on-stage personas. The youthful male audience members and the military in general considered female sexuality an integral part of the troop shows. Describing an Army Show in Italy, *Khaki* magazine wrote that the "pretty girls" provided "a warming memory of pre-war days" to "men away from home."[164]

Servicewomen's participation in these troop shows blurred the lines between acceptable entertainment and disreputable behaviour. One of the troop show dancers complained of unwanted advances in her diary, noting, "One cheeky fellow came up and gave me a terrible smack [kiss]."[165] While the military generally condoned the raucous sexual behaviour of servicemen, it actively discouraged servicewomen from openly displaying their sexuality. Women in the troop shows, and servicewomen more generally, were expected to comport themselves modestly. Chaperones, curfews, modest clothing, and codes of conduct reinforced the need for servicewomen to behave respectably. As

162 Halladay, "Ladies and Gentlemen," 147.
163 Cowburn, interview.
164 "Front Line Music-Halls."
165 Diary of Mary E. Carry, December 1944, CWM 19850350-001.

a result of the whispering campaign that had brought negative public opinion and sluggish enlistment to the women's service branches, the military establishment focused on the purity and demure femininity of servicewomen.[166] Women who overtly presented their sexuality were demonized, but those who eschewed male attention were also suspect.

The military could not, of course, put a lid on servicewomen's sexuality. Women could be, and were, discharged from the military because of sexual misconduct. Pregnancy was grounds for dismissal. Women were sometimes, but rarely, released due to lesbian relationships, and generally, the military moved women caught with same-sex partners to different units.[167] The army deemed lesbianism uncommon.[168] At the time, lesbian sex, while viewed as immoral and an aberration, was not as threatening to the social order as gay male sexuality. Discretion, and keeping up heterosexual appearances, were survival techniques

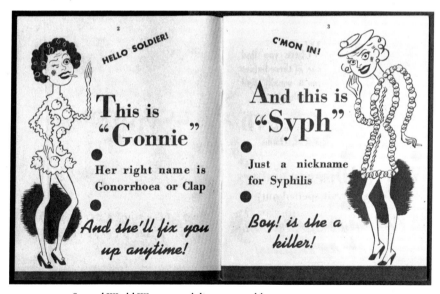

FIGURE 1.29. Second World War venereal disease pamphlet.
Source: George Metcalf Archival Collection, Canadian War Museum 20110057-021.

166   Pierson, *They're Still Women*, 170–175.
167   Greer, *Girls of the King's Navy*, 84.
168   Gossage, *Greatcoats*, 161.

that proved as useful in uniform as out of it. In fact, women who were attracted to women may have found that the military offered them more opportunities to pursue same-sex liaisons than had civilian life.

The military did not distribute birth control or venereal disease prophylactic kits to servicewomen, though it provided condoms and prophylactic "V-packettes" to servicemen.[169] Pregnancies, disease, and abortions did occur. Aside from educational materials that highlighted the need for abstinence and caution, the military provided little concrete help to servicewomen. Sex education pamphlets, such as the one shown in figure 1.29, target a male audience and placed the blame for venereal disease on women; in this literature, men are not responsible for transmitting disease. In the pamphlet, women wear disease as clothing (or, arguably are themselves made of the disease) and lure men with their overt sexuality. "Gonnie" ("Her right name is Gonorrhea or Clap") is heavily made up, stands in high heels, and a very short dress made of pustules. She waves and winks suggestively at the reader, saying, with a cigarette in her mouth, "Hello soldier!" "Syph" ("Just a nickname for Syphilis"), sports a dress made of syphilis bacteria and beckons to the reader from behind a coy hand. "C'mon in!" she welcomes, while the pamphlet caption warns, "Boy! Is she a killer!"[170]

LEADING WREN LORNA STANGER, WOMEN'S ROYAL CANADIAN NAVAL SERVICE CORPS

The insignia depicting a camera on the naval uniform in figure 1.30 points to another field that opened up for women during the Second World War.[171] While many photographers assumed that dark rooms were a domain reserved for men,

OPPOSITE: FIGURE 1.30. Leading Wren Lorna Stanger's uniform.
Source: Canadian War Museum 19790488-001-003, 19790488_005-4.

169   Hogenbirk, "Women Inside the Canadian Military," 180–181; Pratt, "Prostitutes and Prophylaxis," 116; Gossage, *Greatcoats*, 156–162; Pierson, *They're Still Women*, 200–214.

170   VD Pamphlet, Photograph Album of Minnie Eleanor Gray in Europe, CWM 20110057-021.

171   Lorna Stanger's WRCNS Service Dress Cap, Service Dress Jacket, and Service Dress Skirt, CWM 19790488-001, CWM 19790488-002, CWM 19790488-003.

during the war the navy trained women such as Lorna Stanger, who wore this uniform, to take and develop photographs. But Stanger did not start her military career in the darkroom. Following her basic training, Stanger learned that the navy was planning to assign her to a kitchen job. Her reaction to this news was not positive. As Helen Walter had done during her service with the CWAC, Stanger lobbied the WRCNS to change her assignment because she "had no interest in becoming a cook."[172] As a result, Stanger was accepted into a photography course being offered through the Department of National Defence. She may have had a leg up because of prior clerical experience from her work at Statistics Canada, which helped with the more administrative parts of her job.

While non-traditional and an opportunity for postings away from Ottawa in both Halifax and London, England, Stanger's work with Naval Information was fairly staid. Though she did have a pass that allowed her to take photos of war-torn Britain, Stanger recalls only being sent on outdoor photography assignments twice while she was in the United Kingdom. Generally, her unit developed and printed photographs taken by shipboard sailors or printed photographs for death notices in newspapers. In Stanger's published reminiscence about the war, she remembered one instance of working 36 hours straight to assemble and print all of the death notices for the sailors who perished aboard HMCS *Athabaskan*. "Because the Germans were quick to triumphantly announce its sinking, news of the tragedy was published right away and the public was aware of it. So we had to hurry to get the crew's pictures out to their home newspapers—families were waiting anxiously to know whether their loved ones were still alive."[173] Stanger enjoyed her navy work, despite these regular reminders of the human cost of war.

The end of the war brought relief but also sadness because Stanger was unable to continue her work in photography. "Being discharged was a big let-down," she recalled. "It was a sad experience, coming back and being told I wasn't needed anymore. I didn't know what I was going to do. The option of becoming a photojournalist didn't exist back then: there was some restriction against women in darkrooms, and we weren't allowed to work there."[174] Stanger tried to find work in a related field, but even a naval connection who was working at the *Globe and*

---

172 Cooney, "Lorna Cooney," 156.
173 Cooney, "Lorna Cooney," 157.
174 Cooney, "Lorna Cooney," 162.

FIGURE 1.31. Leading Wren Lorna Stanger (*right*).
Source: George Metcalf Archival Collection, Canadian War Museum 19790488_005-10.

Mail could not hire her. Eventually Stanger found work at the Royal Canadian Mint, but her job was abruptly terminated when she married. She remembered, "I didn't need to quit or want to; but when my employers found out I was about to marry, I was told that I had to leave my job. At that time married women weren't allowed to work for the government."[175] Stanger returned to public service work after government policy changed in 1955.

LIEUTENANT JOAN BAMFORD FLETCHER, FIRST AID NURSING YEOMANRY

This seventeenth century Japanese *katana*, or samurai sword (figure 1.32), may seem out of place in a book about Canadian women and the world wars, but it is in fact representative of Joan Bamford Fletcher's exceptional wartime experiences.[176] Though Fletcher had a fairly remarkable upbringing and a taste for adventure,

---

175   Cooney, "Lorna Cooney," 162.
176   Sword given to Joan Bamford Fletcher in 1945, CWM 19800177-001.

no one could have predicted that she would end up in Sumatra (now Indonesia) commanding a detachment of defeated Japanese soldiers. Born in Saskatchewan around 1910, Fletcher spent her youth in two different worlds: her family's prairie ranch and European boarding schools.[177] Cultured and educated, she was equally at home on the range as in the cosmopolitan centres of Europe. According to a postwar *Time* magazine profile, "Cowhands in her native Regina knew brown-eyed, big-voiced Joan Fletcher as a husky, gusty gal who could handle horses with the best of them."[178]

For Joan Bamford Fletcher, and women like her who wanted to perform active, direct service, the choices at the start of the Second World War were limited. The Canadian military had yet to form the women's branches, and Fletcher was not a nurse. She first joined a paramilitary group, the Saskatchewan Auxiliary Territorial Service, and trained to be a driver.[179] In 1941, Fletcher went to Britain and joined the First Aid Nursing Yeomanry (FANY). This women-only para-military organization was a uniformed volunteer group that predated the First World War.[180] On the eve of the Second World War, it became affiliated with the Auxiliary Territorial Service (ATS), the women's branch of the British Army. The FANY handled transport for the ATS, forming the Women's Transport Service, whose members drove field ambulances in Great Britain.

Joining the FANY made sense for a woman like Fletcher. As a full-time volunteer organization, members served without pay (except for food and billets) and therefore had to be largely financially self-sufficient. Many of the FANYs, including Fletcher, came from relatively affluent backgrounds. The group appealed to women who wanted to be actively involved in the war. Some members were attached to the Polish military that had escaped Poland to regroup in France, and then Scotland. FANY members acted as drivers, clerks, cooks, and administrators for the exiled Polish troops.[181] A select group of FANYs were also attached to the Special Operations Executive (SOE) and engaged in espionage, with some operating in occupied Europe.[182]

---

177 Fletcher's birth year remains uncertain.
178 "Gusty Gal," 15.
179 "She Gave Orders," 6.
180 "Goes to England," 7.
181 Popham, *FANY*, chap. 9, Kindle; "Prairie Girl Who Braved Sumatra," 18.
182 Noakes, *Women in the British Army*, 126.

TOP: FIGURE 1.32. Lieutenant Joan Bamford Fletcher's sword.
Source: Canadian War Museum 19800177-001.
BOTTOM: FIGURE 1.33. Lieutenant Joan Bamford Fletcher, ca. 1943.
Source: George Metcalf Archival Collection, Canadian War Museum 19800177-004_1.

Figure 1.33 dates from Fletcher's time in Scotland, where she worked as a driver. She poses in front of a van displaying the words "Polish Forces in Britain Field Ambulance," along with a crest featuring an eagle emblem, a national symbol of Poland. In the photo, Fletcher leans against the vehicle casually, her legs crossed at the ankles. Smiling broadly, she is hatless, adding to the relaxed nature of the image. She is not the main focus of the photo; the ambulance is. Fletcher, who, by all accounts, had a determined personality, is almost overshadowed by the vehicle. Perhaps the novelty (or complexity) of the situation—a Canadian woman serving with a British unit posted to the Polish army stationed in Scotland—appealed to the photographer.

In April 1945, Fletcher was among a draft of FANYs attached to the South-East Asia Welfare Unit, sent to the region to perform humanitarian work, mainly with prisoners-of-war.[183] But in October, she was given a far more dangerous assignment. While formal hostilities had ceased with the official surrender of Japan on September 2, 1945, South East Asia was still in turmoil. The Japanese had taken over much of the area during the war, imprisoning an estimated 130,000 Allied civilians in a series of internment camps. Many of these men, women, and children were from the Dutch East Indies, present-day Indonesia.[184] By the end of the war they had spent years in deplorable conditions in the prison camps, suffering from malnutrition, maltreatment, and illness. With the war over, they needed to be evacuated. The situation was further complicated by the civil unrest that followed the Japanese retreat. Though the internees were no longer threatened by their Japanese captors, they were now at the mercy of pro-Indonesian independence groups who did not want to return to western colonial rule. To be safely evacuated, someone had to transport these internees from their camps to safe areas on the coast. With no Allied soldiers yet available, FANY member Joan Bamford Fletcher was sent to the area to help.[185]

Fletcher arrived in Sumatra in October 1945 and was tasked with evacuating some 2,000 internees from the Bangkinang camp to the city of Padang. To do this, she needed trucks and protection, so she went to the headquarters of the Japanese 25th Army. Amazingly, Fletcher managed to secure a fleet of vehicles

183 Popham, *FANY*, chap. 12, Kindle.
184 Arnold, *The Internment of Western Civilians*, 32.
185 Popham, *FANY*, chap. 12, Kindle.

and several dozen armed Japanese soldiers to act as escorts from the camp to the coast.[186]

The journey from the camp to Padang was 280 miles through 5,000-foot-high mountains. Over six weeks, Fletcher led 21 separate trips to get all the internees to safety. Groups hostile to the Dutch continually harassed her convoys. They erected roadblocks and attacked the vehicles, trying to kidnap internees. "It was fatal to stop," Fletcher recalled, "Those boys didn't waste much time if they got you."[187] Fletcher herself rescued two internees who were being held at knife point and was injured when struck by one of the trucks. Still, she and the soldiers she commanded persisted with the rescue, facing treacherous weather, mechanical breakdowns, and other accidents along the way. And as for the men she was directing? "It shook the Japanese a bit to find themselves under the command of a woman," she later noted.[188] But her grit won them over. At the end of the evacuation, the soldiers themselves told her that she was worthy of command and that they had been honoured to serve under her.[189] The captain of the Japanese company Fletcher had led presented her with his *katana*, a significant tribute that demonstrated just how much her toughness had earned their respect. Fletcher paid a physical price for her service. In addition to the rough conditions she endured in Sumatra, she also contracted a tropical disease that resulted in the removal of part of her lower jaw bone.

In 1946, the British formally recognized Fletcher's heroism by making her a Member of the Order of the British Empire for her service in South East Asia.[190] Still looking for adventure after the war, she took up a position at the British Embassy in Poland, where she worked for several years.[191] Her tenure there came to an abrupt and somewhat spectacular end. After becoming embroiled in an espionage scandal, she fled Warsaw just ahead of the Polish police, again making the news in her home country. "I don't much care for the quiet life," she said upon her return.[192]

---

186 "Woman Describes Sumatra," 12.
187 "Plastic Jaw Souvenir," 1.
188 "They Gave Her a Sword," 19.
189 "J**'s Admire Canadian Woman," 8.
190 "Canadian Woman Made M.B.E.," 5.
191 "B.C. Woman Flees," 31.
192 "Life Behind Iron Curtain," 3.

FIGURE 2.1. Mrs. John J. Morrison's knitting machine.
Source: Canadian Museum of History D-16997.

2 SELFLESS SERVICE
Women and Volunteering in Wartime

*I shall get that box of cake off to little Jem and finish that pair of socks today
likewise. A sock a day is my allowance. Old Mrs. Albert Mead of Harbour
Head manages a pair and a half a day but she has nothing to do but knit. [...]
Even Cousin Sophia has taken to knitting, Mrs. Dr. dear, and it is a good
thing, for she cannot think of quite so many doleful speeches to make when her
hands are busy with her needles instead of being folded on her stomach.*[1]
—Lucy Maud Montgomery, *Rilla of Ingleside*

L ucy Maud Montgomery's 1921 book *RILLA OF INGLESIDE* is a
key Canadian war novel. Taking place on the Canadian home front, the
book centres on women who wage war from their kitchens and parlours,
doing what they can for a war in which they cannot fight but feel compelled to

---

1   Montgomery, *Rilla of Ingleside*. For more on the significance of this book, see McKenzie and
     Ledwell, *L. M. Montgomery and War.*

support, even if they do not always agree with the conflict. The characters in the book live wartime lives and express wartime fears. And they knit; ceaselessly and voluntarily, they knit, turning out sock after sock for those serving overseas. Voluntary contributions to Canada's two world-war efforts by women were vast and wide-ranging—knitting was just one.

In both world wars, volunteering was arguably the most socially acceptable manner for women to support the war effort. But despite the ubiquity of wartime volunteering, we had some difficulty finding stories for this chapter. We had a wealth of museum objects to choose from, but few personal stories to go along with them. This may reflect the nature of volunteer work, which is, in theory, a selfless, often anonymous act. The outcome of the work is more important than receiving recognition for having done it; women knit thousands of socks to keep soldiers' feet warm and dry, not to be heralded as heroes. Another possible contributing factor to the anonymous nature of these artifacts is that most forms of wartime volunteering hewed to established gender norms, reinforcing the notion that women could best serve by embracing the nurturing, caring, comforting role they supposedly embodied. The voluntary activities that most women undertook during wartime were things that women normally did, but on a different scale and, as museum scholars Margaret Anderson and Kylie Winkworth assert in their work on representations of women's labour in museums, "a lifetime's washing and cooking leaves no monuments."[2] This chapter includes a number of stories of individuals whose contributions fall within this maternal sphere.

Though individuals made up the backbone of volunteer contributions, they were often directed by organizations, such as the Canadian Red Cross and the Imperial Order Daughters of the Empire (IODE), or the government. These groups often positioned women's voluntary work (and it *was* work) strategically in terms of caring and mothering, giving "the organization symbolic and moral power, drawing broad public support and large financial contributions."[3] Within these groups some women pushed against boundaries and moved boldly into spaces of male dominance. By mobilizing women for war service, they vaulted themselves into positions of greater public prominence. In general, however, women's volunteering took place quietly, close to home, or even in the home.

2   Anderson and Winkworth, "Museums and Gender," 130.
3   Glassford, "'The Greatest Mother,'" 219.

Women supported the two war efforts by performing deliberate actions, but also by adopting modes of behaviour driven by war needs. Volunteering was a mindset, and Canadian women took it up with no small amount of enthusiasm in both the First and Second World Wars. Without their support, time, and energy, the outcome of the wars would have been very different.

MRS. JOHN J. MORRISON, KNITTER

This machine (figure 2.1), featuring bobbins, cranks, needles, and spools, would have been a familiar sight to many Canadian women in 1914. It fired no bullets, but in its own way, it was a weapon of war, one wielded by a largely unheralded army of home front women. It is a knitting machine from the Canadian Museum of History (CMH) collection and it underscores the challenges many researchers face in examining women, war, and the material they left behind.[4] While knitting was abundant during both world wars, historians generally know little about the individual women who took up their needles in support of the war effort, and we know next to nothing about the woman who owned and used this machine.[5] The sole indication of the owner and wartime use of this machine is a handwritten note that accompanied it. The note reads: "Knitting Machine, owned by Mrs. John J. Morrison of Hamilton, Ontario, used in WWI mainly for making socks for the Canadian Red Cross for the troops overseas."[6]

Our research has uncovered scant information about Mrs. John J. Morrison. We do not even know her first name, and "John J. Morrison" is just common enough, and Hamilton, Ontario, just big enough, to make finding her difficult. Using a husband's first and last name to refer to his wife presents a challenge when researching women's history. An archaic convention now, its prevalence during the era of the world wars adds an extra layer of complexity to the task of tracing women—and their wartime experiences—through the years.

While Morrison might remain a mystery, we know more about her volunteer activity. Knitting was perhaps the most widespread volunteer act in support of the

---

4   Knitting Machine, CMH D-16997 a-y. We are indebted to volunteer Victoire Renaud, who reassembled this knitting machine for the purposes of exhibition in 2015.
5   See Duley, "The Unquiet Knitters."
6   CMH Acquisition File D-16997.

First World War effort. Performed mainly by women, the number of knit comforts produced and sent to military personnel in the field was vast; the number of women knitting—at all hours, in every spare moment—was equally impressive. That said, the total number of items knit in Canada during the First World War is difficult to measure. While women might knit on their own, the items they produced were often distributed by charitable organizations (many of them local or provincial rather than national), and these groups kept their own statistics. The Canadian War Contingent Association (a national umbrella group for hundreds of smaller charitable organizations) reported that they had received a total of 280,000 socks and thousands of other knit articles in 1916 alone.[7]

Knitting was a subset of one of the most potent ways that women contributed to the war effort in both the First and Second World Wars: the sending of comforts. Trench life was harsh, and soldier morale was vital to winning the war. Comforts, or small luxuries, made the lives of servicemen easier. What constituted a comfort? According to the popular Canadian periodical *Everywoman's World*, a comfort was "anything and everything that brings the old home life nearer to them."[8] In practice, that meant sweets, tobacco, reading material, and knit goods. In 1918, Mary Plummer, who ran the Canadian Field Comforts Commission, emphasized that "stationery, tobacco, leather bootlaces, chocolate (good, solid bars), tins of meat or fruit or coffee, seedless raisins, and dates are very welcome."[9] Much needed, she noted, were socks ("emphatically the most valued contribution,") underclothes, and towels. For soldiers serving in the muddy trenches of the First World War, clean, dry socks were indispensable for avoiding trench foot and other serious ailments.

The call for socks began early in the war. In an article about sock knitting and the world wars in the United States and Britain, Rachel P. Maines explains that "few nations in wartime could shift production to knitting mills rapidly enough to make a difference."[10] Indeed, in 1916, the President of the Canadian Bank of Commerce stated, "Socks have been ordered by the million pair at a time, and our mills are far behind in their deliveries."[11] The military turned to civilians and women quickly

---

7   Canadian War Contingent Association, *Field Comforts*, 6.
8   White, "For Tommy in the Trenches," 10.
9   "What Not to Send," 8.
10   Maines, "Socks at War," 68.
11   "The Canadian Bank of Commerce," 1078.

threw themselves into sock production. A 1914 editorial in *Everywoman's World* magazine remarked upon "needles which are now going clickety clack from coast to coast," producing goods for soldiers in response to "[Lord] Kitchener himself [stating] that woollen things are needed."[12] Kitchener, a senior British Army officer, was not the only illustrious figure to call upon women to contribute to the war effort by knitting. The Archbishop of Canterbury gave women permission to knit during Sunday services, and Queen Mary led women around the globe in knitting for Allied troops.[13] The anonymous Mrs. Morrison was part of this sock-knitting army that spanned the British Empire and the Dominions.

While a great many women knit socks and other items by hand, time-saving devices like Morrison's knitting machine allowed wartime knitters to produce a higher volume of socks. Auto knitters, as they were sometimes known, functioned by hand crank, quickly winding wool onto bobbins and then feeding it into a rapidly rotating cylinder of needles where the knitting emerged from the bottom as a long tube. Only a little handwork (turning heels or stitching toes) was required, a boon for women who were producing large number of knit socks, toques, and balaclavas.

Why did Mrs. Morrison have a knitting machine and could this be a clue as to who she was? Unfortunately, knitting machine ownership itself is not a helpful clue. The artifact's manufacturer's plate identifies Creelman Brothers of Georgetown, Ontario, as having made this auto knitter. Models like this one produced hosiery and were marketed to women as a means to make money from home with slogans such as "The Very Best to Put Dollars In Your Hand," "Knit your Hours into Dollars," and "Better than One Hundred Hands."[14] Many working-class women squeezed small paid tasks into their days as a means to supplement their husband's incomes.

Mrs. John J. Morrison may have been a mother of young children, housebound, or of modest means, using her Creelman Brothers auto knitter to contribute to the family's income. However, it is equally possible that she may have been an upper-class woman who participated in regular work bees (a group of volunteers performing a task for a charitable purpose) using the machine to knit batches

12   Doyle, "Canadian Women," 32.
13   Meader, *Knitskrieg!*, 46; "A Hearty Response," 2.
14   Creelman Brothers, "Catalogue 101"; "Auto Knitter Hosiery Company," 7.

FIGURE 2.2. Manitoba women at an IODE sock-knitting event, 1917.
Source: Archives of Manitoba, IODE, 4.3, N 16802.

of socks in the company of her friends. Images, such as figure 2.2 of a Manitoba branch of the IODE, show women gathered to both hand- and machine-knit socks for soldiers overseas. In this semi-posed photograph (everyone is busy, but no one has their back to the camera), woman stand and sit around tables and sewing machines. Two women in the left corner of the photograph examine a third woman's handiwork. The woman at the table in the centre of the photograph is using an auto knitter. Her hand is on the crank mechanism, and a weight pulls the knitting down and away from the machine. The banner behind the tea station reads "I.O.D.E Sock Shower for Soldiers Headquarters," but the women also produce other goods; a cone of yarn holds down a balaclava on the knitting machine table. Women, and sometimes children, gathered in private homes and public spaces to knit, sew, quilt, and package their products for shipment overseas.

These work bees supplemented the individual knitting women did in their own homes in the quiet moments between household tasks. According to a 1917 article in the Toronto *Globe*, the "Knitting Room of the Women's Patriotic" had five knitting machines in war service, some donated for the duration of the conflict.[15] In Hamilton, where Mrs. John J. Morrison lived, the Associated Field Comforts group supplied machines to accomplished knitters who could commit to making between 75 and 100 pairs of socks per month.[16] Women like Mrs. Morrison collectively turned out thousands of socks every month during the war, a vast communal effort that made a material difference in the lives of service personnel overseas.

HONORARY LIEUTENANT MARY ROBERTSON GORDON, CANADIAN FIELD COMFORTS COMMISSION

While some objects in museum collections have little provenance, others arrive with information or stories that are easier to piece together via research. Historically, we tend to know more about objects associated with individuals from wealthy or influential backgrounds, or whose stories are rare rather than representative. Like Mrs. Morrison's knitting machine, the object in figure 2.3, a uniform, relates to women's voluntary efforts during the First World War, and it too is a part of the story of wartime comforts.[17] Unlike the knitting machine, this time we have more information about the woman to whom it belonged.

Few items are as closely associated with war as military uniforms, and unsurprisingly, they make up a significant portion of many military museum collections. Uniforms have a language all their own, and if you speak that language most can be decoded at a glance. Colour, cut, and insignia all say volumes about the wearer: their national allegiance, their branch and unit, and their place within an established hierarchy. This uniform is based on a military style popular during the time of the First World War, but is not official military issue. The skirt is rather plain, with few clues indicating its origin, but the tunic is instructive. It has four pockets and a belt. There are two rank stars (or pips) on each shoulder, along with shoulder titles bearing "CANADA." The pips indicate a lieutenant's rank, while the shoulder titles mark the wearer as Canadian. The four front brass buttons bear

---

15   "Knitting Machines," 8.

16   McMaster University Archives, "Socks for the Boys."

17   Honorary Lieutenant Mary Robertson Gordon's Canadian Field Comforts Commission
      Service Dress Tunic and Service Dress Skirt, CWM 19760445-001, CWM 19760445-002.

the initials "FCC," revealing that the owner of this uniform was a member of the Canadian Field Comforts Commission (CFCC). The CFCC gathered comforts—like the socks Mrs. J. Morrison knit—and distributed them to troops overseas.

The CFCC was just one of a number of organizations that structured women's volunteer efforts. The CFCC, as well as the War Contingent Association and the Canadian Red Cross, collected comforts and distributed them overseas. These agencies also welcomed monetary donations and then arranged for bulk purchases of items that they shared out among the fighting forces. Local branches of organizations such as the IODE and the Women's Institutes branches raised funds and pooled resources to gather materials, knit, purchase comforts, package them, and mail them to local soldiers serving overseas.[18] The IODE in particular had a connection to the comforts question: the organization had been founded in part as a means of sending field comforts to soldiers fighting in the South African War (1899–1902).[19]

The stories of the CFCC and the women most associated with it are relatively well documented. At the outbreak of the war, two Canadian women, Mary Plummer and Joan Arnoldi, anticipated soldiers' need for comforts. As members of the Women's Patriotic League, they went to Valcartier, Quebec, where the Canadian Expeditionary Force (CEF) was training, to check on the distribution of comforts. They lobbied the Minister of Militia and Defence, Sam Hughes, to back an organization that would distribute comforts from home to the soldiers overseas. This unit, they argued, would help avoid the mistakes of the South African War, when comforts sent to troops often failed to reach their destination.[20] Hughes agreed, and the organization operated with the "official recognition" of army authorities.[21] This official support may have been rooted in who Arnoldi and Plummer were as much as it was in what they proposed to do. Arnoldi was a member of the IODE in Canada and its future president.[22] Both were from prominent, affluent families. Mary Plummer's

OPPOSITE: FIGURE 2.3. Honorary Lieutenant Mary Robertson Gordon's Canadian Field Comforts Commission (CFCC) uniform.
Source: Canadian War Museum 19760445-001, 002.

18   Nixon, "What Loving Hands Are Doing," 12, 40.

19   Coops, "Strength in Union," 78.

20   "Connecting Link," 10.

21   Duguid, *Official History of the Canadian Forces*, 132.

22   "Miss Arnoldi Is Voted President," 18.

father, financier James Henry Plummer, led one of Canada's largest steel companies, the Dominion Iron and Steel Corporation.[23] Arnoldi's father, Frank, was a well-known Toronto lawyer and a vice-president of the British Empire League in Canada.[24] Their fathers' prominent positions, as well as their own drive to perform war service, would certainly have smoothed their path with military authorities.

With Sam Hughes's support, Arnoldi and Plummer formed the Canadian Field Comforts Commission.[25] The two then sailed to England with the first contingent of Canadian soldiers sent overseas and set up a CFCC depot near Salisbury Plain, where the Canadian troops were based. They are pictured in their headquarters in figure 2.4. Note the crossed swords and vase made from a shell casing, lending their office a military air. For the next four years, with only a modest staff of civilian women volunteers and a handful of male soldiers, they distributed vast amounts of comforts to troops at the front. The officers of the CFCC were paid, but this should not overshadow the spirit of voluntarism that had led them to offer their services.[26] Commissioned as honorary officers and technically members of the Canadian Army Medical Corps, they served, as historian Richard Holt terms it, in "a bona fide unit of the CEF."[27] Plummer and Arnoldi embodied the upper-middle-class values of their background: patriotism, duty, belief in the moral rightness of the British Empire, and the special role of women as mothers and caregivers within their own "separate sphere."[28] At the same time, something compelled them, and the other women of the CFCC, to move beyond the private, home front–centred works undertaken by most women in their social circle into the male realm of overseas military service.

This uniform, however, did not belong to either Arnoldi or Plummer but to Mary Robertson Gordon (Giblin). Like Arnoldi and Plummer, Gordon came from a prominent family. Her uncle was Reverend Charles W. Gordon, who, under his

23   Roberts and Marchildon, "PLUMMER, JAMES HENRY."

24   Berger, *The Sense of Power*, 38; Johnstone, "Diverging and Contested Feminisms," 77, 79.

25   Nicholson, *Official History of the Canadian Army*, 37; *Canada at War: A Record*, 117.

26   According to their CEF personnel records, Joan Arnoldi was being paid $2.60 a day in 1914–1915, while her brother Errol, also a lieutenant, was making $3.60. Privates in the CEF made $1.10 per day. Lt. Joan Arnoldi, CEF Personnel Record; Lt. Errol Arnoldi, CEF Personnel Record.

27   Holt, *Filling the Ranks*, xxiv.

28   The "separate spheres" theory, as laid out in Cott's *The Bonds of Womanhood*, explored how nineteenth-century women's place was perceived as being in the home and men's in the public domain.

FIGURE 2.4. Honorary Lieutenant Joan Arnoldi and Honorary
Captain Mary Plummer at CFCC headquarters, 1914–1918.
Source: George Metcalf Archival Collection, Canadian War Museum 19930003-702.

pen name Ralph Connor, was one of the most famous Canadian novelists of the day.
Prior to the war, Mary Gordon had been educated in Europe, attending schools in
Edinburgh and Dresden. After war broke out, she sailed to Britain to see if "there
was any part she could play."[29] Like Joan Bamford Fletcher in a later war, she clearly
had the financial means and personal freedom to travel overseas and offer her services; many women would not have been in a position to do the same. In Britain,
she met and became engaged to a Scottish doctor who was later killed in action.[30]
Her uncle Charles Gordon had also gone overseas as a chaplain with the CEF.

Gordon joined the CFCC in August 1916, where her work would have supported the movement of comforts. Bulk parcels of supplies were sent from
Canada to the CFCC depot where members and their soldier-assistants sorted and

29   "Mary Roberson Gordon Giblin," John King Gordon fonds, MG30 C24193, vol. 93, file 12.
30   John King Gordon fonds.

packaged them for delivery to the various fighting units at the front. About 60 percent of the shipments handled by the CFCC were intended for soldiers in general; the other 40 percent were parcels addressed to specific units and forwarded through the comforts commission.[31] This type of work may have been satisfying for a woman like Gordon, with loved ones serving in uniform.

As the rank stars on Gordon's uniform indicate, she was an officer, which distinguished her from the enlisted men. The CFCC officers were few in number and worked within the rough male world of soldiering. Their ranks were honorary, and likely conveyed little actual power of command outside their depot, if at all. Mary Plummer, nominally the head of the CFCC, was a captain (see figure 2.4 for the three pips on her shoulders, indicating this rank), while Joan Arnoldi, Mary Gordon, and other members of the CFCC held lieutenant's ranks. While the ranks and uniforms could command respect, they also caused some controversy. Colonel Walter Gow, Canada's Deputy Minister for Overseas Military Forces, reported the following in a memorandum to his Minister, George Perley:

> The crucial point with the 7 ladies of the Commission is that their right to wear their uniforms should not be questioned. They complain that they have been called "imposters" and even worse and they rightfully resent this. Whatever one may think of the policy which permitted them to assume uniforms in the first instance, it is now, in my judgment, impossible to do otherwise than recognize their right to them.[32]

The CFCC uniforms, like the women who wore them, stood out in the landscape of war populated only by men or nursing sisters in their feminine white veils and "bluebird" uniforms.

The work the women of the CFCC performed was appreciated by the soldiers who received comforts. Both Plummer and Arnoldi had their names "brought to the notice of the Secretary of State for War for valuable services rendered in connection with the War."[33] Whether they changed attitudes or carved new space for

---

31   Report, April 27, 1918, by Captain A. L. MacCalleran, RG9 III-A-I, File 10-13-6.
32   Col. Walter Gow to George Perley, April 5, 1917, RG 9 III-A-I, File DHS-4-57.
33   Canada, Military Honours and Awards Citation Cards, 1900–1961, M. Plummer, date of award August 7, 1917; J. L. Arnoldi, date of award March 13, 1918.

women in wartime or public office is less certain. Arnoldi, Plummer, and Gordon were privileged white women whose war work was still well within the purview of the domestic sphere, except that they had extended that sphere to the military realm. They were not in the military to kill or defend but to offer comfort to the men who were.

SOLDIER'S COMFORT BOX

The writing printed on this box quaintly instructs senders at home how to post comforts to soldiers serving overseas: "Fill me to the brim with good things (not exceeding regulation weight) wrap me in strong brown paper—tie me with strong cord—address me fully and distinctly then send me on my message of love. I'll deliver the goods."[34] This type of box was handy, as many women mailed care packages directly to close friends and relatives along with donating comforts to anonymous soldiers through organizations like the CFCC. Women sending items directly to "their" soldiers had to purchase the comforts, the boxes, and parcelling material, and also had to pay to have them shipped. For families whose primary bread winner was serving overseas, and at a time when the cost of living was rising dramatically, these expenses could mean making sacrifices at home.[35] Lawrence Rogers, a lieutenant with the 5th Canadian Mounted Rifles, acknowledged in a letter home that comforts for him meant his family going without:

FIGURE 2.5. A First World War comfort box.
Source: Canadian War Museum 20030364-001.

> now dear girl I don't want you to send me cake and candy for two
> reasons first it gives you a lot of extra work and secondly everything is

---

34 Tobin's "Peerless" Soldier's Comfort Box, CWM 20030364-001.
35 Morton, *Fight or Pay*, 95.

so expensive I know you will go without yourselves just to be sure that I get something and I don't want that. Don't think dear girl that I don't appreciate the trouble that you go to for I do and also enjoy the cake and fudge but I won't have you and the kiddies doing without for me.[36]

Businesses saw parcels for soldiers as a sales opportunity. Makers of various packable goods touted their suitability as comforts in their advertisements. Wagstaffe, a maker of jams and other preserved sweets, marketed tinned Christmas puddings as just the thing for the boys overseas.[37] C. J. Bodley's of Toronto sold a product called Bodley's Overseas Cake whose packaging featured a soldier brandishing a rifle and a Red Ensign.[38] Some retailers even opened special "Overseas Counters" that were a one-stop shop for comforts, providing the luxuries, the boxes, and even packing them for the consumer.[39] War was expensive for some but profitable for others.

JOANNA ST. CLAIR, EMBROIDERER

Seven hundred hand-embroidered names, as well as the emblems of the City of Moose Jaw and the IODE, decorate this immense wall hanging. The hanging itself is machine-stitched and made from a deep blue silk and cotton, accented with gold and cream-coloured embroidery threads. The embroidery in the bottom right hand of the work identifies the artist and her purpose in making this wall hanging. She signed her work, "Executed by Joanna R. St. Clair as her 'bit' for the I.O.D.E."[40]

---

36 Lawrence Rogers to May Rogers, October 10, 1917, CWM 20040015-005.
37 "Some Novel Lines of Wagstaffe Products," 41.
38 Ad, Bodley's Overseas Cake, 2.
39 "Beating the Regular Christmas Trade," 80.
40 Wall Hanging, WDM-1996-MU-1.

OPPOSITE: FIGURE 2.6. Joanna R. St. Clair's fundraising wall hanging (with details, ABOVE).
Source: Western Development Museum WDM-1996-MJ-1.

Joanna St. Clair's wall hanging may be impressive in scale and beauty, but it is not unique. Shipping comforts overseas was a costly undertaking for organizations as well as individual women. According to historian Rebecca Beausaert, autograph or signature quilts were a popular way of raising funds for war work, being "one of the more common styles adopted by rural women's charitable and benevolent societies."[41] Needle workers charged money to embroider a name on their quilt and the completed piece was then sold or auctioned off.[42] Though not quilted, St. Clair took a similar approach to fundraising with her embroidered wall hanging. Signature quilts and wall hangings like this one are a good example of a confluence of different types of voluntarism. Women volunteered hundreds of hours, stitching late into the night, giving their time and skills while community members donated precious cents to buy handicrafts to help the war effort. Their exertions were important to the Canadian war effort. Fundraising—both canvassing for money and donating it when able—was an immense part of wartime voluntarism.

In addition to raising funds, making and displaying a signature quilt was an opportunity to raise morale, demonstrate patriotism, and commemorate those who had died. Quilts were sometimes worked on as a group activity at quilting bees, which Beausaert describes as a mix of "emotional labour and leisure."[43] The gatherings provided an opportunity for seamstresses to contribute to the war effort, to enjoy a social distraction from the worries of wartime, and, for some women who were mourning a loved one, to work through their grief. For the people paying money to have their names included on the quilts, signatures demonstrated their devotion to the war effort and, sometimes, served as a stitched memorial for those who had died.

The Western Development Museum, which preserves Joanna St. Clair's wall hanging, completed a comprehensive catalogue of the 700 people and organizations who paid to have their names embroidered on it. Most are represented only by a family name and first initial, making detailed research difficult, however, some of the names are traceable because of additional information included on the wall hanging. Nearly 65 military men's names and ranks are embroidered on the wall

---

41 Beausaert, "Red Crosses and White Cotton."
42 Reich, *World War I Quilts*, 13–14.
43 Beausaert, "Red Crosses and White Cotton."

hanging, along with a small number of titled local dignitaries (mayor, ex-mayor, chief, commissioner, doctor). A handful of organizations are also represented, such as the Great War Veteran's Association (GWVA) and the City of Moose Jaw.

From city directories, census, immigration, and travel documents, we learned Joanna St. Clair arrived in Montréal, Quebec, in 1912 from Glasgow, Scotland, with her 23-year-old daughter, Marguerite. Listed in her immigration papers as a 52-year-old widow and housewife, she may have been supported by her daughter, who worked as a stenographer, or by her brother who had previously settled in Winnipeg. By 1913, the St. Clairs had settled in Moose Jaw. The Women's Institute pages of the *Edmonton Bulletin* newspaper briefly refer to St. Clair as a prize-winning seamstress, recognized in 1917 for her hardanger embroidery (traditional Scandinavian white on white embroidery) and a handmade rug.[44]

The wall hanging was a massive undertaking, and not completed until 1927. An IODE newsletter mentions St. Clair's wall hanging (but not her): "A silk banner embroidered with the crest of Moose Jaw, the insignia of the I.O.D.E., and several hundred names of citizens was presented by the Regent to the Canadian Legion at the opening of the New Memorial Hall. This banner was begun during the War, to raise funds, and represents years of work by one of the members of the Chapter."[45] St. Clair died two years after completing the work, having truly "done her bit" for the war effort and veterans.

MARY ANN SUTTON, POET

Textiles were not the only creative way that women raised wartime funds. A set of slides and pamphlets of poetry in the CWM collection points to another creative fundraising endeavour. These belonged to Mary Ann Sutton of Toronto, an amateur poet who used a magic lantern during her readings. Magic lanterns shone light through glass slides bearing images, projecting them for audiences to see. Sutton used the collection of slides and poems as material for war related presentations that she gave in Toronto, selling copies of her poetry to raise funds for the war effort.[46]

---

44   *Edmonton Bulletin*, 4.
45   Imperial Order Daughters of the Empire and Children of the Empire, *Echoes*.
46   CWM Acquisition File 20140301.

FIGURE 2.7. Mary Ann Sutton's copy of *The Last Voyage of the Lusitania* with a slide from her poetry readings.
Source: George Metcalf Archival Collection, Canadian War Museum 20140301-004 and 20140301-005.

The collection of 16 slides and four printed poetry pamphlets depicts a number of wartime topics selected to stir patriotism and urge support for the war effort. One of the subjects was the 1915 sinking of RMS *Lusitania*, a large passenger ship, by a German U-boat. More than 1,100 civilians died in the attack, spurring public outrage, providing fodder for Allied military recruiting campaigns.[47] The slide in figure 2.7 shows people in lifeboats picking up survivors amid the floating bodies of the dead, as the *Lusitania* sinks in the background. The number in the corner of the slide likely indicates its place in the presentation order, and corresponds to annotations in Mary Ann Sutton's personal copy of her poem "The Last Voyage of the Lusitania." Two of the poetry pamphlets at the CWM have printed prices on their covers (one for 10 cents and the other 25 cents, equivalent in 2021 dollars to

47   See Richards, *The Lusitania Sinking*.

between $2 and $5). Although we have no documentation detailing where Sutton donated her fundraising proceeds, there were innumerable possible recipients among local and national charities.

Sutton's poetry and recitations not only fundraised for the war but served as homegrown propaganda for the Allied cause. In addition to the Lusitania poem, the CWM holds "Over the Top or The Taking of Vimy Ridge By The Canadians," "Britain's Joan of Arc—Edith Cavell," and "Football of the War or The Kaiser Would Like to Make it a Draw." Sutton's poems are uncritical of the war, glorifying the Allies and demonizing the Germans. The number 10 in the bottom right of the glass slide pictured in figure 2.7 aligns with a stanza in "The Last Voyage of the Lusitania" that describes dead Allied children and German shame:

Boats brought in many bodies, high on the piers they're piled.
Children in death embraced each other; there's a mother clasping her child.
Unrecognized by those around, for none their bodies claim.
Died victims of pirates' savage lust, to Germany's eternal shame.

The Vimy poem—described as "An official report in rhyme"—leans on words and phrases common in First World War discourse. Soldiers do not die, but "fall gallantly doing their bit," and the Germans were defeated by "British grit endurance and pluck."[48] This approach was typical of the time. Graphic depictions of German violence and uncritical praise of Allied actions were normal in propaganda, newspaper and magazine coverage, political cartoons, and, as witnessed through Sutton's writing, in poetry.

Sutton was one of numerous home front poets, many of whom were women. Though we do not have statistics for Canadian poets, literary historian Claire Buck states that over a quarter of the more than 2,000 poets active in Great Britain during the war were female.[49] At the time of the First World War, poetry was a popular form of public entertainment.[50] Home front poetry was often patriotic, rallying support for enlistment and fundraising. Avid poetry readers purchased

48   Mary Ann Sutton, "Over the Top or the Taking of Vimy Ridge by the Canadians," CWM 20140301-004.

49   Buck, "British Women's," 87.

50   Newman, *Tumult and Tears*, xii.

published anthologies but average citizens also encountered patriotic verse daily in their local and national newspapers and in magazines. Many daily newspapers and weekly magazines, looking to fill column inches, ran poetry competitions for amateurs, offering prizes and modest fame. The vast majority of these poets have long since been forgotten, Mary Ann Sutton among them.[51]

The four poems in the CWM collection seem to be the only poetry of Sutton's that survives. The pamphlets are clearly attributed to Mary Ann Sutton, professionally printed, and marked "all rights reserved." Danforth Press in Toronto printed one of the booklets, but the rest are without a printers' stamp. The glass slides were purchased from the Charles Potter Company in Toronto, sellers of scientific instruments, optical supplies, and "lantern slides of fine quality."[52] While famous entertainers of the era, such as Arctic traveller Agnes Deans Cameron, produced slides from their own image libraries, more modest speakers purchased preprinted slides for their public presentations.[53] At least two slides were specially prepared for Sutton: one bears the words, "The Last Voyage of the Lusitania/Founded on Facts/All Rights Reserved/Written by Mrs. M. A. Sutton," and the second shows Sutton's portrait (figure 2.8).[54] The images on most of the slides appear to have been reproduced from popular publications like the *London Illustrated News* (one of the images has a clearly visible fold line through its centre) or purchased in a set through an educational lantern slide company that sold boxed sets of slides on any number of topics.[55]

We suspect that Mary Ann Sutton was motivated by patriotism and a special connection to the war, rather than the potential for artistic fame and fortune. A biographical sketch at the back of her poem "The Taking of Vimy Ridge by the Canadians" notes that she had several sons in the military.[56] One of her sons, John,

OPPOSITE: FIGURE 2.8. Mary Ann Sutton, 1917.
Source: George Metcalf Archival Collection, Canadian War Museum 20140301-001.

51 The perspective of the soldier often took precedence over all other voices in the postwar era, and amateurs like Mary Ann Sutton were quickly forgotten. See Higonnet, "Ventriloquizing Voices."
52 Smith, "Potter, Charles," 29.
53 See Converse, *Against the Current*.
54 Mary Ann Sutton, Lantern Slides, CWM 20140301-005.
55 Hecht, "Decalcomania," 3–6.
56 Sutton, "The Taking of Vimy Ridge."

was killed in action in 1916. Her own health was precarious, as she was debilitated by rheumatoid arthritis and unable to walk. But she had a personal stake in the war, one that explained her drive to spend so much of her precious energy writing, performing, and fundraising. Mary Ann Sutton died in January 1920, 13 months after the war's end. Her poetry and her slides remain for future generations to study, in the collection of the CWM.

SOUVENIR OF THE PARLIAMENT HILL FIRE

This small block of wood is an inconspicuous artifact, its purpose (a paperweight, perhaps?) obscure at first glance. But a fragile piece of paper pasted to one side is very revealing:

Souvenir of Fire

Parliament Buildings, Ottawa

February 3rd, 1916

Made from wood of Sir Wilfrid Laurier's door and copper from roof. Sold by the Ottawa Women's Canadian Club for the Benefit of the Prisoner of War Fund[57]

Far from ordinary, this object is actually a relic from one of Canada's most dramatic home front moments—the February 1916 fire that destroyed Centre Block of the Parliament buildings. The Ottawa Women's Canadian Club (WCC) made and sold this "Souvenir of Fire" to benefit prisoners of war (POWs). The funds they raised, in part through initiatives like this one, helped purchase comforts for Canadians in German hands. Conditions for POWs could be difficult, and they relied on the extra food and supplies sent through the Canadian Red Cross.[58] This object is an intriguing—if grim—example of the inventive ways women sought to raise money for the war effort.

The fire souvenir fundraising campaign was hatched mere weeks after the devastating blaze, with the WCC arranging to have the materials

---

57   Souvenir, Parliament Hill Fire, 1916, CMH 2011.161.1.

58   Glassford, *Mobilizing Mercy*, 103–104.

set aside, and asking for volunteers to help manufacture "souvenir trays, picture frames and paper weights" from the rubble.[59] One of the women behind the idea was Ottawa's Lillian Freiman (figure 2.12) who, apart from her many other charitable causes, was also a member of the WCC's Prisoners of War Committee.[60] As for how such an unusual project got going, the stature of the women of the WCC arguably helped. These

FIGURE 2.9. Souvenir of the 1916 Canadian Parliament buildings fire. *Source:* Canadian Museum of History 2011.161.1.

women enjoyed high social standing, money, and perhaps most importantly, access to power through their well-placed husbands. Other members included Marie Coats, whose husband was Dominion Statistician Robert H. Coats, and Helena Calvert, whose husband James B. Hunter was the Deputy Minister of Public Works. The wider membership of the group was similarly upper-middle to upper class. While the voluntarism shown by these women arguably sprang from patriotism and good intentions, it was facilitated by the access, wealth, and leisure time their financial security allowed. This souvenir fire block, now in the collection of the CMH, is a tangible reminder of their effort to turn a national tragedy into support for soldiers.

TSUNE YATABE, NURSING AIDE

This artifact, a small sheet of writing paper handwritten in Japanese script, reminds us that Canadian society in the era of the world wars was, as it is today, ethno-culturally diverse. It is the first in a 33-page essay Tsune Yatabe submitted

---

59   Cooper, *Ottawa Women's Canadian Club*, 14.
60   "Sell Souvenirs," 3.

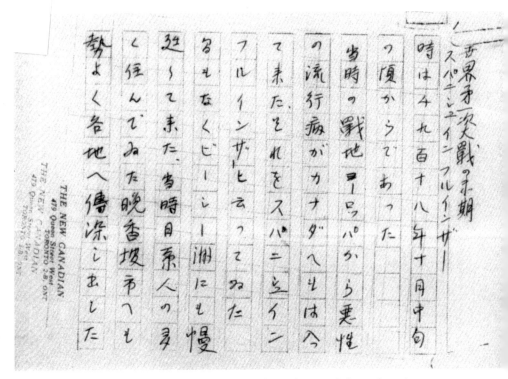

FIGURE 2.10. Tsune Yatabe's memoir of nursing during the Spanish flu pandemic.
Source: Library and Archives Canada, C-12833_0349.

for a Japanese Canadian Citizen's Association (JCCA) memoir and history contest in 1958.[61] The competition, which focused on the experiences of first- and second-generation Japanese Canadians (*Issei* and *Nissei*), was a means for the JCCA to kick start its first national history project and to develop material for a book-length community history. All entries were later microfilmed by Library and Archives Canada when the JCCA deposited its papers with the archives.[62] In 1958, Yatabe had lived in Canada for over 40 years, but the experience she chose to describe was from her time volunteering during the First World War, when she was a young mother and wife living with her husband, two young children, and two other families in a rooming house in Vancouver.[63]

---

61   Yatabe, "History Contest Entry, 16-7." This document was translated by Kazue Kitamura and graciously shared by Tsune Yatabe's granddaughter, Susan Yatabe. All of the Japanese language source materials cited in this article have been identified and translated by others and the authors are very grateful to these many scholars and family researchers for opening these unique sources to non-Japanese readers. All quotes attributed to Yatabe are from this source.

62   16-2 JCCA Revitalization-History Project, March 1, 1958, MG28 V7.

63   See Cooke, "Looking for the Helpers," 3–4.

According to granddaughter Susan Yatabe's research, Tsune Makuta arrived in Canada between about 1910 and 1914. She married Gensaku Yatabe, a gardening contractor, and their first child was born in Canada early in 1915. As was the case with many non-British immigrants to Canada, official documents (census records, ships registers, or military service files) often contained name misspellings, making detailed biographical research difficult. Her story, told in her own voice, is invaluable for researchers and helps us tell a more inclusive story of Canadian women and the world wars.

By 1921, there were just under 16,000 Japanese Canadians in Canada and men vastly outnumbered women.[64] As a result, Japanese Canadian women's voices and wartime perspectives are less often present in the literature. Their lives and relationship to the Canadian war effort are overshadowed, on the one hand, by the stories of male Japanese Canadian veterans and on the other by those of Anglo-Canadian women. Most *Issei* women's life stories have melted into biographical sketches written about their husbands, and only a handful of women's own recollections have survived in public collections or been published in English.[65] Many of the early historians (both academic and community-based) who wrote about Japanese Canadians overlooked individual *Issei* women's contributions while praising their collective forbearance during their early years in Canada. (Michiko) Midge Ayukawa's ground-breaking work in the 1980s and 1990s, which fits into a larger feminist historiography, began to reverse this trend.[66] Amazingly, there are two Japanese Canadian women's memoirs of the Spanish flu at Library and Archives Canada. We focus on Yatabe's experiences here, but a recently translated memoir by Suno Yamazaki also exists.[67]

Yatabe's essay opens with two short but striking sentences: "In mid-October of 1918, a terrible influenza epidemic arrived in Canada from the battlefields of World War I in Europe. It was called the Spanish flu." The Spanish flu was an influenza pandemic that struck in 1918 and 1919, killing between 50 and 100 million people around the globe.[68] It was one of the deadliest disease outbreaks in

---

64   Adachi, *The Enemy That Never Was*, 91.

65   See Ayukawa, *Hiroshima Immigrants*.

66   Ayukawa, "Good Wives," 103–118; Ayukawa, *Hiroshima Immigrants*.

67   Yamazaki, "History Contest Entry, 16–7."

68   Humphries, "The Horror at Home," 236.

human history and killed more people than the First World War. Historians now debate whether the flu came to Canada from the United States or from Europe, but it is likely that the war—thanks to the movement of soldiers—contributed to the spread of the disease.[69] At the beginning of the epidemic, wartime exigencies, including fundraising events, work in war industries, military mobilization, and volunteer work bees trumped public health needs. Wartime secrecy kept the Canadian media from reporting the full extent of the outbreaks. Without official guidance, Canadians continued their daily activities until the disease had spread across the country. Once it became evident that official action needed to be taken, flu response had a huge impact on home front life in Canada. Overwhelmed by the rising death toll, many jurisdictions attempted to limit public events, closing schools, and mandating mask usage.[70] Yatabe writes that in Vancouver "public schools and churches were forced to close to prevent the flu from spreading." Despite these efforts to control the disease, hospitals across Canada suffered from overcrowding and temporary clinics were shoehorned into unusual spaces. Vancouver's municipal government had reacted slowly to the epidemic, but the rising death toll soon forced the Health Department and Relief Department to press various facilities into service as hospitals, including the University of British Columbia auditorium, school gymnasiums, and temporary buildings, even at one point considering converting a downtown hotel. Non-governmental organizations such as the Rotary Club, Canadian Red Cross, IODE, Victorian Order of Nurses (VON), and labour unions fundraised and assisted with staffing, cooking, training, and transportation.[71]

Yatabe volunteered at the Japanese Spanish Flu Special Mission Clinic, a temporary flu hospital that treated members of Vancouver's Japanese community.[72] The establishment of this clinic followed a similar pattern to other Vancouver flu hospitals, with one important difference. With few exceptions, all fundraising, staffing, and volunteering came from within the Japanese Canadian community. The clinic was established at the Strathcona School, where a number of Japanese

69   Humphries, *The Last Plague*, 68–78.
70   Andrews, "Epidemic and Public Health," 29.
71   Andrews, "Epidemic and Public Health," 36, 38.
72   Kawano, *A History of the Japanese Congregations*, 13–14, 124.

Canadians had been students.[73] In her memoir, Yatabe explains that this clinic came about through the initiative of members of the Japanese community and her church, the Vancouver Japanese Methodist Mission, led by Pastor Reverend Yoshimitsu Akagawa and his wife Yasuno, who had trained as a nurse and midwife at the Kyoto Medical College in Japan.[74] Yatabe recalled, "A Japanese pastor from the Methodist church, Mr. Masamitsu Akagawa, and a missionary from his church took the initiative to tackle the epidemic."

Yatabe's essay implies the need for the flu clinic was linked to staff shortages in existing hospitals, stating that "Many patients could not stay in hospitals, as many doctors and nurses had been sent to work at the battlefields." During the flu epidemic, volunteer nursing aides, some with as little as 30 minutes of training, helped to fill in for medical professionals as resources were stretched to the breaking point.[75] Others posited reasons beyond staff shortages and overcrowding for the creation of the Japanese Canadian hospital. The family of clinic Doctor Kozo Shimotakahara later asserted that the need for a separate Japanese Canadian facility was practical and compassionate, to allow Japanese-speaking patients to be cared for by Japanese-speaking caregivers.[76] Still others argued that a separate hospital was established because of racism. According to a United Church history, "Hospitals in Vancouver were filled with Caucasians and there was no place to treat and care for the Orientals who became ill. Many Japanese were included among those who could not receive treatment and died."[77]

Finding racial prejudice in the medical system would not be surprising in First World War–era British Columbia. In the early twentieth century, Japanese-immigrant families suffered from near constant racial discrimination. Racial tensions dissipated somewhat during the First World War, as attitudes hardened towards German and Austrian immigrants and softened towards Canada's Japanese Allies, whose navy was protecting shipping lines along the Pacific Coast.

---

73 Nakayama, *Issei*, 147.

74 Nakayama, *Issei*, 117–119. As with many other Japanese names, translation of old characters by different authors have made for various spellings of the same name. The Akagawas are an example of this phenomenon: Yoshimitsu or Masamitsu Akagawa and his wife, Yasuno or Yasuo have both had their names translated differently in different sources.

75 Andrews, "Epidemic and Public Health," 27–28.

76 Shimotakahara, "Biography of Kozo Shimotakahara,"

77 Kawano, *A History of the Japanese Congregations*, 13–14.

FIGURE 2.11. Tsune Yatabe (*bottom row, second from left*) with her "church friends," four of whom worked at the Special Flu Hospital, ca. 1923.
Source: Courtesy of the Thomas Fisher Rare Book Library, University of Toronto, Rev. Kosaburo Shimizu Papers.

In *The Enemy That Never Was: A History of the Japanese Canadians*, Ken Adachi suggests this was a fragile peace, frequently broken by labour conflicts, immigration debates, and anti-Asian prejudice.[78] Whether the need for a separate Japanese Canadian facility was due to racial prejudice or because of kindness is unclear. While some scholars have argued that the flu built bridges between diverse populations, work remains to be done on racial segregation in flu hospitals. In recent decades, flu historians have investigated lesser-researched aspects of the influenza pandemic, including class, race, and gender. Tsune Yatabe's memoir is a small window into a larger phenomenon that requires further study.[79]

Racism may well have been an important factor in the establishment of a separate hospital for Japanese Canadian patients, but it also ensured that the clinic was relatively well staffed by Japanese Canadian professionals who were not eligible or welcome to practise in Vancouver's established hospital system. Dr.

78   Adachi, *The Enemy That Never Was*, 100–104.
79   Bogaert, "Military and Maritime Evidence," 44–63; Kelm, "British Columbia First Nations," 23–48.

Kozo Shimotakahara, who had studied in the United States, was among them. Shimotakahara was able to prescribe medication through his private practice and was therefore an asset to the clinic.[80] Other clinicians at the Japanese Spanish Flu Special Mission Clinic, including between four and six doctors and a few nurses, had trained in Japan. They worked alongside a larger group of volunteer kitchen aides, maintenance men, nursing aides, and orderlies. Only two volunteers, Miss Etta DeWolfe and Miss Howe (or Howie), members of the Women's Missionary Society, were not Japanese.

Whatever the reason for the special clinic's existence, it was certainly needed to treat the large number of Japanese Canadians who were dying from the flu. In 1958, Yatabe remembered that, "Although more and more patients arrived at the hospital, few nurses applied for the work. They feared getting infected... We saw Mr. and Mrs. Akagawa working very hard." As a member of the congregation and the church's women's group, Yatabe would have been aware of the clinic's struggles. This awareness motivated her to volunteer: "As healthy people we felt we should do something to help... Some of us said that we should not risk becoming infected. Others said we could help the Akagawas [who were in charge of the hospital] by giving them things they needed without directly contacting the patients." When Tsune Yatabe's husband, Gensaku Yatabe, was rejected as a hospital volunteer because the clinic wanted female nurses, she offered her services. "After learning that I applied, two church friends also applied. I was very glad." Some of the women with whom Yatabe worked in the clinic are pictured in figure 2.11, including Suno Yamazaki, author of the second 1918 flu memoir held by Library and Archives Canada. In this group portrait, taken several years later at the Powell Street Japanese Methodist Church, where the women worshipped, volunteered, and socialized, members of the Women's Missionary Society pose in their Sunday best. Miss Howie and Miss DeWolfe, two flu hospital volunteers, are likely among the three non-Japanese women posed at the centre of the photograph.

Tsune Yatabe and her friends worked 12-hour shifts in the kitchen and the patients' rooms. She was overwhelmed by the work, writing that they "were not prepared for such an experience." Her essay focuses on the emotional and mental pressures she felt: "I had never seen a dead body before I worked in the hospital, but there I saw many bodies every day. The funeral parlour was too busy to

80   Nakayama, *Issei*, 62.

remove the bodies immediately, so the bodies were left on the beds. I was initially shocked to see so many of them." She was particularly struck by the plight of families and children. She describes a family who arrived at the clinic with their child. Though all three appeared in good health, the mother and father died three days after arriving: "Their child was orphaned." Other personal accounts confirm the horrific nature of work in the flu hospital. One eyewitness, whose recollections were included in an edited collection, wrote that some of the patients "became mentally ill because of high fever and jumped out of the window. Others planned suicide, and still others began to shout and scream. It was truly a scene from hell."[81] By the end of the outbreak, 28 of the 194 patients who were treated at the Strathcona School hospital had died.[82]

One thing that leaps from the pages is the devotion Tsune Yatabe and others at the hospital felt towards their community. Staff members looked after the child who was orphaned in the clinic and an elderly woman urged, "because I have enough money, please look after the child, no matter the cost."[83] Often, and not unsurprisingly for a community of first-generation immigrants separated from Anglo-Canadian society by language, culture, and racism, Japanese Canadian women directed their wartime contributions towards their own community, packing comforts for Japanese Canadian members of the CEF; translating official military/government correspondence for family and friends (in Canada and Japan) who could not read English; fundraising; and supporting the families of Japanese Canadian soldiers who were injured or killed.[84]

Tsune Yatabe eventually fell victim to the disease. She remembered, "The ambulance came to my house and took me to the hospital. I had a high fever at the time. My oldest child cried when he heard that anyone who was taken to the hospital by ambulance died." Her husband and their 18-month-old son also contracted the illness and were brought to the hospital. Yatabe was very sick: "Four doctors lost hope and gave up on me. I was told I was going to die. Many patients visited me after learning I was not going to live much longer." Luckily, the entire

81   Kawano, *A History of the Japanese Congregations*, 14. It is unclear whose memories are included in this history as they are not attributed specifically to one person by the editor.

82   Kawano, *A History of the Japanese Congregations*, 13.

83   Yatabe, "History Contest Entry," 16–7.

84   Okawa, "Nippon Fujinkai," 8–9; Kaye Kishibe, *Battlefield at Last*, 37.

family survived the epidemic. To date, there has been no broad study on volunteer nursing aides like Tsune Yatabe, who were not a part of large organizations, such as the Canadian Red Cross or Victorian Order of Nurses, which might have tracked mortality rates nationally.

Tsune Yatabe recalled the last day of the war, spent in the flu hospital as a patient:

> Mrs. Hokkyo kept calling the staff but nobody came to our room. She began to cry... I felt sorry for her, so I got out of bed and crawled all the way to the office. I later learned the reason why no one came to our room... News from the battlefield often came to the hospital, and the three staff members were excited to hear the news about the end of the war. Many people were honking their car horns and making celebratory noises. I was allowed to return home on that exciting day. I was in a car decorated with flags from different countries. It was November 11, 1918, a historic day not only for the world but also for me.[85]

Yatabe, like thousands of other Canadians and millions worldwide, spent the days surrounding the Armistice fighting the flu pandemic that was an unintended consequence of a global mobilization for war. The flu was her fundamental First World War story, holding resonance long after the conflict, immortalized in memoir much as soldiers later chose to capture their battlefield stories.

LILLIAN BILSKY FREIMAN, PHILANTHROPIST AND VETERANS' ADVOCATE

Though the First World War ended in November 1918, volunteer efforts did not, as many veterans returning home needed support for physical and psychological injuries. One symbol that remains from those early years is the small poppy badge pictured in figure 2.12a.[86] Most Canadians today will recognize it; simply made with a pin, paper, and felt, it very closely resembles the modern versions worn every November to commemorate those killed in war. The seasonal ritual of poppy-wearing started in the aftermath of the First World War, when Moina Michael, an American, took inspiration from Canadian Lt. Col. John McCrae's 1915 poem

---

85   Yatabe, "History Contest Entry," 16–7.
86   Poppy Badge, 1920–25, CWM 19760167-008.

LEFT: FIGURE 2.12a. A Vetcraft poppy, mid-1920s.
RIGHT: FIGURE 2.12b. Back of Vetcraft poppy showing logos.
Source: Canadian War Museum 19760167-008.

"In Flanders Fields" to begin a poppy campaign. Anna Guerin, a French woman, then began selling poppy reproductions to raise funds for children in war-torn France.[87] In 1921, Guerin came to Canada and met with the Great War Veterans Association (GWVA), where she urged them to make November 11, then called Armistice Day, "poppy day throughout Canada."[88] On the heels of this, the GWVA, which merged with other veterans groups to become the Canadian Legion in 1925, began to run its own poppy fundraising campaign. A prominent Ottawa woman named Lillian Bilsky Freiman was in charge of Ottawa's first poppy day, and she would continue to be a poppy campaign stalwart for the next two decades. She is pictured here (figure 2.13) with a group of poppy day volunteers in 1921.

Lillian Freiman was a philanthropic, patriotic whirlwind in First World War–era Ottawa. The wife of an affluent local businessman, A. J. Freiman, she was well known in Ottawa society and within the Canadian Jewish community.[89] Thanks to the Freimans' wealth and her own substantial spirit of voluntarism, she was a driving force behind multiple charitable causes and a member of many women's organizations. At the outbreak of the war in 1914, she immediately turned her

87   Fox, "Poppy Politics," 24.
88   "Plans to Make Armistice Day," 7.
89   Lo, "The Path from Peddling," 245.

FIGURE 2.13. Lillian Freiman (*eighth from left*) with a group of poppy-campaign volunteers, 1921.
Source: Ottawa Jewish Archives 01-1157.

energy towards the war effort, and began volunteer work with the Canadian Red Cross.[90] She converted part of the large Freiman home on Somerset Street into a wartime workshop for the production of comforts, setting up sewing machines and hosting up to 200 volunteers daily. Through her membership in the Ottawa Women's Canadian Club, she spent the war years organizing and working on a number of fundraising activities, including the aforementioned Parliament buildings fire souvenir campaign.[91] The mayor of Ottawa also recruited her help during the 1918 Spanish influenza pandemic. Freiman directed some 1,500 volunteers who cared for the sick in special flu hospitals. During the war, she became particularly concerned with the needs of returning soldiers, and in 1917, got involved with the GWVA. Through advocacy and philanthropic initiatives like the "Keeping Faith Fund," designed to help ex-soldiers and their families who were facing financial hardship, Freiman made veterans one of her priorities.[92]

Freiman was an early supporter of the poppy campaigns. The first poppies used in Canada—65,000 for Ottawa alone—were purchased from France, but later they were Canadian-made.[93] By 1923, poppies for remembrance were being made

90   "Active Committees Red Cross Societies," 17.
91   Cooper, *Ottawa Women's Canadian Club*, 10.
92   "Many Pitiful Cases," 9; "Keeping Faith Fund Drive," 3.
93   "Heard Around Town," 3.

by veterans in "Vetcraft" shops around Canada.[94] The markings on the back of this poppy (figure 2.12b) show that it was made by Vetcraft. Created by the Department of Soldier's Civil Re-Establishment, Vetcraft gave injured veterans opportunities to make income through manufacturing various items. In the words of the *Ottawa Journal*, the program enabled the "moral and economic rescue of veterans who came home almost too badly disabled to find anything in ordinary industrial and commercial life which they could do."[95] The poppies they made were an important symbol of remembrance and a key fundraising tool, but as Freiman noted in 1929, they were also a vital source of income for the veterans who made them.[96] As one veteran declared in 1946, while he once despised seeing the poppy ("to us they represented a graveyard flower") they were now "the means of [his] livelihood."[97]

Lillian Bilsky Freiman died in 1940, but not before she was recognized for her work. She was named an officer of the Order of the British Empire in 1934, the first Jewish Canadian to receive this honour. Freiman and her husband were strong supporters of Jewish causes, and in the aftermath of the First World War, she organized the movement of European-Jewish orphans to Canada, which included her own adopted daughter, Gladys. She was also the President of Canadian Hadassah, a Jewish women's organization.[98] In 2008, Parks Canada recognized Freiman as a "Person of National Historic Significance," and a plaque now stands outside the former Freiman home in Ottawa, which today houses the Canadian Army Officer's Mess.

MARY ZINIUK, KNITTER

The label on this skein of yarn, picturing the Union Jack and bearing the words "Military Service Yarns," identifies this wool as being intended for knitting comforts for servicemen and women.[99] As we have seen, during the First World War, providing socks for men serving in the muddy, wet trenches was a practical necessity. The soldiers, sailors, and aircrew fighting the Second World War also needed

---

94 "Veterans' Poppies," 2.
95 "Public Gets Opportunity," 19.
96 "Order Poppies in Advance," 5.
97 "Poppies Made by Eastern Vetcraft," 14.
98 Berman, "Bilsky (Freiman), Lillian."
99 Military Service Yarn, Second World War, CWM 20050085-002.

woollen comforts, and for a second time knitting became a significant volunteer activity on the home front. The numbers of items produced in Canada under Canadian Red Cross auspices alone is staggering: the organization estimated that some 750,000 volunteers knit 50 million pieces.[100] Making clothes brought the knitter close to those who had marched away by allowing them to contribute in a physical manner to the well-being of the troops.

Mobilizing women for volunteer war work at the outbreak of the Second World War largely followed patterns set during the First World War, which had ended a scant 20 years earlier. Many women remembered their previous war work and

FIGURE 2.14. Mary Ziniuk's service yarn.
Source: Canadian War Museum 20050085-002.

set about renewing old contacts and re-establishing familiar routines.[101] On the home front, charitable organizations that had begun in 1914 as local committees and grown into national powerhouses by 1918 re-established themselves rather than beginning from scratch, including those that organized and distributed knitting. There were, however, differences between the knitting campaigns of the two wars. By 1941 and 1942, home front knitters were knitting for women in the services as well as men, a reality reflected in Second World War pattern books. That said, very few knit goods made for women have survived in public collections.[102] Individual families with servicewomen may have knit for their loved ones or, as is visible in some photographs, military women knit for themselves, but in the public imagination, knitters were female and the lucky recipients were male.

---

100 Walker, "Over the Top," 31.
101 Glassford, "Volunteering in the First and Second World Wars."
102 Wills, *Close-Knit Circle*, 23.

FIGURE 2.15. Mary Ziniuk with her fiancé, Wesley Johnson (*left*), and her brother William, ca. 1939. *Source:* Courtesy of Linda Dierker and Genie Berger.

What really differentiates Second World War knitting from that of the First World War is standardization and regulation, some of which came about as part of interwar industry developments. During the Second World War, knitters' yarns for military use came in standardized colours, weights, materials, and even labels. A Depression-era resurgence in the popularity of hand knitting meant that by 1939 a wide variety of wool was readily available.[103] Differences were also due to government wartime regulations. Military leaders, politicians, and volunteer organizers alike took to heart the lessons learned through the First World War, bringing an increased formality and structure to the waging of the Second World War. Whereas the First World War effort often began with local or ad hoc committees (often with bumps in the road around governance, structure, and funding), early in the Second World War, the federal government stepped in to regulate voluntary activities through the Department of National War Services.[104] Wool itself was regulated. Before the war, Canada had imported most of its wool supply, but the hostilities made imports difficult. Demand for wool increased as the ability to obtain it from foreign sources decreased. In response, the government established the Canadian Wool Board in March 1942.[105]

The daughter of its original owner, Mary Ziniuk, donated this (highly regulated) yarn to the CWM. It is one of three skeins that were left over from her wartime efforts. Ziniuk was only a teenager when her brothers and fiancé enlisted

103 Wills, *Close-Knit Circle*, 22.
104 *Department of National War Services Act; Annual Report of National War Services.*
105 Agricultural Supplies Board, *Canada Urgently Needs*; "Canadian Wool Board Will Take Over," 3.

in the military. In figure 2.15, she stands with her fiancé, Wesley Johnson, and her brother William.[106] Unlike many women across Canada, she would not have remembered the massive knitting efforts of the First World War. But like those women, Ziniuk may have felt motivated to knit because she had loved ones in uniform. In an op-ed prompted by the *World War Women* exhibition, her daughter recalled that she "knit for them all, scarves and socks and vests and gloves."[107] We were fortunate to have information about Ziniuk's knitting from her family, but even without these accounts, the skein of yarn itself would have provided some clues. Thanks to colour standardization, the yarn tells us the service for which knit items were destined. Military service yarn was dyed to match the Canadian uniforms, including khaki, grey, navy, and, like this skein, air force blue.[108] Indeed, Ziniuk's three brothers served in the air force. Each skein contained enough yarn for one pair of service socks, and came with a pattern on the label or in a supplementary pamphlet, depending on the brand of the yarn. Knitters like Ziniuk could produce other garments from the same wool following special wartime patterns companies such as Monarch, Beehive, and Lux published or from the free booklets that the Red Cross supplied.

During the Second World War, the Canadian Red Cross and other volunteer organizations associated with knitting attempted to exert some measure of control over the production and distribution of knit goods for the military, which they had not done to the same degree during the First World War. Ziniuk would have been affected by some of these controls but not all of them, since she knit for family members and would have given what she produced directly to her brothers and fiancé rather than sending them through a charitable organization. The types of garments Ziniuk knit, and the patterns she chose, may have been influenced by what these organizations recommended in their publications, depending on the seasons and fluctuating needs. A Monarch wartime knitting pattern book assured knitters that there was an "actual need" for every item in the publication.[109] One constant was socks. One newspaper reported that "the army needs socks, socks,

---

106   Genie Berger lent copies of her family photographs and provided invaluable information during the course of this project. The authors would like to acknowledge her contribution.
107   Berger, "Three Balls of Yarn."
108   Service yarn advertisements, 10, 11.
109   *Monarch Book No. 87*, 28.

and more socks. No one need fear that the socks they knit will not be needed. They will be welcomed even though they are the ten thousandth pair."[110] The Canadian Red Cross also turned out goods designed for specific war needs (leg cast covers for cold climates, for example) and made much of the organization's professionalism, noting that "branches do not work on projects they feel like working on. They are assigned the immediate and pressing needs and comply with instructions sent out to their divisions from national headquarters."[111]

The Canadian Red Cross assigned expert knitters to review incoming donations, examining them for imperfections, such as malformed seams in socks that could cause blisters. In many cases, these experts ripped out the seams and fixed them before the items were bundled for shipment. If they could not be fixed, they were rejected. Mrs. N. Brown, known as "Mrs. Fixit" at Canadian Red Cross headquarters in Ottawa, was lauded for her expertise in correcting flawed knitting.[112] When knitting directly for her family, Ziniuk would not have been affected by attempts to control quality, however, if she also contributed to local work bees, she would have had to be careful to meet the organizations' exacting standards.

Unlike Ziniuk's brothers, many of the soldiers and sailors who received knit goods from Canada would not have known the name of the knitter who made their vest or hat. Sometimes charities sewed labels into larger items such as blankets, balaclavas, or vests, identifying the organization that sent them, but knitters themselves usually remained anonymous. Occasionally, women tucked a note inside their knit goods, offering support to soldiers and sailors far from home. One Canadian knitter who had made sure to include her name with her knitting received a letter in reply that was later published in the newspaper. The soldier, Private Howard Main, wrote that he "happened to be the lucky one to get yours with your name and address tucked away in one of the fingers."[113] One of Mary Ziniuk's hand knit items, a vest her younger brother Bill wore during his military service, was still in his closet when he passed away in 2018.

110   "What Happens Behind the Lines – Socks Are Needed Still."
111   "Red Cross Organization Resembles Vast Factory."
112   "Woman Thrives on Knitting Problems," 7.
113   "Behind the Lines: Articles Knitted by Hamilton Women."

KATE AITKEN,
BROADCASTER AND HOMEMAKING EXPERT

"SEW....SAVE....SERVE." The text of this 1943 booklet (figure 2.16), *The Miracle of Making Old Things New Again: A Re-make Revue*, frames everyday home economics as a way to support the war. The cover messages are direct: "Speed up the day of Victory! Give your old garments a new life... and save buying new. Enlist in the fabric conservation programme."[114] The booklet was part of a nationwide campaign to encourage women to conserve clothing, a necessity when fabrics were scarce and needed for wartime uses. The Wartime Prices and Trade Board (WPTB), an enormous government agency that controlled the home front economy, issued the pamphlet, distributing copies to audiences of the Re-Make Revue. Part travelling fashion show, part workshop, the revue presented models wearing dozens of outfits that had been altered and remade, turning old clothes into something new.[115]

For many women, one of their most significant voluntary efforts involved changing their everyday habits to match wartime needs. While some women enlisted in the military, and others took on paid war work, most, if not all, women of the day shouldered the burdens of domestic duty, in addition to the added outside obligations they took on in wartime. They were responsible for cleaning, cooking, shopping, and childcare, and the war affected all of these tasks in one way or another. Canadians had to follow an ever-growing list of regulations enacted by the WPTB, such as food rationing. These mandatory rules were accompanied by an equally long list of suggested behavioural modifications.[116] Vast quantities of patriotic encouragement flowed from official and non-official sources, urging women to buy Victory Bonds, collect books for soldiers, save cooking fat, restrict telephone use, and even melt down used tubes of lipstick to make new ones. War needs trumped personal comfort. Radio shows, newspaper editorials, newsreels, women's magazines, schoolbooks, and advertisements pressed Canadians to conform to a wartime way of life. Overindulgence or attempts to circumvent restrictions placed Canadians in the awkward position of having their

---

114   Wartime Prices and Trade Board, *The Miracle of Making*.
115   "Consumer Branch Launches Drive," 4.
116   See Broad, *A Small Price*; and Keshen, *Saints*.

FIGURE 2.16. *The Miracle of Making Old Things New: A Re-Make Revue* booklet.
Source: Canadian War Museum Library REF PAM TT 705 M46_1.

loyalty questioned. One WPTB proclamation characterized the sin of using too much sugar as "a betrayal of the war effort and consequently an offence against decency."[117] For some women, integrating wartime restrictions into their day-to-day lives was more a case of being "voluntold" than of true selfless voluntarism.[118] Nevertheless, following the growing list of rules and regulations set forth by the WPTB was a meaningful contribution to Canada's war effort and a sacrifice many women willingly made.

Clothing—both themselves and their family—was largely a woman's task, and it was one more slice of the regular domestic routine complicated by the war. While scarcity could, and at times did, limit choices, Canadians did not have to cope with coupon rationing of clothing. In Britain, material shortages led to increasingly strict clothing rationing, austerity rules, and the advent of "Utility" clothes.[119] In Canada, the WPTB enacted a raft of regulations governing apparel manufacturing, streamlining available styles and uses of material, which then affected consumer choice.[120] Consumer education—teaching women how to cope with the challenges of the wartime wardrobe—was key, and the WPTB had just the woman in mind to do it.

Kate Aitken, broadcaster, teacher, farmer, journalist, and home economics expert, headed the wartime home conservation initiative, leveraging her public profile in support of the war effort. By the time the WPTB named her Supervisor of Conservation in February 1943, Aitken was already a household name.[121] Born in Beeton, Ontario, in 1891, she taught school then ran a successful poultry farm with her husband. In the early 1920s, she began giving talks and demonstrations on subjects related to farming, cooking, and homemaking and eventually became the Women's Director for the Canadian National Exhibition. The cooking classes she conducted there were extremely popular, and in 1934 she started broadcasting on CFRB radio in Toronto. The program, pitched mainly at women, was a mix of household advice and current affairs. Her food column for the *Montreal Standard* contained recipes and domestic tips. Given her background, fame, and areas of

---

117 "The Purchase of Sugar," 19.

118 See Keshen, "One for All."

119 For more on the British experience of clothes rationing, see Hargreaves and Gowing, *History of the Second World War*; and Summers, *Fashion on the Ration*.

120 Keshen, *Saints*, 104–105; "Ottawa Decrees Sharp Decrease," 5; "Short on Cloth," 5.

121 "Toronto Woman is Appointed," 10.

expertise, Aitken must have seemed a natural fit to conduct a nationwide campaign encouraging domestic conservation.[122]

Because of her experience, the Consumer Branch (a division of the WPTB designed to enlist the cooperation of women in supporting the board's rules) tapped Aitken to take on the role of conservation supervisor. The Branch was headed by another well-known media personality, Byrne Hope Sanders, the editor of *Chatelaine* magazine. With the help of women's organizations across the country, local committees made up of volunteers communicated between individual women and the WPTB, transmitting information and relaying concerns women may have had back to Ottawa.[123] Sanders had taken a leave of absence from her regular job to lead the Consumer Branch, and Aitken did the same.

One of Aitken's first projects was directing the Re-Make Revue, which aimed to teach women how to make something new from old clothing. Similar to Britain's popular "Make-Do and Mend" campaign, the revue encouraged Canadian women to conserve their way to victory.[124] The Re-Make Revue booklets were handed to audience members when they entered the venue. As the outfits were paraded and discussed onstage, audience members could follow along and consult the patterns and instructions.[125] The booklet is filled with before and after examples of clothes (and domestic textiles like drapes and tablecloths) refashioned into new, chic garments. Out-of-style evening dresses become new, fashionable day dresses; a father's worn coat can be made into a smart school blazer for the son; and a weary bathrobe is transformed into warm overalls. With this booklet, women had a guilt-free way of keeping their family's clothes current. Most pages include a diagram showing how to lay out pattern pieces on old, disassembled garments. Multiple showings took place in the cities and towns the revue visited, with some targeted at specific audiences, such as teenaged girls. Local women modelled the outfits, and Kate Aitken supplied the commentary.[126]

OPPOSITE: FIGURE 2.17. Kate Aitken's cooking school presentation, ca. 1938.
Source: Canadian National Exhibition Archives MG4-S2-IA14227.

122   Zankowicz, "How to Keep a Husband."
123   Broad, *A Small Price*, 32.
124   *The Miracle of Making*, front cover; Caton, "Fashion and War," 256.
125   "Plans Completed for Re-Make Revue," 11.
126   "Re-Make Revue Will Feature Fashions," 11.

The free performances were community affairs, with local women affiliated with Consumer Branch committees participating, along with groups such as the Girl Guides, the Canadian Legion, and service personnel.[127] In addition to the revue, remake centres and sewing clinics were set up under the sponsorship of the Consumer Branch.[128] By April 1944, some 60 remake centres were operating across Canada that, according to Aitken, saw 800 "volunteer seamstresses" help 16,000 women refashion 48,000 articles of clothing, saving some 200,000 yards of fabric.[129] In addition to these numbers, countless women were independently putting the principles of clothing conservation into practice in their own homes.

In 1944, Aitken returned to her radio show and Irene Gougeon took over as Supervisor of Conservation for the WPTB. Her public service was not finished, however. In 1945, the British Ministry of Food invited Aitken to tour the UK and Europe, to appraise the postwar food situation abroad.[130] That same year, her *Canadian Cookbook* was released, and it quickly became a staple in kitchens across the country. Aitken made the jump to television in the 1950s before retiring from broadcasting—radio and TV—in 1957, devoting herself to writing.

THE REMAINING MUFFIN TIN

This muffin tin represents the small domestic contributions many women made to help the war effort. It belonged to Miriam Cooper, who used it to make baked goods at her home in Victoria, British Columbia.[131] Her daughter, who later donated the pan to CMH, recalled that her mother had given up most of her aluminum ware during Second World War scrap metal recycling drives. But Cooper had held on to this one.[132]

In 1941, the Department of National War Services began a Canada-wide salvage drive of materials useful for war needs, such as metals.[133] The recycling drives and tight controls over many materials had a direct impact on

127 "Mrs. R.F. McWilliams to Open," 10.
128 "Sewing Clinic Opens," 5; "Re-Make Centre Opens," 8.
129 "48,000 Garments Re-Made," 15.
130 "Mrs. Aitken to Speak," 4; "Plight of Europe Described," 4.
131 Muffin Tin, CMH 985.39.6.
132 CMH Acquisition File 985.39.6.
133 "Salvage Drive to Be Started," 13.

FIGURE 2.18. A muffin tin saved from the scrap heap.
Source: Canadian Museum of History 985.39.6.

the lives of Canadian women, who were forced to care for their families with less. Canada's Minister of Munitions and Supply, C. D. Howe, assured consumers that their sacrifices were essential, stating that, "Every dollar saved, every purchase delayed, every ounce of material saved [...] will go to increase the fighting power of those in the forefront of the battle."[134]

Scrap drives had the added benefit of raising morale. Every Canadian could participate and feel that they were being of use to the war effort. By 1945, almost 1,700 salvage groups—formed by women's organizations, businesses, and school children—had run drives across the country, collecting mountains of recyclables.[135] In 1941, the Canadian Red Cross organized a national aluminum gathering campaign. Newspapers across the country profiled the drive, calling on every family to donate at least one aluminum kitchen tool to the recycling effort.[136] The salvage drives collected pots and pans, muffin tins, scrap car parts, and, in Hamilton, Ontario, even old beauty shop equipment. As one salvage volunteer coordinator remarked, "When these people saw a shining new

134   Bellamy, *Profiting the Crown*, 29.
135   Keshen, *Saints*, 38.
136   "Récupération de l'aluminium."

plane with gleaming aluminum parts flying away to fight Hitler they would have the satisfaction of saying to themselves: 'There goes part of my old permanent waving machine or dryer.'"[137] Whether or not the aluminum collected was of sufficient quality to be used in airplane manufacture or a worthwhile use of resources (as some debated) seems to have been beside the point.[138] Mobilizing women in the fight on the domestic front was an asset to the war effort.

BARBARA MCNUTT, WAR SAVINGS STAMP CANVASSER

This bright red apron was a familiar sight in Canadian cities and towns during the Second World War.[139] A maple leaf and the words "Miss Canada" are printed across the bib. Miss Canada was the name given to canvassers—usually adolescent girls—who volunteered to raise money for the war effort by selling War Savings Stamps. The aprons' pockets held stamps, the booklets in which to paste them, and money received from the sale of the stamps. A blue wedge cap went along with the uniform, giving the outfit a sprinkling of military panache. War Savings Stamps were one of the methods the Canadian government employed to raise money for the war. The stamps were a form of internal borrowing first used during the First World War and then reintroduced in 1940. One war savings stamp cost 25 cents, and 16 (or four dollars' worth) pasted into a booklet could be redeemed for a five-dollar War Savings Certificate. The accumulated certificates would be cashed in after the war. Because of their lower cost, the stamps were marketed to children as well as adults with less disposable income.[140] At stores, shoppers were encouraged to take their change in stamps.[141]

This particular apron was altered to fit; the straps have been shortened and the skirt hemmed, suggesting it was worn by someone smaller than the average

OPPOSITE: FIGURE 2.19. Barbara McNutt's Miss Canada uniform.
Source: Canadian War Museum 20070060-002a.

137 "Beauty Parlour Equipment."
138 Thorsheim, *Waste into Weapons*, 69–70.
139 Barbara McNutt's Miss Canada Apron, CWM 20070060-002.
140 Keshen, *Saints*, 31; "On Sale Today!," 4.
141 National War Finance Committee advertisement, 6.

Miss Canada. Indeed, it belonged to Barbara McNutt, shown in figure 2.20, who at age 11–12 was younger than most program volunteers. Canvassers were usually in their teens, but McNutt and a friend joined anyway, taking over an older sister's route in their hometown of Dartmouth, Nova Scotia. The elder sister, hoping to increase her sales from $5 per week to $20 per week, had moved on to a more affluent area.[142] Before she began canvassing as a Miss Canada, McNutt had collected cooking fat and scrap metal.[143] Children too, were a part of the war effort, and they undertook their activities with no small enthusiasm. Years after the war, McNutt recalled that, "Raising money to help win the war was a very responsible job... and we took it seriously."[144] McNutt was awarded a Miss Canada lapel pin and she later speculated that it might have been for good behaviour or attendance, adding that she sometimes filled in for her elder sister along with completing her own route.[145]

The Miss Canada scheme began in 1942, when the National War Finance Committee decided to increase the sales of War Savings Stamps by mobilizing a fleet of young women to sell them across the country. Before that, the stamps were sold at "investment dealers, brokers, banks and post offices," along with grocery and drug stores.[146] As a young girl, McNutt was different from the considerably older Miss Canadas featured in ads and on posters. The publicity campaign framed the army of red-aproned Miss Canadas as the embodiment of youthful good health and wholesome patriotism. The campaign blatantly traded on femininity to sell the stamps (there were no "Mr. Canadas") and the use of young, pretty women as sales bait was certainly not new or novel. An advertisement for Eaton's department store in Winnipeg heralded the arrival of Miss Canada in almost mythic terms as "a symbolic figure which will appear to you in the form of an attractive young woman garbed in a scarlet jumper apron and blue service cap."[147] Almost every article mentioning the women referred to their youth and good looks or alluded

OPPOSITE: FIGURE 2.20. Barbara McNutt in her Miss Canada uniform, ca. 1945. *Source:* George Metcalf Archival Collection, Canadian War Museum 20150269-001_600.

142 CWM Acquisition File 20070060.
143 Pope, "New Exhibit Features Women."
144 Pope, "New Exhibit Features Women."
145 CWM Acquisition File 20070060.
146 Wood Gundy advertisement, 14; "Map Out Program," 13.
147 Eaton's advertisement, 20.

to their feminine attributes. Whether this was effective is difficult to measure, but one writer for the Saskatoon *Star-Phoenix* noted, "You can't avoid them and you can't resist their salesmanship. And Canada needs the money."[148]

In reality, the Miss Canadas could not always count on an enthusiastic response. Canadians, already pushed to buy Victory Bonds, to conserve, to drive less, to work more, and now to ration food (sugar in July, tea and coffee in August, with more to come) were showing signs of war weariness. According to the *Ottawa Journal*, "Miss Canada, eh?" followed by a chuckle, was "Ottawa's No. 1 formula for polite refusal," followed by "Thanks, but I just bought some."[149] Barbara McNutt used her canvassing time wisely, going only to the homes where she was reasonably sure the occupants would buy stamps. She later remembered "going to every house for a few weeks until we settled into just calling at homes where we knew someone would buy a stamp or two... Many of our customers were people we knew from the church and community, and we sometimes got invited in to sample fresh-made cookies."[150] McNutt's strategy, and the work of other Miss Canadas across the country, paid off. During the Second World War, the stamps raised $318 million. While this was much less than the staggering $12.5 billion raised by the better-known Victory Bonds, it was certainly not an insignificant amount.[151] As with the conservation campaign, the push to sell War Savings Stamps had non-monetary value as well, in how it pulled young people, such as Barbara McNutt, into the war effort.

JEANNETTE CONNON "CONNIE" LAIDLAW, VENTRILOQUIST

As artifacts go, the object in figure 2.21 is perhaps one of the oddest to appear in the collection of a military history museum.[152] Standing about three-and-a-half feet tall, wearing a flower-print dress and proper white gloves, "Charlotte" was brought to life by a teenage ventriloquist known as Connie Laidlaw during the

---

148   "Girl Would Meet Boy," 3.
149   "Miss Canadas Won't Take No," 10.
150   CWM Acquisition File 20070060.
151   Keshen, *Saints*, 31–32.
152   Connie Laidlaw's Ventriloquist Figure, CWM 20130158-001.

Second World War. With Charlotte perched on her lap, Laidlaw performed shows for military personnel as a member of the Victory Entertainers troupe. Although no comprehensive list exists of Canadian wartime amateur entertainment troupes, one theatre historian, Patrick O'Neill, estimated their number to be in the hundreds.[153] With around one million Canadians in uniform over the course of the Second World War, these groups helped amuse troops during the leisure time they had on the home front, while they trained and waited for deployment. Only a few amateur troupes travelled overseas; most, Victory Entertainers included, stayed in Canada.

Canadians showed interest in entertaining the troops almost as soon as the war started. The Victory Entertainers, founded in Hamilton, performed their first show a mere 18 days after the declaration of war, at the Stanley Barracks in Toronto.[154] So many people were willing to entertain troops that the Department of National Defence established a special division to handle all those who wanted to offer their services.[155] Some of these performers were professionals (some were even enlisted military members themselves), but most, like Laidlaw, were civilian amateurs. These groups travelled the country, performing where troops were present, offering a distraction from the tensions and boredom of wartime. Laidlaw was not a part of the Victory Entertainers from its start, though she was apparently performing for soldiers as early as 1941, at age 12.[156] She joined the Victory Entertainers as a teenager, using Charlotte as her act.

While some of the entertainment groups had their roots in local amateur theatre companies, many appear to have been organized quickly by those who wanted to do something useful to help the war effort. Many troupes sported patriotic or

FOLLOWING PAGE (LEFT): FIGURE 2.21. Jeannette Connon Laidlaw's ventriloquist figure "Charlotte."
Source: Canadian War Museum 20130158-001.
FOLLOWING PAGE (RIGHT): FIGURE 2.22. Jeannette Connon Laidlaw with "Charlotte," 1940–1948.
Source: City of Toronto Archives, fonds 1266, item 125798.

153 O'Neill, "The Halifax Concert Party."
154 O'Neill "The Halifax Concert Party."
155 O'Neill "The Halifax Concert Party."
156 "Chorley Park Concert," 10.

military-inspired names (including the Tin Hats and the Bluebell Bullets) and there was a distinct "do it yourself" element to the costuming, choreography, and sets. Charlotte's clothes have this make-do feel. While her dress and hat appear to be specially made, her gloves, brooch, and shoes (decades out-of-style) are real and probably someone's discards. Margaret Tollefsen (née Hendstridge), a teen-aged entertainer with the Highlights Revue, recalled that her whole family was involved in the show. Her father and his friend (both First World War veterans who were too old to enlist but wanted to contribute) dreamed up the idea for the show and her mother and her friend worked behind the scenes.[157]

In an effort to entertain thousands of military personnel, week after week, these "Victory shows" usually featured an array of dancers, comedians, acrobats, musical acts, and other novelties. An advertisement for a troop show performance in Wetaskiwin, Alberta, drew audience members by promising "A Breezy Riotous Fun-Fest: Wit, Music, Vaudeville, Burlesque, Song."[158] Connie Laidlaw was cer-tainly a novel act: one of the few women performing as ventriloquists in North America, and possibly the only one in Toronto. She made the news, including in this press photograph (figure 2.22), which was later published in the *Globe and Mail* along with an article. Towards the end of the war, the Victory Entertainers were recognized for their years of hard work in a ceremony held at Exhibition Park, where they received "army medals [...] for [the troupe's] 266 camp shows."[159]

Laidlaw continued working with Charlotte after the war, still a rarity in the niche world of ventriloquism. The *Globe and Mail* called her "Canada's only girl Bergen," in reference to famous ventriloquist Edgar Bergen.[160] She also competed in the Miss Canada beauty pageant, finishing in the top 10 in 1948 and again in 1951.[161] She eventually married and moved to Australia, where she became a cultural officer at the Canadian Consulate in Sydney. Charlotte, the ventriloquist figure, came into the care of a fellow performer in the Victory Entertainers. Charlotte now resides in the collection of the Canadian War Museum.

---

157 Tollefsen, interview.
158 "Lever Brothers Lifebuoy Follies," 9.
159 "Connie and Charlotte," CWM Acquisition File 20130158.
160 "Canada's Only Girl 'Bergen,'" 4.
161 "Slender Halifax Blonde," 9; "Appearance – In Street Clothes," 18.

3

BACKING THE ATTACK
Women Workers at War

NOT EVERYONE MAKES THE NEWS WHEN THEY START A NEW job. In May 1942, 28-year-old Ethel Harvey did just that when she began working at a shipyard in Victoria, British Columbia. Harvey was the first woman welder in the city, and her employment raised the ire of the local Boilermakers' Union. A union spokesman was adamant that "as long as there are men available there is no need for women.[1]" He argued there were other, much more appropriate ways women could help support the war, such as "nursing, cooking, sewing, or even joining the army."[2] For her part, Harvey had no intention of giving up her job. "This is my war effort," she argued in response, "and I am proving that women can do this class of work satisfactorily."[3] Other labour leaders were

OPPOSITE: FIGURE 3.1. *On the Land*, 1918–1919, Florence Wyle.
Source: Beaverbrook War Art, Collection Canadian War Museum 19710261-0421.

1   "Woman Welder Meets Labour," 19.
2   "Woman Welder Meets Labour," 19.
3   "Woman Welder Meets Labour," 19.

supportive of Harvey, citing the needs of war production.[4] The Boilermaker's Union changed their stance a few months later, voting to accept women members as long as they were paid the same as male workers.[5] But it was no victory for Ethel Harvey. By that point, she was no longer at the shipyard, union hostility having forced her out.

Women pushed against many barriers during the world wars, breaking through some and weakening others, and the labour force was one of them. Many Canadian women spent their wars working for pay, in jobs directly or indirectly linked to the two war efforts. As men left the workforce for the military, demand for food, munitions, and other war supplies ramped up. One answer to wartime labour shortages was obvious: employ more women. And women were available. They entered the workforce for multiple reasons: financial need, patriotism, and boredom, to name just a few. As the stories told here show, much of their work was performed in munitions factories, on farms, or in clerical settings. For other women, the war opened up opportunities to develop their talents in more unusual ways, career paths that peacetime might not have offered.

The women in this chapter came from a variety of backgrounds, although most were from working- or middle-class families. Their wartime workforce experiences include pride and praise, as well as harassment and gendered rules and regulations. What happened to their jobs at the end of the wars is folded into their wartime stories. Most women were let go as the men—now veterans—returned looking to resume their peacetime lives. For some, we know quite a bit about their lives and experiences, while others left only traces behind. Together, they illustrate a number of ways the wars created opportunities for women to make a living while contributing to Canada's two war efforts.

FLORENCE WYLE AND FRANCES LORING, WAR ARTISTS

These bronze sculptures are powerful and graceful all at once. *On the Land* (figure 3.1) by Florence Wyle depicts a young woman, shovel in hand, putting her back into farm work.[6] The woman captured in Frances Loring's *The Shell Finisher* (fig-

OPPOSITE: FIGURE 3.2. *The Shell Finisher*, 1918–1919, Frances Loring.
Source: Beaverbrook War Art, Collection Canadian War Museum 19710261-0414.

4   "Labour Leaders Support," 13.
5   "Union Accepts Women," 14.
6   Wyle, *On the Land* and Loring, *The Shell Finisher*.

ure 3.2) hoists munitions onto her shoulders. Both are from a series of 14 sculptures of civilian war workers created by Loring and Wyle, two of Canada's foremost sculptors. The women depicted in these works are strapping, forceful, yet still unmistakeably feminine; they have strong jaws, necks, and calves but their work clothes, while loose, cling and drape from their bodies so that the viewer cannot mistake their hips, breasts, and thighs. They were symbolic of a new labour force and, by extension, new work for women. As men went off to fight, women streamed into the workforce, filling positions that had been vacated by male workers and occupying new ones. Between 1911, three years before the outbreak of the First World War, and 1921, the number of women in the paid workforce grew by approximately one third.[7] In addition, the types of labour women were allowed to do expanded. Before the war, most Canadian women who worked were employed in a narrow group of jobs considered acceptable for women, including teaching, nursing, and domestic service. While the work women did could be physical and strenuous, they were generally excluded from jobs requiring heavy physical work. This changed with the war. These 14 sculptures show women (and a few men) occupied in hard, manual labour. Their physical postures and facial expressions evoke long hours of work in demanding circumstances. A relief panel by Loring, titled *Noon Hour in a Munitions Plant*, captured a wartime workplace where women and men worked alongside each other, dirty and exhausted but strong and determined.[8]

Their clothes—trousered legs at a time when most women wore skirts; sleeves rolled up—denote physical labour requiring practical attire. In her study of trousers and British munitions workers, Jennifer Roberts notes that "trousers were expressly distributed for work involving very dirty work, climbing ladders or to the crane drivers to preserve the women's decency when working up high."[9] As figure 3.5, a photograph of Toronto area munitions workers, shows, not all women in war work, or even in munitions plants, wore trousers. During both world wars, individual factories advised their workers which uniforms were suitable, and labourers sourced their clothing locally. For historians, as a result, there is little standardization to be found across the country, within one industry, or even when looking at photographs of women working side by side in the same workplace.

7   Street, "Patriotic, Not Permanent," 149.
8   Cameron, *And Beauty Answers*, 114.
9   Roberts, "A Biography of the Trousered."

The Canadian War Memorials Fund commissioned these sculptures in 1918. Max Aitken (later Lord Beaverbrook) was the force behind the fund. Wealthy and influential, Aitken had already created the Canadian War Records Office out of a desire to document and publicize Canada's war effort, and the fund was an extension of that initiative. Under the program, over 100 artists—civilian and military—were commissioned to capture Canada's wartime experiences in their work.[10] Some, like future Group of Seven members A. Y. Jackson and Frederick Varley, served in the military and painted front line scenes, while others remained behind the lines or on the home front, depicting training, war work, and other activities that supported the war effort. This was Canada's first official war art program, and it established a precedent that would continue during the Second World War.[11]

The first works the fund commissioned focused on the military. But by 1918, they had extended the scope of the program to include home front subjects.[12] In 1918, Eric Brown, the Director of the National Gallery of Canada, approached Wyle and Loring on behalf of the chairman of the Gallery's board of trustees, Sir Edmund Walker, who also sat on the Committee of the Canadian War Records Office. They hoped that Wyle and Loring would undertake a series of works documenting war workers, particularly women, in Canada. Brown had been inspired by the sight of women war workers he had seen in Toronto. He had seen "the various types of girl war workers in their working clothes, munitions makers, aeroplane girls, land workers, fruit pickers, etc.," and he believed that they would be "very fine subjects for a series of small bronzes."[13] Arguably, the commissioning of these sculptures indicated official recognition of women war workers as a significant part of Canada's wartime experience.

Despite this, rarely do women appear as the main subjects in Canada's First World War art. The works of Edward Manly McDonald, Gerald Moira, and Mabel May are among the few exceptions, along with Loring and Wyle. The latter's work also stands out within this select group for other reasons. Art historian Catherine Speck described their sculptures as "the most transgressive artworks representing

---

10   Brandon, *Art and War*, 45.
11   Brandon, "A Unique and Important Asset," 67–74.
12   Tippett, *Art at the Service of War*, 49–51; Butlin, "Women Making Shells," 42.
13   Boyanoski, *Loring and Wyle*, 21.

FIGURE 3.3. Sculptors Frances Loring and Florence Wyle, 1950.
Source: Photograph by Gilbert A. Milne. Archives of Ontario C 3-1-0-0-666.

female labour during the First World War. [...] The women fill the space they occupy, with bronze an ideal sculptural medium to highlight muscles and bodies moving, and folds in clothing."[14] Loring and Wyle's women are not fragile; they are (quite literally) solid depictions of women who are taking an active role in war. They are not depicted as passive, waiting for their men to return home, or weeping over a fallen soldier. They suggest movement and purpose. The Art Gallery of Toronto exhibited a number of the sculptures upon their completion in a special exhibition of war memorials in the fall of 1919. Critics at the time praised the

14   Speck, *Beyond the Battlefield*, 34–35.

work. One reviewer wrote that "the dress and attitude of women workers in field and factory, from being the subject of 'farmerette' jokes, has here been turned to account as the source of a beauty that is finely nervous and supple."[15]

While the sculptures represent a particular field of women's war work, the story of the artists who created these pieces depicts another, if less common way that women contributed to the war effort. Florence Wyle and Frances Loring, who appear in figure 3.3, were American-born artists who had moved to Toronto shortly before the First World War.[16] They had a very close partnership, both professionally and personally. Historians and biographers have speculated about their sexual orientation, but they lived at a time when same-sex relations were socially unacceptable and actively hidden from view. We know they lived and worked together for 50 years, dying within weeks of each other.[17] And we know they left behind sculptures that emphasize—almost reverently—powerful female bodies performing uncommon pursuits for women.

Sculpting itself was an unusual choice at the time. A 1914 *Women's Saturday Night* article listed Loring and Wyle as two of the three known female sculptors in Canada.[18] In addition, few of the artists who received commissions from the fund were women. Of the 123 Canadian War Memorials Fund artists listed by R. F. Wodehouse in his *A Check List of the War Collections of World War I, 1914-1918 and World War II, 1939-1945* only 14 were women.[19] A handful portrayed women in their works. When the Art Gallery of Toronto exhibited Loring and Wyle's sculptures, viewers not only applauded the representation of the subjects, but of the skill of the artists themselves, praising their abilities above those of their male contemporaries. Eric Brown congratulated the two artists and, in his letter, included a comment by A. Y. Jackson, writing, "He says you have done a series of bronzes which make him wish to knock down all the statues in Toronto and let you replace them with anything you wish."[20]

Loring and Wyle's wartime contributions were not limited to these sculptures; both women created other patriotic war art during the First World War. Wyle

15   Boyanoski, *Loring and Wyle*, 23.
16   Boyanoski, *Loring and Wyle*, 10.
17   "Loss to Sculpture," D5.
18   Sisler, *The Girls*, 24.
19   Wodehouse, *Check List*.
20   Boyanoski, *Loring and Wyle*, 23.

concentrated on smaller pieces, including a bronze relief commemorating the martyred nursing sister Edith Cavell, displayed at the Toronto General Hospital.[21] Loring, on the other hand, created numerous monumental pieces during and following the war. One of the earliest, *Miss Canada*, which Loring constructed in 1917 for the main entrance of the T. Eaton Co. on Yonge Street, was visually stunning but purely ephemeral. Constructed of plaster, the 16-foot figure represented Canada as a triumph of the British Empire upon the 50th anniversary of Confederation. In wartime Toronto, the public and the press applauded the sculpture's patriotic motifs (red ensign, provincial coats of arms, laurel, and maple leaves) as symbols of "the brave and dauntless spirit of Canada's young men and women."[22]

If their sculptures contributed to the war effort, the war also contributed to Loring and Wyle's career. The First World War was a high-water mark for them, bringing both public recognition and financial stability. As biographer Elspeth Cameron writes, "The First World War was probably the best thing that could have happened to Florence Wyle and Frances Loring, although at first glance it seemed inimical to their lives and art."[23] The public appetite for patriotic sculptures augmented rather than diminished at the end of the First World War. The end of the war in 1918 brought work to sculptors and stone masons across the country as towns built memorials to commemorate their local dead. Hundreds of small cenotaphs and imposing monuments dotted the landscape by 1930, and with fundraising efforts foundering during the Great Depression, many monuments were completed only years before the outbreak of the Second World War. The need for a large number of sculptors to create public monuments was unprecedented and fed Loring and Wyle's careers in a way that would not have been possible without the First World War. Loring's large-scale works lent themselves well to war memorials.[24] The call for war memorials was so overwhelming that Loring eventually expressed frustration with the work, preferring the breadth of her earlier sculptures of war workers produced for the Canadian War Memorials Fund.

---

21   Boyanoski, *Loring and Wyle*, 22. Edith Cavell was a British nurse executed as a spy by the Germans in 1915 after helping servicemen to escape occupied Belgium. Depicted as a martyr throughout the Allied nations, her story was used as a means of promoting recruitment, stirring patriotic sentiment, and raising funds for the war effort.

22   Cameron, *And Beauty Answers*, 107.

23   Cameron, *And Beauty Answers*, 109.

24   Boyanoski, *Loring and Wyle*, 31.

She found the memorials repetitious and eventually uninspiring, noting in a letter, "We have wasted a lot of time on fool monuments that we would have preferred putting on war records."[25] Regardless of Loring's frustration with the repetitiveness of the war memorial sculptures, they did represent a period of visibility and financial stability that was not assured into the future.

The Second World War and postwar period were not as fruitful for Loring and Wyle. Though they had continued to make their living as sculptors through the Great Depression, the government had significantly reduced its spending on public art and the artists' situation was financially precarious. The outbreak of the Second World War was not met with the same patriotic fervour as during the First World War. The artistic community, noting a reluctance on the part of the Canadian government to invest in the arts, met in Kingston in 1941 to discuss the issue. Loring and Wyle were among the 150 artists, patrons, scholars, and gallery directors in attendance at the conference. Loring argued that the association should undertake to "counteract the feeling, which is rather general, that it is a disgrace to in any way patronize art until the war is over."[26] Artists, she continued, should be valued and engaged in the war effort.[27] Eventually Canada did create a war artist program, however, it was not established until 1943, and it was smaller than during the First World War, with only 32 artists being given official status.[28] Loring and Wyle's Second World War commissions were small in number as a result of shifting artistic fashion and the limited amount of paid sculpture work available. Indeed, both politically and stylistically, the world was shifting away from the type of artistic work that Loring and Wyle produced.[29]

As a result, the pair broadened the ways they supported the war effort through art, devoting much time and effort to art education. In addition to their role as mentors to young artists, Loring and Wyle raised awareness of the arts in Canada through their various associations. Shortly into the war, Loring wrote a teaching booklet as part of a series intended to provide servicemen with artistic training to help them to pass the time while serving or recuperating in hospitals.[30] Renowned

---

25   Cameron, *And Beauty Answers*, 133.
26   Sisler, *The Girls*, 70.
27   Cameron, *And Beauty Answers*, 208.
28   Brandon, *Art and War*, 68–69.
29   Boyanoski, *Loring and Wyle*, 53, 59, 65.
30   Cameron, *And Beauty Answers*, 205.

painters and friends A. Y. Jackson and Arthur Lismer had written the first two booklets in the series. The YMCA War Services and Canadian Legion Educational Services published Loring's book, *How to Get Started: Woodcarving for Pleasure*.

Loring and Wyle both died in 1968.[31] Between their public monuments, educational products, and dozens of critically acclaimed works held in public collections, their legacy should have been assured. However, as Canadian Women Artists' History Initiative scholar Janice Anderson has argued, "Like many of the country's women artists, Loring and Wyle have been overlooked in the history of Canadian art."[32] Perhaps that legacy was less important to the artists than their own satisfaction with their work. Wyle once noted that "few are permanently famous. But if you want to create beauty in lasting form, then sculpture is worthwhile."[33]

MARY CAMPBELL, MUNITIONS WORKER

While Loring and Wyle's sculptures of women engaging in hard physical toil is an artistic reflection of women's admission into heavy industry, the small bronze badge (only 4.6 cm × 3 cm) in figure 3.4 leads us to the women workers themselves.[34] The motif on this badge focuses on munitions, and reminds us of the nature of the relationship between Canada and Britain during the First World War. It is emblazoned with the words "Imperial Munitions Board," "Woman Worker," and at the bottom "Canada"; the royal crown sits atop the badge. In the middle, standing upright, is a stylized shell. A bar proclaiming "six months service" hangs from the bottom of the badge. In 1914, Canada was a self-governing dominion of the United Kingdom and did not control its own foreign policy. When Britain declared war on Germany, Canada was at war as well. The Canadian response to the war was largely tied to British needs: men, food, and munitions. Artillery ruled the conflict, forcing armies into the ground in lines of trenches. Once dug in, troops were stuck in a frustrating deadlock that both sides tried to break with ever more artillery. The guns

31   Boyanoski, *Loring and Wyle*, 65.
32   Anderson, "The Forgotten Artists."
33   Sisler, *The Girls*, 117.
34   Mary Campbell Mays' Imperial Munitions Board Woman War Worker Badge, CWM 19800471-001.

of the First World War required massive amounts of ammunition, more than Britain could manufacture on its own.[35]

In 1915, the British Ministry of Munitions created the Imperial Munitions Board (IMB). Under the direction of businessman J. W. Flavelle, this government agency coordinated the production of war material in Canada, using a combination of private contractors and its own manufacturing plants. Canada produced an immense number of shells during the war—one quarter to a third of those fired by Britain.[36] This level of manufacturing required huge numbers of workers. At the start of the war, Canada had been in

FIGURE 3.4. Mary Campbell's Imperial Munitions Board Woman War Worker badge. *Source:* Canadian War Museum 19800471-001.

a recession. Initially, factories could draw on their existing industrial workforce as well as a large pool of unemployed workers. However, as the war progressed, production increased, men enlisted, and heavy industry struggled to find labour. With the wartime economy growing, factories that had previously only employed men now opened their doors to women. Historian Kori Street, who studied women's paid work during the war, estimates that between 11,000 and 13,000 worked for the IMB alone.[37] Women not only worked in munitions production, but they also worked in plants overseen by the IMB that manufactured chemicals, ships, and airplanes.

The IMB issued this badge to Mary Campbell. As a young woman, Campbell had taken a job as a munitions inspector in Toronto.[38] Her work testing artillery

---

35   Carnegie, *History of Munitions Supply*, x-xi.
36   Carnegie, *History of Munitions Supply*, 133.
37   Street, "Bankers and Bomb Makers," 91.
38   Mary (Campbell) Mays to Canadian War Museum, May 17, 1980, CWM Acquisition File 19800471.

shells for defects was crucial, since defective shells could malfunction, injuring or killing Allied soldiers. Other women on the production lines filled shells with explosives, pressed metal sheets into tube shaped cartridges, drilled or turned shells on lathes, and checked delicate fuses.[39] While her badge contains one "six months service" bar, she stated that she actually earned three bars, indicating a longer term of service.[40]

We do not know exactly why Mary Campbell decided to work in munitions, but other women were motivated by war industry's comparatively high wages. She may have been from a working-class background, as were most women in the factories, with limited paid-work options available to her. Wartime munitions jobs were dirty, unhealthy, and dangerous, but the wages women could earn formed a powerful inducement, particularly in light of increasing wartime inflation that made it difficult to make ends meet.

Campbell may also have been motivated by patriotism and a desire to contribute to the war effort in a tangible way. She clearly valued her work and the service badge she received, having kept it carefully for 64 years and referring to it as a medal.[41] Medals are closely associated with war service, imbuing the recipient with a sense of pride and serving as a visual marker of service. Usually—but not exclusively—they are reserved for those in the military, but occasionally civilians engaged in vital war work have also received recognition in medal form. During the First World War, members of the military were eligible to receive medals for their service in Europe, for brave acts, and for their important contribution to Canada's war effort. Since women were only able to join the military as nurses, only Canadian Nursing Sisters were able to earn military medals. At a time when war service on all fronts was prized and proudly displayed, badges such as these gave war workers a chance to publicly prove their patriotism.

Campbell's pride is also evident in the postcard she donated to the CWM. On its front is a studio photograph of Campbell and a friend in their factory uniforms.

OPPOSITE: FIGURE 3.5. Mary Campbell (*left*) with a friend, 1914–1917.
Source: George Metcalf Archival Collection, Canadian War Museum 19800471-002.

---

39   See Imperial Munitions Board, *Women in the Production.*
40   Mary (Campbell) Mays to CWM, June 10, 1980.
41   Mary (Campbell) Mays to CWM, May 17, 1980.

M.M. Our Uniform

She originally sent the card to a soldier in France, and later annotated it with "M.M. Our Uniform / This is me biting my lip." ("M.M." being Campbell's initials after her marriage.) Countless romantic picture postcards were mailed between soldiers and their love interests during the First World War. In an era when studio photography had not yet been supplanted by amateur photography, women like Mary Campbell could purchase inexpensive portrait postcards to send to their loved ones overseas. Campbell's postcard picturing her in her uniform mirrored the practice of soldiers sending portrait postcards of themselves in uniform to loved ones back home. As photography historian Hélène Samson argues, studio portraits allowed those who purchased them to "picture and reflect on themselves, their families and their communities-both real and imagined."[42] Some women paid to have portraits taken of themselves in their uniforms, "popular mementoes of their time in the factories."[43] The pose and clothing that Mary Campbell chose, wearing her factory uniform and mob cap, along with her later handwritten note that brings attention to the uniform, reflects a desire to showcase her wartime contributions. Sociologist Nathan Joseph calls these uniforms an indicator of women's "emotional investment in the war and the visual indication of their work outside of the domestic sphere."[44] The man to whom Mary Campbell was writing, Corporal Charles Burnett Walker, may never have received the card, as it was returned to Campbell's home in Toronto.[45] During the war, soldiers were very mobile, and romantic allegiances shifted quickly. As Walker survived the war, we do not know what caused this postcard to be returned, but we do know that in May 1917, Mary Campbell married another man, Joseph Mays.

During the First World War, industrial workers often wore lapel pins that served as identification for workplace security and as a means of protecting male workers (who were sometimes seen as shirkers or slackers out of military uniforms) from public scrutiny. The CWM collection contains dozens of war worker badges, from both world wars, from a variety of Canadian companies. The badges, bearing the company names, often emphasize the wearer's status through terms

42   Samson and Sauvage, *Notman*, 82.

43   Roberts, "A Biography of the Trousered."

44   Roberts, "A Biography of the Trousered," citing Joseph, *Uniforms and Nonuniforms*, 155.

45   The postcard was sent from M. Campbell, 76 McCaul Street, Toronto. She later wrote on the back, "This was sent to France and came back to me." M. Campbell to Cpl. Walker, CWM 19800471-002.

such as "war worker," "in service," or "munitions worker," presumably to make their connection to war work more obvious. This IMB war worker badge stands out because it emphasizes the wearer's gender. The IMB badges may have been part of a broader push to normalize women's work in wartime industry, at least for the duration of the war, so as to increase the labour pool. Previously, women in factories enjoyed little public recognition, union participation, or government policies that acknowledged their particular circumstances.[46] Important as both a recruitment tool and a validation of women's work in an essential war industry, the badges embodied a change in attitudes towards women's work.

In addition to convincing the Canadian public of the suitability of women in wartime production factories, the IMB worked to influence potential employers. *Women in the Production of Munitions in Canada*, an IMB publication, emphasized "the practicability of woman labour in the production of munitions of war" and went on to praise the "womanhood of Canada, nobly backed by the workmen concerned [who] have rallied to the force behind the man behind the gun."[47] The booklet showed successful and productive munitions factories staffed by women. It described the types of suitable work, acknowledging and refuting prejudices against women in industry: "The tool room presents every advantage for female labour, in spite of the fact that engineering history tells us that it is the department for highly trained mechanics" and "it has been clearly demonstrated that women, under the guidance of trained toolmakers, are efficient and useful."[48] The last page of the publication displayed the IMB women war worker badge, noting that it was issued after one month's service.[49]

While praising women as potential workers, the publication nonetheless presented them as emotionally and physiologically inferior to men. *Women in the Production of Munitions in Canada* suggested that women flourished in particular work environments, implying that men were heartier. Mats, it was noted, helped workers who had to stand on greasy floors as the dampness was "particularly prejudicial to the continued efficiency of female labour."[50] The booklet also noted how

46 See Frager and Patrias, *Discounted Labour.*
47 Imperial Munitions Board, *Women in the Production,* 5.
48 Imperial Munitions Board, *Women in the Production,* 21.
49 Imperial Munitions Board, *Women in the Production,* 64.
50 Imperial Munitions Board, *Women in the Production,* 32.

important it was to consider women's welfare to ensure productivity. Plants often employed women specifically to supervise the health and well-being of female workers. These women, known as matrons, were "almost indispensable as a means of adjusting the many small irritations that are magnified in a women's mind by neglect or inability to make them known to one of her own sex."[51] The fact that women workers were portrayed as having particularly female needs also allowed promoters to emphasize how women's bodies or psychology were especially suited to munitions work. Women were said to be particularly adept at tooling because the work was repetitious.[52] This supposed female aptitude for repetitive work comes up again during the Second World War. An article in *La Presse* explained that women could "maintain production at an even pace long after male workers would have succumbed to boredom. Women are used to monotonous work; setting the table and doing the dishes three times every day and wiping dust from the same furniture all year long."[53]

The number of women employed in munitions factories likely peaked in 1917.[54] As the war drew to a close, the industry started to contract as the demand for munitions, airplanes, and military vehicles slowed. The day after the Armistice, the *Toronto Globe* published an article outlining the possible labour problem that would follow the layoffs.[55] The Canadian workforce faced a potentially rough readjustment to peacetime. Thousands of munitions workers would soon lose their jobs and need new ones, and soldiers returning home would need civilian jobs too. Workers (male and, to a much smaller degree, female), empowered by their vital contribution to the war effort, let go of their newfound importance reluctantly and the postwar period was rocked by a number of labour actions, including the 1919 Winnipeg General Strike.[56] In general, women remained on the sidelines of these strikes, having accepted that their wartime industrial production work was temporary.[57] Trade unions and the Canadian public, who had (often grudgingly) supported the employment of women in munitions for the duration of the war,

51   Imperial Munitions Board, *Women in the Production*, 57.
52   Imperial Munitions Board, *Women in the Production*, 21.
53   Auger and Lamothe, *De la poêle à frire*, 122.
54   Street, "Bankers and Bomb Makers," 87.
55   "Must Soon Lose Jobs," 3.
56   Kealey, *Enlisting Women*, 152; Heron, *The Canadian Labour Movement*, 51–53.
57   Kealey, *Enlisting Women*, 153, 156.

would not accept women staying on in jobs that could be filled by thousands of returning veterans, many of whom found themselves without sufficient work.

A few women petitioned their employers to stay on and a small number of female workers expressed their concern to factory matrons about losing their jobs, but these instances were rare.[58] Very few women remained employed in metalworking or heavy industry in the years after the First World War yet public discourse minimized any anger or anxiety women felt about losing work. One magazine author characterized working women's dissatisfaction as mere "bubbles bound to rise when the current turns, and just as sure to disappear."[59]

And, for the most part, these "bub-bles" did disappear into the general Canadian postwar unrest, economic boom, and later Depression bust, until they rose again during the Second World War, when another labour crisis materialized.

LOIS ALLAN, FARM SERVICE CORPS

Figure 3.6 shows another tiny badge (just 2.5 cm high), found in the Library and Archives Canada collection, and it reminds us that Canada was a source of more than just military personnel and munitions.[60] The badge bears the words "Farm Service Corps /1918" and embossed upon it is a woman in a broad-brimmed hat, tunic, and bloomers holding a shield representing the province of Ontario

FIGURE 3.6. Lois Allan's Farm Service Corps badge.
Source: Photograph by Tom Thompson. Library and Archives Canada MG30-C173.

58   Street, "Bankers and Bomb Makers," 101–102.
59   Street, "Bankers and Bomb Makers," 101.
60   Lois Allan's Ontario Farm Service Corps Badge, MG30-C173.

in one hand, and a sheaf of wheat in the other. Beside her lean a hoe and a rake. During both world wars, Canadian food producers provided a vast quantity of foodstuffs for the Allied war effort, despite serious challenges. While mechanization had begun to transform agriculture in the early twentieth century, the industry remained labour intensive. But wartime producers had to increase their output at a time when help was scarce. Worker shortages worsened after April 1918, when the Canadian government rescinded the conscription exemptions that had been granted to farmers, throwing more uncertainty into the sector.[61] Federal and provincial governments created a number of schemes to direct labour to farmers, drawing on non-traditional sources, such as older boys and teens, and women of all ages.

The badge is stuck in a small journal (smaller than 21 cm × 28 cm) that belonged to Lois Allan. All of the journal's contents relate to Allan's time with the Ontario Farm Service Corps. The Farm Service Corps was a 1917–1918 program aimed partly at young women. A provincial initiative, it supplemented the federal Soldiers of the Soil (SOS) program, which sent between 22,000 and 25,000 teenage boys to help farmers. Though the boys of the SOS enlisted and worked across the country, Ontario farms by far employed the most "soldiers of the soil."[62] As for the young women of the Farm Service Corps, known as farmerettes, many were students during the year. Allan studied at Queen's University.[63]

An Ontario Trades and Labour Branch pamphlet in the Lois Allan fonds at Library and Archives Canada indicates there were five ways in which women could contribute labour.[64] Entitled *Women's Work on the Land: How You May Assist in Food Production this Summer*, the pamphlet states, "In the campaign for greater production of food in Canada women workers are needed in Ontario for five kinds of Work:—On fruit and vegetable farms./ In the camps to cook for the workers./On mixed and dairy farms./In the farmhouses, to help feed those who are raising the crops./In canneries, to preserve the fruit and vegetables./To take charge of milk routes."

OPPOSITE: FIGURE 3.7. Lois Allan at a Farm Service Force camp in Winona, Ontario, 1918. *Source:* Photograph by Tom Thompson. Library and Archives Canada MG30-C173.

---

61   Granatstein, "Conscription in the Great War," 68.

62   Canada Food Board, *Report*.

63   Lois Allan, note tucked into 1918 scrapbook, MG30-C173.

64   *Women's Work on the Land*.

This was not volunteer work; the women were paid. Fruit picking, according to *Women's Work on the Land*, was piece work, but women were guaranteed one dollar per day, "rain or shine—six days a week—unless the earnings in any particular week are over $9." Women earned different amounts for different fruits. Strawberries, blackberries, and gooseberries were lower earners at two cents a quart, while farmerettes could make 40 cents picking a quart of black currants. Wage regulations accounted for slow days (or workers): "When picking on piece rates if the majority in a group [is] not earning at the rate of 15 cents, the pickers will be paid at the flat rate of 15 cents per hour."[65] Tucked in near the back of the scrapbook is Allan's first pay envelope and a pay stub ($4.80) from later in the summer. Beside the envelope, Allan wrote, "Do you recall that delicious feeling when you received your first pay envelope?"

Allan also pasted photos from her time with the Farm Service Corps into her scrapbook. They show smiling young women, enjoying their work (as well as some spare time) in the countryside. In one candid snapshot (figure 3.7), 18-year-old Allan stands in her farmerette attire, squinting just a little against the sun, holding a basket in one hand, a branch in the other. Her dress includes wrinkled bloomers and a baggy tunic, much like the clothing worn by the woman on her badge. In an era where photographs were often formal and taken in studios, Allan's willingness to be captured at work, in worn clothes, implies a pride and even pleasure in her hard work. To twenty-first-century viewers, her clothing stands out as from another age, but it was something to talk about for people of the time as well. During the First World War, the media drew attention to the clothing adopted by women working in agriculture. "Farmerettes Don Novel Costumes," read one headline above a photo of two young women from Toronto wielding farm implements. One sported khaki "riding breeches," while the other was attired in "bloomers."[66] The novelty here, of course, was that the women were wearing pants, not skirts, a rare sight prior to the war. Trousers on women were seen as a "gender transgression" that stirred commentary in the press and even between private correspondents.[67] One Canadian soldier describing working women in a 1917 letter wrote: "Some of them wear trousers or riding breeches, just the same as men.

---

65   *Women's Work on the Land*, 4.
66   "Farmerettes Don," 6.
67   Woollacott, "Dressed to Kill," 199–200.

They look comical."[68] One- or two-piece garments were marketed to women performing farm labour, and in the interwar years "farmerette" was sometimes used to describe a style of clothing worn by and sold to women and girls for outdoor, sporty pursuits.[69] Fruit pickers' clothes were, of course, intended to be practical, and dictated by Ontario's Trades and Labour branch. *Women's Work on the Farm* instructs fruit pickers that "the dress recommended is a navy blue or khaki belted smock and bloomers, and shoes with low heels. A broad hat is worn, except when the work is in the trees. A bandana handkerchief is then used."[70] With the exception of the hat (which she wears in some of the other photographs in the album), Allan's clothing appears to have conformed to these guidelines.

A note in the Allan fonds, apparently written after the war, provides an overview of her farm work. She picked strawberries, tomatoes, raspberries, and cherries as well as "pulling flax, to be made into wings for airplanes."[71] She also describes time spent at the E. D. Smith's Winona jam factory hulling imported strawberries. She wrote that the young women with whom she worked were motivated by patriotism, "filled with enthusiasm for the cause" and anxious "to do their 'bit.'"[72] Days were long, with women working 10 to 12 hours. Nonetheless, the women seemingly enjoyed their work and maintained a camp-like holiday spirit. Allan and her friends "[enlivened] the monotony of the work" by singing parodies of popular songs.[73] Her diary is filled with handwritten lyrics, including a song they wrote, sung to the tune of "Clementine," which read: "O the tall ones, O the small ones,/O the busy farmerettes/They are workers, they're no shirkers/Each earns every cent she gets."[74] The accommodations likely contributed to the summer-holiday feel. The YWCA, or other trustworthy organizations, ran and supervised camps in which young women working with fruits and vegetables often lived. The camp had "a house for cooking, eating, storing clothes, and bedrooms for a small number" as well as military tents with cots.[75] Allan and her friend Alice Goodwin

---

68   G. A. Lumsden to Margaret Dobson, 1917, Margaret Dobson fonds.

69   Ad, McGowan and Co., 2; Canadian Department Stores Ltd. advertisement, 3.

70   *Women's Work on the Land*, 2.

71   Allan, note tucked into 1918 scrapbook, 2.

72   Allan, 1918 scrapbook, 1.

73   Allan, 1918 scrapbook, 1.

74   Allan, hand written song sheets tucked into the 1918 scrapbook, 1–2.

75   *Women's Work on the Land*, 3–4.

chose a tent.[76] When Allan's time with the Farm Service Corps came to an end, she found she had "lost most of the money" she had earned and had to write home for train fare.[77] She closes her note saying, "First 2 [E. D. Smith and fruit picking] were enjoyable made friends for life."

CECELIA MCTAGGART, REGISTRAR'S OFFICE

This piece of paper (figure 3.8), tucked inside a leather wallet along with a lucky four-leaf clover, is a National Registration card.[78] It indicates that the bearer had registered with the federal government's Canada Registration Board (CRB) and is emblematic of Canada's labour problems during the First World War. As the war dragged on, the government became increasingly concerned about labour shortages, and it wanted to know what workers, with which skills, they could mobilize for war purposes. On February 22, 1918, it passed an Order-in-Council creating the CRB, with compulsory enrollment planned for the spring. On June 22, over 5 million Canadians aged 16 and over registered at 25,000 locations across the country, staffed by some 150,000 registrars.[79]

This card is made out in the name of, and signed by, Miss Cecelia McTaggart, of 534 Queens Avenue, London, Ontario. She came from a privileged background, living in an affluent neighbourhood filled with the large homes of well-off professionals.[80] Her father, Alexander McTaggart, was a physician and her maternal grandfather was Imperial Oil founder William Spencer. The women in McTaggart's family did not have to hold paid employment. As befit their social standing, they spent their days doing intricate needlework or performing good works through the YMCA and the Methodist Church. Cecelia McTaggart had a different life in mind. Before the war, she wanted to enroll at university and study journalism, but her parents disapproved, believing university attendance

OPPOSITE: FIGURE 3.8. Cecelia McTaggart's 1918 National Registration Card.
Source: Canadian Museum of History 2008-H0027.32.

---

76   Allan, 1918 scrapbook, 1.
77   Allan, note tucked into 1918 scrapbook, 2.
78   Cecelia McTaggart's National Registration Card, 1918, Brookbank Collection.
79   *Canada's War Effort,* 25; *Canada Yearbook 1918,* 662–663; "This Scheme," 1.
80   *1921 Census of Canada,* London, Ontario, Sub-District 4.

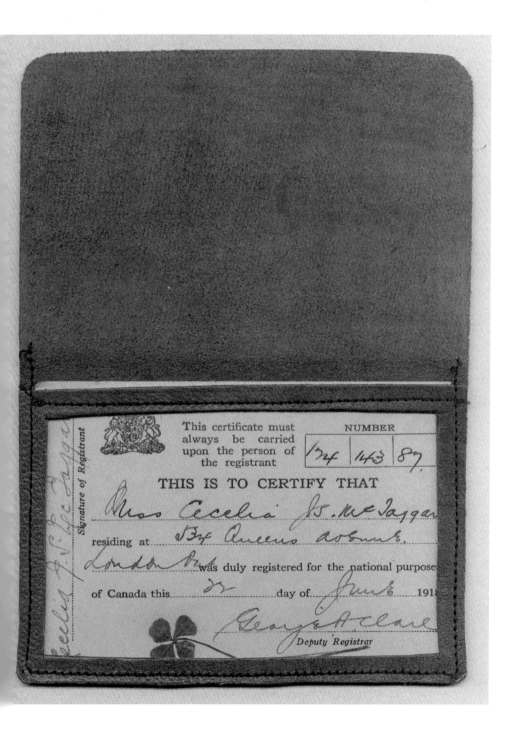

unsuitable for a young woman of her class.[81] Familial responsibility and social expectation played an important role in the options available to Cecelia, and other young women of similar backgrounds, even after she reached the age of maturity.

The war temporarily changed what society deemed acceptable for upper-class women like McTaggart. As one National Registration advertisement states, it was crucial that "every available unit of human energy [...] be utilized to the best advantage."[82] While working-class women had long done paid labour to help support their families, during the war, patriotism rather than economics likely motivated upper-class women to work. For a young woman like Cecelia McTaggart, coming of age in the era of the boundary-pushing "New Woman," the war provided an opportunity to escape her conventional upbringing, even in a very limited way. At the outbreak of the First World War, McTaggart took an automotive course with the goal of driving overseas, but her family again discouraged her ambitions.[83] So she began working in the London office of W. E. Wismer, a deputy registrar for the Province of Ontario. Wismer and his officers were responsible for the registration of the citizens of London for military service and wartime employment.[84] Although little is known of McTaggart's exact role at the Registrar's office, we suspect she was a clerical worker, given her gender and background.

Clerking had once been skilled work for literate men, but it was increasingly a feminine domain.[85] As new machines such as punch card sorters and typewriters automated clerical tasks, male clerks rejected the changing work environment and women began to replace them. As historian Leah Price notes, one speaker at a stenographers' club meeting in 1901 argued that it was "degrading for a strong, healthy man to be occupied all day long in using the pen upon what was little more than copying words."[86] The First World War accelerated the trend of clerical work becoming a women's profession. Between 1911 and 1921, the percentage of women who held such jobs in Canada doubled. By 1921, women occupied over 41 percent of all Canadian clerical jobs.[87]

---

81   Godin, "The Brookbank Collection," 15.
82   "Canada's Registration," 1.
83   Godin, "The Brookbank Collection," 15.
84   "Quebec Registrar Ordered to Quit," 3.
85   Lowe, "Women, Work and the Office," 361.
86   Price, "Diary: The Death of Stenography."
87   England and Boyer, "Women's Work," 309; Street, "Bankers and Bomb Makers," 52–53.

Social

Mrs Sherwood Fox and Daughter

Mrs John Smallman

All photographs by Norrall Studio

Mrs. George Ellis

FIGURE 3.9. Cecilia (McTaggart) Ellis (*right*) after her marriage, 1922.
Source: Toronto Sunday World, August 6, 1922, Canadian
Museum of History 2008-H0027.36_001.

Cecelia McTaggart, and other young women like her, played an important role in the registration offices, given the vast amount of information that required processing and the dwindling supply of male clerks, many of whom had enlisted in the military. According to a 1918 government pamphlet, about 75,000 women worked on the National Registration effort in 1918 and between 5,000 and 6,000 had found paid employment in the wartime civil service.[88]

McTaggart travelled to Québec City in the spring of 1918 to work with the Registry Office. Just a month prior, the city had been rocked by violent anti-conscription protests that turned into a deadly riot. The protesters, most of whom were French Canadian, felt alienated from the Anglo-Canadian majority and the British war effort, and they objected to being forced to serve in the military. Street battles left four civilians dead, dozens injured, and the Military Service Registry

88   *Canada's War Effort*, 24–25.

Office was sacked.[89] The federal government appointed a new official, Alleyn Taschereau, to replace the ousted Québec City Registrar. Taschereau enlisted the help of London Registrar W. E. Wismer in setting up a new office. [90] To assist him, Wismer brought along "a few of the best members of his London staff" including "Miss C. McTaggart."[91] According to her mother's 1918 diary, McTaggart worked with the Conscription Office in Québec City from April through July 1918 and then moved to Ottawa to continue her work until October 1918 when she returned home to London.[92] She appears to have been busy with her conscription-related duties and missed the rollout of the National Registration program in June 1918.

Unfortunately, neither her mother's diary nor newspaper accounts give any detail about what her duties with the Conscription Office entailed. Family lore focused instead on the romantic tale of her meeting with her future husband. According to her descendants, she "had an active social life in the upper echelons of Québec City society and it was in that milieu that she met George Ellis."[93] The couple married in 1921. The portrait photograph (figure 3.9) was taken soon after their marriage and published in the society pages of the *Toronto Sunday World*. Cecelia McTaggart's wartime work, and indeed her clerical work, was over. During the Second World War, McTaggart again supported the war effort, this time driving a salvage truck, something she had been forbidden by her family to do during the First World War.[94]

ADA SYLVESTER, CANADIAN CAR AND FOUNDRY

Ada Sylvester used the mallet in figure 3.10 at the Canadian Car and Foundry (Can Car) plant in Fort William, Ontario, during the Second World War, where she manufactured aircraft parts.[95] The mallet, with its wooden handle and unusual hammer head featuring two end caps, is not something that would normally grace

---

89   Nicholson, *Official History of the Canadian Army*, 347–348.

90   "Quebec Registrar Loses"; "Dominion Police May Be Replaced"; "After a Storm Comes a Calm"; "That the Government Intends Not to Relapse."

91   *L'Événement*, April 26, 1918.

92   Josephine Maud McTaggart, Diaries, CMH 2009-H0016.

93   Godin, "The Brookbank Collection," 15.

94   Godin, "The Brookbank Collection," 15.

95   Ada Sylvester's Can Car Mallet, CMH 2007.86.3.

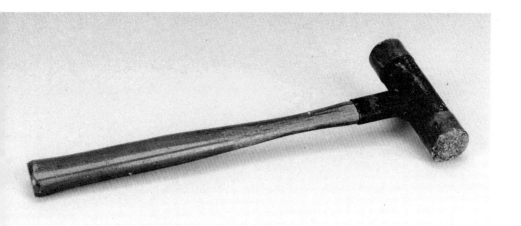

FIGURE 3.10. Metalworking mallet used by Ada Sylvester, 1943.
Source: Canadian Museum of History 2007.86.3.

a household toolbox, though that is exactly where it was before it came to CMH in 2007. The mallet's unusual construction is a clue to its former life—metalworkers shaping soft or thin sheet metals chose mallets like these to avoid puncturing or denting their work.

The Can Car factory is representative of Canadian wartime industry, growing from having only a handful of female production staff in 1938 to a workforce consisting of more than 40 percent women over the course of the war.[96] As in the First World War, Canada's productive capacity was retooled to provide the material needed to wage war. The types of products needed—munitions, vehicles, textiles, food—was broadly similar, but this time the Canadian government was more organized in its approach to the regulation of industry and labour. Unlike the 1914–1918 period, Canada was now an independent nation, joining the war of its own volition. There was no Imperial Munitions Board; instead, the federal government established a Department of Munitions and Supply and also a Wartime Industries Control Board. The Canadian government was far more willing to control the economy than it had been during the First World War, and it took the reins on almost everything. Under the direction of the government, many industries grew exponentially, including airplane manufacture. From 4,000 workers

96   Smith and Wakewich, "'I Was Not Afraid of Work,'" 229. Much of the research on Canadian Car and Foundry in Fort William was developed by Wakewich and Smith over the course of a decade of oral histories and publications. A material culture and oral history-based research project at the CMH initiated by Krista Cooke benefitted greatly from their research and the work of Kelly Saxberg, documentary film maker of *Rosies of the North* (National Film Board, 1999).

producing 40 planes a year, during the war, Canadian production grew to 4,000 airplanes a year turned out by 116,000 workers.[97] Women like Ada Sylvester were a part of this growth.

As in the previous conflict, the Second World War brought jobs to a population enduring tough economic times. Canadian Car and Foundry had thrived during the First World War as a shipbuilder, but the Great Depression altered the company's fortunes. The Montréal-based company closed its Fort William facilities from 1921 to 1937 and, like many industries, Can Car shifted focus to adapt to market demand. From ships, to streetcars, and on to airplanes during the Second World War, Can Car modified their production lines, machinery, and workforce as markets contracted and expanded.[98] Can Car reopened the Fort William plant in 1937 and began airplane production in 1939, bringing new economic vitality to a region suffering economically. Ada (Sylvester) Dlholucky recalled seeing unemployed men race to the local dockyards in hope of work: "They really had to rush for a job. When the boats would come in, you would see hundreds of bicycles from the east end going down Simpson Street to get to the island to get the boat to get a job. They weren't paid much, but just to get something."[99] In oral histories of women who worked at Can Car during the Second World War, many recalled the relief and jubilation when the war began and local manufacturing plants stepped up production, bringing prosperity to the depressed area.[100]

As had been the case during the First World War, factories were soon short of men to hire. The economy grew, requiring more labour at the same time as men enlisted to go overseas. Employers like Can Car had to look beyond their existing labour pool and hire women workers to do what had traditionally been considered men's jobs. One woman whose family was suffering financially recalled that her father insisted she work at Can Car as soon as he could. "My dad drove, dragged, me in to the Canada Car to work. I wasn't even 16. But he had a little bit of influence there. He was the crane driver in the final assembly... So he got me in there and I started as a rivet chaser."[101] A rivet chaser worked as a part of the riveting team,

97   Ball, *Mind, Heart, and Vision*, 95.
98   See Burkowski, *Can-Car*.
99   Dlholucky, interview.
100 Kovac, interview; Dlholucky, interview.
101 Kovac, interview.

often five or six people working together to fasten two large pieces of sheet metal together. Hundreds, eventually thousands, of other women soon joined her on the assembly lines at Can Car.

Women were in such demand that Can Car recruited from across Ontario and the Prairies and built a dormitory, called Winston Hall, to house them. They helped build approximately 2,200 Hawker Hurricanes and Curtiss Helldivers over the course of the war. The women of Can Car had a role model in Elsie MacGill, the plant's Chief Aeronautical Engineer and the first woman to hold such a position. MacGill, whose life and work have been chronicled by historian Crystal Sissons, earned the nickname "Queen of the Hurricanes" for

FIGURE 3.11. Ada Sylvester, ca. 1943.
Source: Canadian Museum of History 2009-0458-0003-Dm.

her efforts at Can Car.[102] Other firms across the country saw similar increases in the number of women they employed building trucks, tanks, rail cars, airplanes, guns, ammunition, ships, and other armaments. Still more worked in supporting industries such as food processing factories, lumber mills, military uniform manufacturers, and chemical plants. By 1944, around 370,000 women held jobs related to the war effort, many in traditionally male sectors such as heavy industry.[103] This number of women workers represented a huge increase over the approximately 13,000 industrial production workers of the First World War.[104] This time, in addition to munitions workers, the Canadian government encouraged women's paid

---

102   Sissons, *Queen of the Hurricanes.*
103   Keshen, *Saints,* 149.
104   Street, "Bankers and Bomb Makers," 91.

employment in many sectors through National Selective Service, a means of regulating the civilian workforce. Women's labour had become essential to the smooth functioning of the Canadian war effort.

As was the case during the First World War, higher wages attracted women to jobs in industry. Most of these new female factory employees came from working-class families, so paid work itself was not a new experience. Prior to the war, parts of the industrial sector were largely closed to women, shut out of male-dominated industrial production jobs.[105] Employers paid these male employees a "family wage" (enough for a man to support his wife and children), and many industrial workers were protected by trade unions or professional associations.[106] Women who worked in industry during the war did not necessarily make the same high wages as the men, but they made more than they would have otherwise. Frozina (Sportak) Dysievick, who worked at Can Car, recalled the dramatic wartime wage increases, noting, "Now with girls working, they were able to get more, invest more. Some of them even got so far as to have a car if they earned enough which before they never dreamed of because they never earned enough. So things kind of bettered themselves to a point."[107]

Ada Sylvester came from a working-class family of eight children who were either serving in the military or working. Everyone in the household contributed to their family's financial well-being. Sylvester had left school to find paid work and later said, "We would like to have had an education, but I was lucky to get to grade nine. We had to go to work."[108] Before the war, teenaged Sylvester helped neighbouring families with babysitting and housework and her sister worked in a grocery store. Her mother stayed home to keep the house and took in a married couple as boarders. Sylvester recalled that the family could not afford a car or a washing machine and she was proud that "the first thing I bought with my money from the Canada Car was a washing machine for my mother. We were always [doing laundry] with the [washboard]. We couldn't afford them [machines]."[109]

---

105   McCullough, "Introduction: Part Six," 331.
106   Peterson and Lewis, *Elgar Companion*, 342–345.
107   Dysievick, interview.
108   Dlholucky, interview.
109   Dlholucky, interview.

Beyond the financial incentive that drew women like Ada Sylvester to wartime factories, patriotism was a strong motivator. Many of the women at Can Car had family in uniform. Three of Ada Sylvester's four brothers and her future husband served in the military. The workers were proud of their contributions and Sylvester recalled one instance where they volunteered their time on the weekends. "We were so dedicated we went there two Sundays in a row and worked for nothing. To make sure we got those airplanes going. It was the Hawker Hurricane... One day it snowed [and] the street cars weren't even running. You know what we did? We walked up to there, no kidding! We walked up there [about 60–90 minutes]. To work for free!"[110] Advertising campaigns implored women from across the country to join the industrial workforce, pitching women's participation as patriotic. The text of a 1943 National Selective Service newspaper advertisement read: "Girls, you are needed now as never before. This is an emergency. Your co-operation now will help to shorten the war. Swing into action today."[111]

Only three women in the production side of the factory were kept on past war's end, and Ada Sylvester was laid off in August 1945.[112] She was sorry to lose her job at the plant. The work, she said, "was good. It was clean. It had supervisors [who kept workers safe]. I wouldn't mind working there all the time! That was good. Wouldn't mind that at all."[113]

NORA (GIBSON) ELRICK, CANADIAN CAR AND FOUNDRY

Women, of course, worked and lived alongside men. Scholars of women's history can learn much from studying their lives together and by comparing their respective experiences and material. We can read these two lunchboxes, belonging to Nora Gibson (figure 3.12) and Jock Elrick (figure 3.13), as material evidence of the gendered experiences of war work.[114] On the surface, their two lunchboxes tell a relatively simple story. Women and men, across the nation, going to work in factories to support their country in wartime. However, through a careful study of

---

110 Dlholucky, interview.
111 National Selective Service advertisement, 32.
112 Wakewich and Smith, "The Politics of 'Selective' Memory," 56.
113 Dlholucky, interview.
114 Nora (Gibson) Elrick and John (Jock) Elrick's Can Car Lunch Boxes, CMH 2007.94.2.1 and CMH 2007.94.3.

the lunchboxes, we can discern that, while both worked at Can Car, the two had very different work experiences during the war.

Nora Gibson's lunchbox is covered in "graffiti." One of her friends riveted name plates onto the front of the lunchbox with Gibson's name and phone number on it, while others in her department left notes and scrawled signatures. Autographed by all of Gibson's friends in the riveting department, it seems to be the equivalent of a high school yearbook, a lasting memory from a brief time in her life. Gibson's use of her lunchbox as a memento may reflect society's, industry's, and possibly her own assumption that women would only be in the industrial workforce temporarily. In comparison, her husband Jock Elrick's lunchbox is battered and well used, but without signatures and notes. Whereas Gibson's work might have been a temporary wartime adventure that required a souvenir to remind her of the friendships she had made, Elrick worked in the factory before the war, and he planned on continuing work there afterwards. Industrial work would be his daily reality for years.

Can Car, and other plants, arranged the work and training of men and women in a way that made it clear that men were expected to have long careers, while women were helping out temporarily. When Gibson began work at Can Car in 1941, she had no relevant experience or knowledge. She had left school early to work as a hairdresser to support her younger siblings. Gibson disliked hairdressing and was happy to leave it for Can Car, which presented a dramatic wage increase. Can Car offered Gibson six months of vocational school training that prepared her to work as an assistant in the riveting department, building tail sections for Hawker Hurricane fighter planes. (Ada Sylvester, who started later in the war, recalled being in training for "about a week" before starting work at Can Car.[115]) Gibson and the other wartime students were trained for a specific type of work. Her job was narrowly focused and there was no expectation that she would develop her skills for a long career. In comparison, Jock Elrick started working at

OPPOSITE TOP: FIGURE 3.12. Nora Gibson's lunch box.
Source: Canadian Museum of History 2007.94.2.1.
OPPOSITE BOTTOM: FIGURE 3.13. Jock Elrick's lunch box.
Source: Canadian Museum of History 2007.94.3.

115   Dlholucky, interview.

Can Car straight out of school as a 17-year-old apprentice in 1937. Male employees like Elrick often moved from department to department after beginning as young apprentices, learning trades and developing their skills for what was expected to be a lifelong career. Jock Elrick carried his lunchbox to work at Can Car from 1937 to 1962. Nora Gibson used hers from 1941 to 1945, when she left the factory, pregnant with her first child, near the end of the war. The couple posed for this photograph (figure 3.14) during their courtship. Interestingly, both Nora Gibson and Jock Elrick are wearing trousers, belted high, falling softly from pleated fronts, tapering down to rolled hems. Evidently, the perceived problems associated with women wearing pants (during the First World War and again, for military women, in the Second World War) had been upended by fashion.

Women were frequently reminded that their employment was a temporary deviation from the norm. A poster with regulations for women war workers at a Boeing Aircraft plant directed them to "Remember you are the first large group of women to enter War Work in Western Canada. Your general conduct and ability is [*sic*] being closely watched. You are not here to permanently replace men but to assist in the manufacture of aircraft to defend these coasts. Don't abuse privileges, keep your mind on your work and—Let's get on with the job!"[116] Some plants drove home the point that manufacturing was, in the long run, men's work with the rule that women could not keep their job if they married. At Can Car, company rules allowed Nora (Gibson) Elrick to keep working in spite of her 1943 marriage to Jock Elrick, Gibson's shift supervisor in the riveting department. Upon marriage, she left Can Car of her own volition, but only for a few months. Missing the work, her friends, and the paycheque, she soon returned to the plant, and the company gave her a job in the electrical department, where Jock would not be her supervisor.

Historians may also consider Gibson's lunchbox as an object useful for discussions about the treatment women faced in industry during the Second World War. Though First World War women workers had set a precedent, the arrival of women in many plants in the 1940s nonetheless caused friction with existing male workers. Women often encountered inequality and harassment in their new

OPPOSITE: FIGURE 3.14. Nora Gibson and Jock Elrick, ca. 1942.
Source: Canadian Museum of History IMG 2015-0145-0004-Dm.

---

116 "Plant Regulations for Women Employees," CWM 20020045-1224.

workplaces. One of the reasons Nora Gibson brought her lunch to work in this box was to avoid the long walk through the staff cafeteria.[117] According to Gibson, many women resorted to packing lunches rather than braving whistles and cat-calls from male co-workers. Jock Elrick recalled similar behaviour. "The men [...] used to holler and whistle at them and all that."[118] Men also used to send Gibson on false errands to the tool crib, which presented opportunities for harassment. After facing the long walk across the plant floor, through a barrage of whistles and remarks, she would return to find the tool she had fetched was not needed after all. Gibson felt unsafe with this overt sexual attention. Her mother, suspicious of the work environment and large numbers of male workers riding the streetcar after their shifts, insisted upon meeting her daughter at the station to walk her home.

Studying past workplace harassment can be difficult, as not all women encountered the same behaviour, and people interpret and remember interactions in different ways. Past generations of women were often habituated to a level of sexual harassment and inappropriate behaviour that would be unacceptable today. Oral historian Carole Thornton interviewed a number of wartime shipyard workers and found that the women did not recall any incidents of harassment on the job. A male interview subject from the same shipyard, on the other hand, "explained the opposite—that the men blatantly harassed the women. He [thought the women] may have ignored or downplayed the men's behaviour since they had been conditioned, in their day, to see this type of behaviour as normal and acceptable."[119]

Though companies seemed unconcerned about the harassment women faced, they were very concerned about women's propriety. In a 2008 interview, Jock Elrick recalled that at Can Car, women were supervised at work to reduce impropriety among co-workers. "They had this matron who would go through the plant and watch [so] there'd be no hanky-panky going on. And then there was a night foreman by the name of Mr. Carpenter... He was making his rounds every half hour or an hour just to keep things moving. You know, things could get out of hand with guys and women working together."[120]

117   Several other interview subjects also mentioned bringing their meals rather than having to wait in line to buy expensive cafeteria lunches. Dlholucky, interview; Dysievick, interview.

118   Elrick, interview.

119   Thornton, "And the Men Just Stood," 599.

120   Jock Elrick, interview.

Attitudes about women workers and those at Can Car specifically were complicated, filled with double standards, and reflective of society's expectations of women. As scholars Helen Smith and Pamela Wakewich have argued in their detailed study of Can Car's worker newsletter, *Aircrafter*, employees were bombarded with messages that "conveyed an ambivalent attitude that both praised and questioned women's war work in traditionally male jobs, thus reinforcing prewar women's roles and socially prescribed forms of femininity."[121] Examples drawn from *Aircrafter* illustrate this ambivalence, on the one hand, sexualizing and trivializing Can Car's female workers (with pin ups and cartoons featuring underdressed female workers) and, on the other hand, praising women for their essential war work and focusing on moral behaviour for women. This left Can Car women negotiating, in the words of Smith and Wakewich, "a delicate balance between moral and immoral decorativeness."[122]

"MISS WAR WORKER"

This photograph (figure 3.15) shows five women with sashes bearing the titles Miss Fabric (Grace Roberts), Miss Assembly (Doreen MacDonald), Miss Prairie Airways (Mary E. Scott), Miss Sheet Metal (Kathleen Diemert), and Miss War Worker (Aurelie Ballavance). They were the 1942 Moose Jaw, Saskatchewan, winners of the Miss War Worker beauty pageant. The man in the photograph is Peter E. Mazza, the director of athletics and social activities at Prairie Airways Limited (Aircraft Division) who had helped to organize the pageant. He later went on to work for Can Car in Fort William. Mazza purchased this photograph and others from Can Car in the immediate postwar period.[123]

War worker beauty pageants may seem anomalous now, an era when Rosie the Riveter is seen as a symbol of female empowerment and beauty pageants anything but, however, during the Second World War, the pageants were immensely popular. Canadians, searching for light entertainment and good news, flocked to greet pageant contestants,

---

121 Smith and Wakewich, "'Beauty and the Helldivers,'" 72.
122 Smith and Wakewich, "'Beauty and the Helldivers,'" 97.
123 CMH Acquisition File 2007.87.

FIGURE 3.15. The 1942 Moose Jaw, Saskatchewan, winners
of the Miss War Worker Beauty Pageant.
Source: Canadian Museum of History IMG2016-0138-0005-Dm.

while industrial leaders viewed the pageants as unbeatable recruitment, advertising, and public relations opportunities. Internal correspondence between officials at Ontario's John Inglis factory noted that the goal of their war worker pageant was to recruit more women, "especially office workers and housewives," stating, "the idea being to have the impression that it might be good business for some of these girls to quit their present jobs and come here."[124]

The pageants not only met explicitly stated recruitment goals but also normalized women's industrial work and combatted social anxiety about the erosion of women's femininity in a male workplace. As Patrizia Gentile notes, "Beauty pageants such as Miss War Worker, Miss Civil Service, and Miss Secretary of Canada eroticized and challenged women's presence in the workplace."[125] Pageants held across the country brought together women judged by their own colleagues to be perfect representations of wartime femininity. One factory newsletter, headlined "Beauty and the Helldivers," celebrated Can Car pin up Virginia Dunlop as being "graceful" and "alluring" but also "efficient."[126] In Toronto, hundreds of competitors from across the region gathered in 1942, 1943, and 1944 to promote their workplaces and vie for the chance to be crowned Miss War Worker. Magazines and newspapers featured the winner of the 1942 Toronto pageant.[127]

Scholars have studied beauty culture and its importance in the workplace as represented in war worker newsletters and other corporate publications. One study, by Helen Smith and Pamela Wakewich, found numerous articles, images, photo captions, and cartoons that emphasized female workers' feminine attributes in "their dual role in the warplant as both worker and decorative morale booster."[128] The General Engineering Company (GECO) newsletter, *The Fusilier*, promoted their company beauty contest and cheered the eight successful candidates who showed "super feminine pulchritude" and who were off to compete in the upcoming provincial contest in Toronto.[129] Beauty pageants were a small but important part of a widely held social belief in the need to keep women feminine even while they performed what was considered men's work in factories, laboratories, and even in the military.

LORIDA (LANDRY) LANGLOIS, SINGER MANUFACTURING COMPANY

This brooch (figure 3.16) was Lorida Landry's first purchase with the income she earned from her first job.[130] This small extravagance, a sterling-silver filigree framed cameo with a pale peach background, was a symbol of Landry's newfound financial

---

125 Gentile, *Queen of the Maple Leaf,* 90.
126 Smith and Wakewich, "'Beauty and the Helldivers,'" 89.
127 For more on war worker pageants, see Van Vugt, "Beauty on the Job."
128 Smith and Wakewich, "'Beauty and the Helldivers,'" 101.
129 *The Fusilier,* June 20, 1942, 1, no.7, General Engineering Company (Canada) fonds.
130 Lorida Landry's Brooch, CMH 2010.214.5.

FIGURE 3.16. Lorida Landry's cameo brooch.
Source: Canadian Museum
of History 2010.214.5.

freedom. She had been raised in a traditional Quebec Catholic environment and her father forbade her from working outside the home until she turned 21. Though as a young woman she had taken in paid sewing work at home, she was thrilled when wartime labour shortages, combined with her age of independence, allowed her to earn a steady paycheque. Landry began working at the Singer Manufacturing Company in 1941. During the war, Singer moved from building sewing machines to explosive shells and airplane propellers, expanding their workforce to include women.[131] Landry saved the brooch, along with other Singer souvenirs, and the CMH acquired the collection from her family in 2010.

Quality control was vital to ensuring safety for the factory workers and for the soldiers who would use Singer's wartime products. Inspectors ensured that the materials produced were not defective, something that could have devastating consequences. Lorida Landry worked as bomb detonator inspector on the production line, a job similar to that performed by Mary Campbell during the First World War. Her task was to check the needles for the detonators used in bombs and to verify proper assembly. Landry had started out as a clerical worker, but moved to the factory floor when she could, as wages there were higher. The work on the line moved quickly and could be hazardous. One of Lorida (Landry) Langlois's children later reported that "[My mother] used to say that [munitions] work was harder than working in the office since they really had to move it on the

OPPOSITE: FIGURE 3.17. Elphège and Lorida (Landry) Langlois on their wedding day, 1943.
Source: Canadian Museum of History CMH IMG2015-0159-0002-Dm.

131   Prud'homme, *Singer*, 29.

line, but the difference in pay was worth it."[132] In many wartime industrial plants, the rapid hiring of inexperienced workers led to an increase in workplace accidents and illnesses. A wartime survey of female industrial workers in Quebec by the Jeunesse ouvrière catholique (JOC) found that over 42 percent of the women had shifts that were longer than eight hours and over 35 percent regularly worked night shifts.[133] One Quebec woman recalled her exhaustion on the job in a factory, stating, "At the Arsenal, I worked seven days a week with only one-half hour for lunch. No holidays, civil or religious. The machines had to function all the time. I found it very hard, especially at night."[134] At Singer in Saint-Jean-sur-Richelieu, workers remembered long and exhausting hours in the factory. Almost all departments had to work full tilt to complete the factory's military orders.[135]

As a very religious young woman living in rural Quebec, Landry would have been subject to heightened pressure and conflicting social messages from both the wartime media and the Catholic clergy. Quebec society in particular was still very repressive towards women. In this era, the church exerted a strong influence on what was considered proper conduct. Quebec women only won the right to vote provincially in 1941 and their desire to take on paid war work was a contentious issue. Prominent politician Jean Drapeau described the use of women in war industry as a federal government plot to destroy Quebec.[136] In spite of the rhetoric, Quebec's central role in Canadian industrial production ensured high levels of female employment.

Some war plants remained very traditional, despite employing women. When she married her co-worker Elphège Langlois in 1943, Lorida (Landry) Langlois was let go from her job. This image (figure 3.17) was taken on their wedding day. At the time, company regulations prohibited married women at the Saint-Jean-sur-Richelieu plant from working.[137] After her marriage in 1943, Langlois stayed home, raised children, built the family home with her husband, and continued to sew for herself and her family.

132   CMH Acquisition File 2010.214.
133   Auger and Lamothe, *De la poêle à frire*, 134.
134   Auger and Lamothe, *De la poêle à frire*, 134. Translation by authors.
135   Prud'homme, *Singer*, 31.
136   Auger and Lamothe, *De la poêle à frire*, 128.
137   The Singer plant in Saint-Jean-sur-Richelieu was a branch of a larger multinational company. It is not clear whether this rule applied specifically to Quebec or if it was also in force at the American and Scottish Singer war plants.

FIGURE 3.18. Verda Sharp (*left*) and Dominion Bridge Company co-workers, 1940–1941.
Source: George Metcalf Archival Collection, Canadian War Museum 20190008-001.

VERDA SHARP, DOMINION BRIDGE

The photograph in figure 3.18 shows a group of women in coveralls and head-scarves, clothing typical of Second World War factory workers.[138] The patches on the coveralls depict the letters *D* and *B*, indicating that these women worked at the Dominion Bridge Company, which produced ships, bridges, cranes, and heavy machinery. In the background, to the right, large shell casings are racked, waiting to be filled. Like many other industrial firms, Dominion Bridge expanded into munitions production during the Second World War.

There are a few hints that this is a candid photo taken by an individual rather than an official propaganda image. The women appear casual and relaxed. Their smiles seem genuine, not awkward poses struck for an official photographer. The racial diversity in the image is a further clue that this photograph is from a private collection since wartime promotional material rarely featured Black women.

138 Verda Sharp and Other Female Employees of Dominion Bridge Company, CWM 20190008-001.

American labour historian Jacqueline Jones argues that governments and mainstream media outlets in the United States aimed their wartime industrial production recruitment almost exclusively at white women, and the same can be said for Canada.[139] In southern Ontario industrial production centres (where a relatively high percentage of Black Canadians lived due to earlier waves of immigration from the United States), the presumption that all wartime factory workers were white is, and was, incorrect. This photograph, taken in Toronto in about 1940–1941, shows photographic evidence of Black women in the wartime industrial production workforce, a group of war workers who remain largely invisible in the historical record. The woman at the far left of the picture is Verda Sharp, from Toronto.[140]

While Sharp began working in war production relatively early, this was not the typical experience for Black women. Racism had shut them out of many industries prior to the war, and this tendency lingered into the war years. In October 1942, articles in the *Globe and Mail* reported that "racial and religious discrimination is quite rampant in Ontario" regardless of the efforts of the National Selective Service (NSS) to ensure full employment for all eligible workers.[141] The NSS, a government body that enumerated and tracked Canadians to assess their usefulness as potential workers, did not force companies to hire all available workers, instead allowing each corporation the latitude to restrict employment by race.[142] According to the *Globe and Mail*, there was an "ethnic crisis" in Ontario, with many companies refusing to hire Black workers.[143] The NSS eventually imposed new rules, forcing employers to forgo racial restrictions for new recruits.[144] By 1943, when the war was in full swing and labour shortages were nearing their height, a few non-white women did appear in government propaganda produced by the Wartime Information Board, but their presence is so noticeable and exceptional that they are now recognizable to historians by name, for instance Cecilia Butler, Agnes Wong, and Mrs. Martin Malti.[145]

139 Brand, *No Burden to Carry*, 24.
140 Verda Sharp was married but separated. She may have been known at the time as Verda Thompson.
141 "Color Line is Drawn," 15; "War Effort Racial Ban," 4.
142 Brand, *No Burden to Carry*, 21.
143 "Color Line is Drawn," 15.
144 Brand, *No Burden to Carry*, 21.
145 Library and Archives Canada online database: MIKAN 3197070 (Cecilia Butler,...

In 1945, Dominion Bridge, where the women in this photograph worked, published a book celebrating its wartime contributions. The book featured dozens of images of male and female war workers, all of them white.[146] Another nearby munitions factory, General Engineering Company (GECO) in Scarborough, published a company newsletter that was exceptional because it included their diverse workforce in the company newsletter, the *Fusilier*.[147] GECO, a government-sponsored shell-filling plant, was one of the largest munitions facilities in Canada with over 170 buildings, and employing over 21,000 people (mainly women).[148] The location of the plant, in close proximity to racially diverse Toronto, may have explained the relatively high visibility of Black women in their workforce. Many munitions plants recruited women from across the country, focusing on rural areas, which tended to be less culturally diverse than urban production centres. Whatever the case, the presence of Black women in the GECO official corporate record, as embodied by the *Fusilier*, is unusually strong. Numerous photographs in the newsletter feature Black women in their GECO uniforms at work, enjoying social occasions, and in the pin ups section, often with text that includes their names, job titles, and personal details. Oral histories conducted with Black women also attest to the fact that they were present in the GECO workforce, helping the war effort as they could, alongside the women whose photographs were featured in the press as recruitment tools.

Verda Sharp's photograph, the GECO *Fusilier*, and the above-mentioned interviews, which the Immigrant Women's Job Placement Centre conducted and were later published by Dionne Brand in *No Burden to Carry*, document Black women's presence in Canada's wartime munitions production workforce. Despite this, historians have had difficulty estimating their number. Local and corporate archives across the country sometimes hold employment records for individual companies, however, no one has conducted a comprehensive study to see how

---

...December 1943), 3191599 (Agnes Wong, April 1944) and 3990863 (Mrs. Martin Malti, January 1943). Whether these publicity images were included in promotional films or publications remains a question for further research.

146 Dominion Bridge, *Of Tasks Accomplished*.

147 While many large industrial production firms, military bases and training schools, banks, and department stores had regular newsletters for their staff, rarely do these publications feature women (or men) who are Black, Indigenous, or Asian.

148 Dickson, *Bomb Girls*, preface and chap. 10, Kindle.

many companies recorded the racial background of employees. Oral histories provide conflicting information. Bertha McAleer, a Black woman working at GECO, remembered that there were "some," but not a lot, of Black employees at the plant.[149] Another Black worker, Marjorie Lewsey, stated the opposite, "I have pictures of some of us that were out there [at GECO]... There were many Black women out there."[150]

According to her son, Norman Cook, Verda Sharp's job at Dominion Bridge was the first time that she had ever worked alongside that many women of different backgrounds.[151] Until the Second World War, many traditionally female jobs like typing, teaching, and nursing remained closed to women from minority communities as employers often refused to hire Black candidates, either male or female, due to racial prejudice. In the years leading up to the Second World War, most Black Canadian women in the workforce, Verda Sharp among them, were domestic servants. Historians James St. G. Walker and Dionne Brand write that "in 1941, 80% of Black adult females in Montréal were employed as domestic servants," numbers similar to those in Toronto.[152] Until labour shortages disrupted traditional hiring patterns, there were few other choices for Black women.[153] Sharp grew up believing that her only future lay in domestic service and as a teen had been "discouraged from continuing her schooling and told that she would find employment only in domestic work."[154] When she met her husband, she left school early to marry, later stating, "I didn't finish school. It wasn't necessary for girls to finish. You just got married and had babies, which was exactly what I did. I was 15 when I had Danny and 17 when I had Barbara."[155] She and her husband separated, leaving Sharp on her own with two small children. Her mother or other female relatives took care of the children while Sharp worked, first in domestic service, and then later as a clerk and switchboard operator for the doctor who had delivered her second baby.

149   Brand, *No Burden to Carry*, 83.

150   Brand, *No Burden to Carry*, 243.

151   The authors would like to thank Norman Cook for sharing family stories about Verda Sharp. Norman Cook, notes from conversation and interview.

152   Brand, "We Weren't Allowed to Go into Factory Work," 181.

153   Brand, *No Burden to Carry*, 15, 22.

154   Braithwaite and Benn-Ireland, *Some Black Women*, 29.

155   Hill, *Women of Vision*, 42.

Verda Sharp started at Dominion Bridge in 1939. Her children had reached school age, and industrial work was higher paying than administrative work. Norman Cook recalls that his mother took pleasure in her new friendships with other Dominion Bridge war workers, particularly the French Canadian women.[156] Several of the women in the Dominion Bridge photograph were Verda Sharp's close friends who had come from Quebec to work in Toronto. According to Norman Cook, his mother believed the war to be a "great integrator of the country" and an experience that "widened [her] world view."[157] Another Black woman, Viola Berry Aylestock, voiced similar thoughts: "I think the whole thing opened up with the war: more was demanded and consequently they had to have more people in jobs; this was the turning point for Blacks."[158]

In the photograph of Verda Sharp and her Dominion Bridge friends, the women wear protective coveralls. Factory workers at most industrial production plants purchased specific clothing, designed to be tough, washable, close-fitting for safety around heavy machinery, and for those working with munitions, non-static to reduce fire hazards.[159] Sharp's coveralls would also have protected her from burns when she worked as part of a riveting team. This work sometimes frightened her: some of the women she worked with suffered burns from the hot rivets. Sharp, who was very conscious of safety, did not enjoy it.[160]

In 1940, Dominion Bridge expanded and began making munitions. Sharp moved from riveting to producing 3.7-inch brass anti-aircraft cartridge cases. The plant manufactured several different types of casings, shipping over 25 million overseas by October 1944.[161] Like riveting, this work could be dangerous, and Sharp worried about explosions or accidents at the factory. Anne Wilmot, a Black worker at GECO, recalled that tetryl, a dangerous explosive used to fill the shell casings, was highly flammable. It also caused a chemical reaction that discoloured her skin.[162] Another worker, Bertha McAleer, recalled, "I guess if I was thinking about it today, maybe I wouldn't have done that... But at the time it was good

156 Cook, notes from conversation and interview.
157 Cook, interview.
158 Brand, *No Burden to Carry*, 96.
159 General Engineering, *Scarboro*.
160 Cook, interview.
161 Dominion Bridge, *Of Tasks Accomplished*, 42.
162 Dickson, *Bomb Girls*, chap. 7, Kindle.

money; we were really filling these shells... My goodness the place could've blown up!"[163] Some Black war workers believed that, like the other women, they were given lesser paid or more menial jobs than male colleagues, but also that they were assigned more dangerous tasks. Fern Shadd Shreve recalled, "I remember in the munitions factory—Chatco Steel in Chatham—that was where there were more Blacks than any other job that I think that I worked on... I guess if I wanted to make a case of it, I could probably say that the Blacks were doing the dirtier work, but I can't prove that."[164]

Verda Sharp did not work in munitions for the duration of the war. She remarried, and afterwards found jobs in restaurants, retail establishments, and as an office cleaner. After attending secretarial school, she rose to a high-level position with the YMCA. Sharp, now Verda Cook, became a leader in the community, one of the founders of the Congress of Black Women and the National Black Coalition.[165]

PRACTICE BUZZER

The object in figure 3.19 looks like an industrial component of some kind, but it is in fact a window into a significant wartime problem for many women workers: childcare. Twelve-year-old Raymond Tartre used this device, a Morse code practice buzzer, while he lived at the Saint Arsène Orphanage boarding house in Montréal.[166] Tapping the round black button (key lever) on the right with one finger, Raymond would listen to the buzzer (activated by batteries held in the tube on the left) sounding out his code rhythms. When used with a friend, one child could be sending Morse code, while the other learned how to decode messages. Practice buzzers like this one taught children a potentially valuable skill, and perhaps more importantly, kept them occupied for hours. Raymond served in the orphanage's army cadet corps and was given this device as part of his training. His mother, who worked at the Montréal Locomotive Works producing tanks, had no access to childcare and had to send

163 Brand, *No Burden to Carry*, 83.
164 Brand, *No Burden to Carry*, 276.
165 Braithwaite and Benn-Ireland, *Some Black Women*, 29.
166 Raymond Tarte's Morse Code Practice Buzzer, CWM 20060047-001.

FIGURE 3.19. A child's Morse Code practice buzzer.
Source: Canadian War Museum 20060047-001.

her son to board in an orphanage. He was allowed to visit his family only one weekend a month.[167] Childcare was an enormous barrier for women who were eager to earn the high wages war industry promised but whose children were too young to care for themselves.

Childcare was a problem for employers as well as mothers. The popular press, which fed social anxiety over the presence of women in the workforce, frequently referred to the fates that befell children left alone while mothers worked outside the home. One article, published in *Chatelaine* magazine, reported that juvenile delinquency for children 12 years old and under, had increased by 100 percent since 1939 and pointed at war plants in the heavily industrialized provinces of Ontario and Quebec as the culprits.[168] Much like the whispering campaign that threatened to reduce recruitment of military women, so too did fears of disintegrating families fuel suspicion of working mothers.[169]

Faced with the prospect of labour shortages in essential war industries, the Canadian government established a wartime day nursery

---

167   CWM Acquisition File 20060047.
168   "Is Home Life Breaking Up?," 8–9.
169   Pasolli, "'I Ask You, Mr. Mitchell,'" 7.

program to help working mothers and their employers. Twenty-eight nurseries in Ontario and six in Quebec looked after around 4,000 children between 1942 and 1946. Another 2,500 children were enrolled in other care programs.[170] The day nursery's establishment sent a clear public message: the labour of working mothers was valuable to the war effort, and Canadian women who chose to work in war factories should have access to safe, reliable childcare. The day nurseries closed in 1946, having been sold to the public as a temporary means of facilitating war workers in a national emergency. While working mothers still existed, their childcare needs were no longer a government priority.

INGE OSWALD, ONTARIO FARM SERVICE FORCE

"Farm Service Force—We Lend A Hand." So reads the emblem on this sweatshirt, signalling that its wearer was a member of the Ontario Farm Service Force (OFSF), a wartime organization dedicated to increasing the amount of food produced for the war.[171] As had been the case during the previous war, Second World War–era farmers suffered labour shortages. With their usual workforce engaged in military or other better-paying wartime pursuits, farmers needed help lest their coming crops rot for want of hands to harvest them for, as an article at the time stated, "fruit, like time, waits for no man."[172] Following the model of the First World War, they once again turned to young women for help.

While the sweatshirt is rather androgynous in appearance, it belonged to a young woman, a farmerette named Inge Oswald. It looks baggy and loose, as sweatshirts often are, and is rather small. Oswald was only a teen when she bought it, probably as a souvenir of her time as a farmerette rather than as an official

OPPOSITE TOP: FIGURE 3.20. Inge Oswald's Ontario Farm Service Force sweatshirt. *Source:* Canadian War Museum 20120014-002.
OPPOSITE BOTTOM: FIGURE 3.21. Inge Oswald's Ontario Farm Service Force cap. *Source:* Canadian War Museum 20120014-001.

---

170   Pasolli, "'I Ask You, Mr. Mitchell,'" 2.
171   Inge (Oswald) Cumberland's Ontario Farm Service Force Sweatshirt and Cap, CWM 20120014-001; 20120014-002.
172   "Ottawa Girls Spend Summer," 7.

uniform piece. Sweatshirts had recently come into fashion for young people in active or athletic pursuits, and there are several examples in Canadian museum collections and period photographs. Oswald did not often wear the sweatshirt while working, as it was far too hot in the sweltering southern Ontario fruit belt. According to information received from her family along with the sweatshirt, she did, however, wear it for many years after the war, including on her honeymoon.

Originally from Austria, Oswald had immigrated to Canada with her family in 1936. Once the war began, the Oswalds found that they were now considered enemy aliens. They had to report regularly to the police station, something that embarrassed young Oswald, who worried about what her peers would say if they found out. In an essay she later wrote for the *Globe and Mail* newspaper, Oswald recalled that coming to Canada, learning a new language, and assimilating to a new culture had already been difficult for her—the war and her Austrian background now added to her anxiety.[173]

In the early 1940s, Oswald (figure 3.22, *right*) joined the OFSF with her best friend, Nora Cumberland (*left*), and went to work on a fruit farm near Beamsville in the Niagara region of southern Ontario. Oswald's summer as a farmerette was cut short after she had a serious allergic reaction to peaches—a problem on a fruit farm. She then went to work at a Campbell's Soup factory, an occupation she liked far less than working in the orchards. Oswald's experience—minus the allergic reaction—generally mirrored that of the thousands of young women who also enrolled in the OFSF. They were there because the loss of male labourers meant that, once again, women were among those marshalled into brigades of farm help.

In April 1941, the Government of Ontario had announced a farm service force modelled on the groups formed during the First World War.[174] The OFSF was made up of separate divisions according to the age and gender of the participants, and entailed varying levels of commitment. The most casual was the Farm Commando Brigade, where adult men and women worked as "spare-time farm hands," helping out whenever they could, on a fairly ad hoc basis. It was unlikely

OPPOSITE: FIGURE 3.22. Inge Oswald (*left*) with Nora Cumberland, ca. 1942.
Source: George Metcalf Archival Collection, Canadian War Museum 20120014-004.

173   Cumberland, "Knitting Our Country," A30.
174   "Will Organize Youth," 20.

that they were there for the money. They were paid 25 cents an hour, which they could, according to an OFSF advertisement, pass along to their "favourite charities."[175] The Holiday Service Brigade was for "salaried persons who have a week to a month of holidays with pay." These folks were encouraged to seek out farmer friends and relatives who needed their help, or else the OFSF would set them up with "a congenial farmer." The Women's Land Brigade was for women 20 years of age or older, who would work for six months to a year in agriculture, engaged in "milking, feeding, and care of stock, field work, haying, stooking grain, threshing, working with horses and tractors."[176] Teenagers were not left out of the farming fun; the Farm Cadet Brigade was for young men age 15 and up who would work on their summer holidays from school. Finally, the Farmerette Brigade was set up to accommodate young women age 16 and up who would work mainly in fruit and vegetable cultivation.

Many of the thousands of teenagers who made up this group lived in camps under the YWCA's supervision, going out during the day to work with the province's many fruit and vegetable growers. Each farmerette was given a pledge card to sign, where she agreed to uphold a code of behaviour that included a promise to remain, "physically fit, mentally alert and at all times to conduct [herself] in an acceptable manner."[177] They were encouraged to position the card where they could be inspired by the pledge as well as a motivating poem by Edgar Guest that was supposed to "stimulate [the farmerettes] to further endeavor."[178]

There were many incentives for young women like Inge Oswald to join the Farmerette Brigade. If their school grades were satisfactory, they were excused from year-end exams so they could leave school early to go out to farms in the spring. Then there was the patriotic appeal of farm service. Seventeen-year-old Yvonne Frere spoke of getting a "victory tan" over the summer, framing her farmerette work as war service.[179] With so many Canadians engaging in all sorts of causes to support the war effort, spending the summer as a farmerette was an exciting yet safe way to join in for teenage girls. Parents could be assured that their

---

175   Ontario Farm Service Force advertisement, 18.
176   Dominion-Provincial Committee on Farm Labour advertisement, 10.
177   Ontario Farm Service Force Pledge Certificate, Marilyn Clark, CWM 20130108-002.
178   Ontario Farm Service Force Pledge Certificate.
179   "Mattawa Farmerettes," 31.

underage daughters were being supervised—at least in theory—by the YWCA chaperones and the girls themselves would benefit from living and working in a healthy, happy atmosphere surrounded by their peers. The YWCA also provided a nurse and recreational secretary who travelled around the dozens of camps dotting the Ontario countryside.[180] The summer camp feel of the scheme was used as a selling point with one advertisement even calling the work "a vacation that will hasten victory."[181]

Of course, farm work was strenuous and far from being a vacation. While the young women of the OFSF made money for their hard work, no farmerette was getting rich. They worked 9 to 10 hours a day and received approximately $15 a week (around $235 in 2021), although more was possible if they worked extra hours. They supplied their own work clothes, soap, towels, and personal supplies. From their pay, $4.50 a week went to room and board and they had to purchase their own dress uniform to be worn after hours, which cost $7.50.[182] Oswald and Cumberland wear this uniform in figure 3.22 and they each appear to have hemmed them to fit (their skirts are different lengths). The farmerettes were encouraged to wear the dress uniform to foster a sense of "camp spirit," but it was also a nod to the differing socio-economic backgrounds of the farmerettes. As the *Ottawa Journal* explained it, "If one were able to doll up in fancy sports clothes after the day's work while another wore shoddy clothing, the democratic aspect of the camp life might suffer."[183] Dressing alike, much like soldiers, with their military-style wedge cap, epaulettes, and service badge, also reinforced the notion that this was war service of a real and valuable sort. The uniform may also have served as a means to further distinguish the farmerettes from seasonal farm labourers, many of whom were racialized minorities looked upon by some locals as "more menial than housemaids."[184] It is arguable that providing uniforms, special camps, souvenir sweatshirts, and entertainment to the farmerettes helped with recruitment efforts for those who might have considered their (largely) middle-class daughters too good for farm or food processing work.

180   "National Y.W. Increases Camps," 5.
181   "Des vacances," 7.
182   "Harvesting to Beat Hitler," 23.
183   "Harvesting to Beat Hitler," 23.
184   Patrias, "More Menial than Housemaids," 69.

The OFSF continued to operate into the postwar years. As the war ended, the need for food did not immediately lessen; a ravaged Europe needed time to rehabilitate its agricultural capacity. Nor did the farm labour crisis stop with the fighting. Accordingly, the appeals made to potential farm service recruits shifted from winning the war to winning the peace, to humanitarian rather than martial goals.[185] Oswald never made this shift to postwar farm work, but she continued to wear her farmerette sweatshirt in the years afterward, a memory of her wartime service.[186]

NORMA ETTA LEE, QUEBEC AIRWAYS

This certificate, titled *British Commonwealth Air Training Plan*, encapsulates one woman's wartime work.[187] What it lacks in visual appeal it more than made up for in meaning, at least to its recipient, Norma Etta Lee. The certificate is proof of her wartime service and a holder of memories. She kept it, with reams of wartime documents, photographs, newspaper clippings and her "whiz wheel" (a basic flight computer) in a large, annotated scrapbook that was donated to the CWM after her death. For historians, it is a springboard to a key part of Canada's war effort.

The BCATP was a massive program that trained a significant portion of the Commonwealth's pilots, navigators, bombers, gunners, wireless operators, and flight engineers—130,000 aircrew in total.[188] Canada had trained aviators during the First World War and that history, combined with political expedience, led to the BCATP. In Canada, politicians thought that the country might not need to supply as many fighting men as it had during the First World War if it instead provided the Allies with food, munitions, airplanes, and training.[189] However, the plan's success had the consequence of bringing large numbers of Canadian aviators directly into the line of fire. Over 72,000 Canadian graduates of the plan, about half of those who trained, helped to fill RCAF and RAF squadrons, bringing Canadian pilots into action, and resulting in a large number of Canadian casualties.[190] The

---

185 "Young Canadians!," 13.

186 CWM Acquisition File 20120014.

187 Norma Etta Lee, British Commonwealth Air Training Plan Certificate, 1945, CWM 20060058-002.

188 Hatch, *Aerodrome of Democracy*, xv.

189 Cook, *Necessary War*, 161.

190 Hatch, *Aerodrome of Democracy*, 202.

BRITISH COMMONWEALTH AIR TRAINING PLAN

This is to Certify

THAT   Miss Norma Lee

served at this unit, operated under and forming part of the British Commonwealth Air Training Plan

From April 2nd, 1942   *To*   March 31st, 1945

In the capacity of:

Control Tower Operator

Description:

Age 27 *Years*   *Height* 5 *Feet* 5 *Ins*

Colour of: Eyes Hazel   *Hair* Auburn

Specimen Signature

Conduct and Character whilst serving:

Very Good

Reason for Discharge:

School Closing

Signed:

Manager No. 6   *Air Observer School*

Countersigned:

Dept. of National Defence for Air

General Supervisor Air Observer Schools

Nᵒ 282

FIGURE 3.23. Norma Etta Lee's British Commonwealth Air Training Plan certificate.
Source: George Metcalf Archival Collection, Canadian War Museum 20060058-002.

BCATP earned Canada the nickname "the Aerodrome of Democracy," and it left a significant mark on the nation's social and economic fabric.[191] Much of the wartime infrastructure built for the program (hangars, runways, air traffic control towers, and airports) formed the basis for Canada's postwar commercial aviation industry. Marriages and friendships between foreign aircrews and Canadian women and their families were another enduring legacy of the program. British, Australian, and New Zealand airmen met Canadian wives while in training.[192]

Seemingly simple details of the certificate tell us important information about the BCATP and the woman to whom the certificate was given. Signed by officials from the Department of National Defence for Air, the General Supervisor for Air Observer Schools, and the Manager of the No. 8 Air Observer School, the certificate, No. 282, was issued to Miss Norma Lee. Despite the military objectives of the BCATP, it employed many civilians, such as Lee. Responsible for basic pilot and navigation training, many of the Elementary Flying Training Schools (EFTS) and Air Observer Schools (AOS) were run by civilian companies. With civilian staff and infrastructure, the military was able to establish and develop the BCATP much faster than if it had been obliged to begin building infrastructure and a workforce from scratch. The certificate also tells us that women, as well as men, worked for the BCATP in a variety of capacities at wartime airfields, both as members of the RCAF-WD and as civilians. From administrative and support duties like cooking, nursing, and clerking to more specialized tasks related to communications, aircraft maintenance, or instruction, women were essential to running the massive number of BCATP sites across the country. While there were many women whose labour contributed to the smooth running of civilian and military airfields across Canada, Lee's work was exceptional for a woman of her time.

According to the certificate, Lee started with the BCATP on April 2, 1942, and was employed as a control tower operator. Other documents, including reference letters from supervisors, work schedules, runway diagrams, and maps in Lee's fonds at the CWM's George Metcalf Archival Collection flesh out the details of her wartime career. She began her career at Quebec Airways at L'Ancienne Lorette airport in Québec City. L'Ancienne Lorette was a BCATP hub that was expanding

191   Hatch, *Aerodrome of Democracy,* iv. The phrase was apparently coined by Lester B. Pearson in a letter he drafted for President F. D. Roosevelt.
192   Kozar, *Canada's War Grooms,* 3.

and changing rapidly. Lee worked with the No. 8 AOS, which had opened in 1941. Canadian Pacific Air Lines sponsored the school and a combination of civilian and military staff operated it. RCAF instructors taught ground school, where student pilots learned basic aeronautical skills and flight procedures, but civilian staff filled many of the other administrative, communications, mechanical, and facilities management positions, described by one Department of Defence historian as "housekeeping functions."[193] In spite of what was supposed to be a clear distinction between civilian and military, the lines were quite often blurred, with aviation companies hiring civilian pilots to provide in-flight training and civilians conducting some ground instruction. Civilian flight instructor positions were occasionally even staffed by women, including one "Mrs. D. Grosfils" who instructed on the Link Trainer at L'Ancienne Lorette.[194] Another woman, who taught at the bombing and gunnery school at Mont Joli, was noteworthy enough to be mentioned in a history of the airfield, though her name was not included.[195]

According to Peter Wood, a nephew of Lee's, she had responded in March 1942 to a call for workers from the airport at L'Ancienne Lorette.[196] At the time, Lee was a member of the Quebec Women's Volunteer Reserve Corps, a women's paramilitary group, and was looking for a new challenge as well as another way to help the war effort. She was hired as an air traffic control tender operator, a position for which she received on-the-job training. Her summary of employment describes this job as controlling the aircraft of No. 8 AOS "by means of the Aldis lamp and Very pistol," which means she used a signal lamp and a flare gun to direct aircraft belonging to the BCATP.[197] Lee had only been in this position for two months when it was cut.

Lee then requested a transfer to the parachute section. She learned to pack and maintain parachutes in Toronto, then returned to No. 8 AOS. Rather than pack parachutes, she now became one of four control tower operators, the rest of whom were men (see figure 3.24). In this photograph, Lee stands with three co-workers

---

193 Hatch, *Aerodrome of Democracy*, 43.

194 *The Last Flight*, 118.

195 Dornier, *Des bombardiers au-dessus du fleuve*, 24.

196 Wood, correspondence. The authors would like to thank Peter Wood for sharing family stories about Norma Etta Lee.

197 Norma Etta Lee—Summary of Employment, Scrapbook of Norma Etta Lee, 1939–1945, CWM 20060058-006.

FIGURE 3.24. Norma Etta Lee with her control tower operator colleagues, ca. 1944.
Source: George Metcalf Archival Collection, Canadian War Museum 20060₅8-014.

in the control tower. To the left is an air traffic control desk, with radio receivers, clock, and handheld radio transmitters. Hanging from the ceiling to the right is the Aldis lamp, used for signalling incoming aircraft. None of the four employees are wearing a uniform, but Lee's fonds contains a fabric badge bearing the winged Quebec Airways insignia, which may once have been sewn to a jacket. Lee's work in the tower included operating the radio to manage air traffic, keeping track of all flight plans into and out of the airport, compiling aircraft reports, tracking the weather, and making sure all equipment was in order, including emergency backups. She carefully noted her various tasks in a summary of her work at Quebec Airways.[198]

In 1943, the growth of aviation in Canada led the government to create a role for women in control towers, calling this new designation air traffic control assistant.[199] A few women, of whom Lee was one, were able to continue their work as full-fledged air traffic control operators because of their prior experience, but women beginning in the field were funnelled through an assistant's training

198 Norma Etta Lee—Summary of Employment.
199 "Thirty Young Women," 8.

program. Without some kind of national registry of airport employees, it is difficult to say exactly how many women may have been working in air traffic control in Canada during the war. With the field in its infancy and not yet centralized or regulated, women working in control towers may have had different titles or performed only parts of the job, working as radio operators or assistants. Without a comprehensive study of early airports and staffing practices, it is impossible to know how many women may have worked in this role. Whether or not Lee was the "first" or the "only" as she believed herself to be, we may never know. What we do know is that Lee worked as an air traffic controller at a time when this was a rarity for women.

Lee's work with the BCATP ended on March 31, 1945. When the need for newly trained pilots and aircrew decreased towards the end of the war, the BCATP began to shut down its training schools, including the No. 8 AOS. When Lee left, she left the world of aviation forever. She was unable to continue as an air traffic controller as the need for women in aviation dried up in the postwar era. Lee apparently hoped to continue in this field, gathering reference letters and writing a long summary of her work history at L'Ancienne Lorette. Her fonds also contains a blank Civil Service application form. But the massive number of returning veterans who had been trained by the BCATP more than filled any air traffic control positions, even in a postwar boom in civil aviation. Aviation was once more considered a man's world. Even though she had been held back, Lee remained interested in the fate of women working as air traffic controllers. Long after the war, Lee kept an annotated scrapbook of clippings showing the slow advancement of Canadian women into the profession.

KATHLEEN MCGRATH,
CHRISTIE ST. VETERANS' AND SUNNYBROOK HOSPITALS

Two mismatched eyes peer eerily out of a box (figure 3.25). One is blue, the other brown. Though they closely resemble human eyes, they are not fully spherical and are, in fact, prosthetics. The box is rather fancy, like a jewelry case. These are the last two artificial eyes ocularist Kathleen McGrath crafted. She considered them to be among her best work.[200]

---

200 Artificial Eyes, CWM 20110152-025.

FIGURE 3.25. Artificial eyes made by Kathleen McGrath.
Source: Canadian War Museum 20110152-025.

Wars do horrible things to human bodies. In addition to those killed during the Second World War, over 50,000 Canadians were wounded.[201] Some of the injuries were life-altering, requiring specialized care. Prosthetics then, of all kinds, were important during and after the Second World War, smoothing the transition to peacetime for thousands of injured veterans. By 1948, over 29,000 had enrolled in rehabilitation programs offered by the Department of Veterans Affairs.[202] Of those, 1,769 had suffered "partial and total losses of hearing and sight."[203] Among that number were those who had suffered an enucleation—loss of an eyeball—and for them, it was vital to obtain a properly fitted and aesthetically harmonious artificial eye. As an article from the First World War noted, prosthetic eyes were more than a simple cosmetic improvement: "Far from being a mere esthetic question, this, in fact, is a matter of the highest practical, hygienical importance, a hollow socket being a continual annoyance to the patient, on account of the secretion produced by the dropping eye-lids, which is liable even to affect the sound eye."[204] Artificial eyes fulfilled a physical and psychological need for those coming to terms with the effects of such a devastating injury.

McGrath (pictured in figure 3.26 in 1933) did not start the war making prosthetic eyes. A trained nurse, she was working as a laboratory technologist for the Dominion Government in Toronto when she came to the attention of Dr. Clifford Taylor, a ground-breaking ophthalmologist. Taylor was a veteran

OPPOSITE: FIGURE 3.26. Kathleen McGrath, 1933.
Source: George Metcalf Archival Collection, Canadian War Museum 20110152-017.

201 Cook, *Fight to the Finish*, 436–437.
202 Tremblay, "Going Back to Main Street," 161; see also Durflinger, *Veterans with a Vision.*
203 Tremblay, "Going Back to Main Street," 172.
204 Davro, "Artificial Eyes," 47.

of the First World War Canadian Army Medical Corps, and his research at the National Research Council in Ottawa led to innovative synthetic eye prosthetics for wounded servicemen. He hired McGrath as a technician in 1941.[205]

The brutal injuries of war often lead to advances in rehabilitative technology. Although experimentation to reconstruct the faces and eyes of injured soldiers had begun centuries earlier, it was not until the mid-nineteenth century that hollow glass prosthetic eyes had become possible. They became much lighter, more comfortable, and more realistic than previous attempts at glass eyes. German engineering and materials were at the heart of these prosthetics, but the two world wars forced Allied doctors to experiment with new techniques and materials.[206] The sand traditionally used to make glass eyes came largely from Germany, so Allied doctors needed to find replacement material. The first synthetic eye prosthetics were made in 1943 by a team of three US Army dentists, and ocularists built on their work, creating other facial prosthetics that advanced the field during the Second World War.[207] Taylor and McGrath worked with new synthetic compounds to produce safe and accurate replicas of damaged eyeballs for returning veterans. By 1946, the Canadian government had already provided over 800 ocular prosthetics to blinded servicemen through Taylor's clinic.

McGrath and Taylor worked out of the ophthalmic divisions of Toronto's Christie St. Veterans' and Sunnybrook hospitals, but they also travelled across the country fitting prosthetic eyes for their patients. Although specialized companies manufactured ready-made prosthetic eyes, custom-fitted versions such as those Taylor and McGrath made were of superior quality. Taylor advertised their services, stating that contacting him was "an opportunity for those that cannot be fitted satisfactorily with stock eyes, to receive expert service."[208] Among the tools and materials McGrath kept are jars of polymer powders, along with curettes and droppers. With equipment such as this, Taylor and McGrath created prosthetics for those who needed specialized products. In addition to ensuring a customized fit, they hand painted the prosthetics to match a veteran's natural eye colour, using minute brushes.

---

205 CWM Acquisition File 20110152.
206 Flascha, "Prosthetics Under Trials of War."
207 Erpf, Dietz, and Wirtz, "Opthalmoprosthesis," 406.
208 "Announcement! Artificial Eyes Made to Order," CWM 20110152-002.

When McGrath began working for Taylor in 1941, she fitted prosthetic eyes. Later, as she gained experience, she manufactured them herself. Letters of recommendation she saved describe her work as exemplary.[209] The nature of her job kept McGrath in the workforce longer than most of the women featured in this chapter, for whom the end of war meant an end to their wartime occupations. But injuries did not miraculously heal when the war ended; rehabilitating service personnel needed ongoing care, and McGrath continued working until the mid-1950s. In 1955, she quit the paid workforce to start a family. She kept her tools, her papers, and her boxes of practice eyes, remnants of her war service that now remain for posterity in the collection of the CWM.

209 Dr. Ross Millar to Kathleen McGrath, May 28, 1941, CWM 20110152-005.

FIGURE 4.1. Lieutenant William Robert Boucher's personal effects box.
Source: George Metcalf Archival Collection, Canadian War Museum 20050205-011.

4 "DEEPLY REGRET TO INFORM YOU"
Women, Worry, and Loss

I N EXAMINING WOMEN'S CONTRIBUTIONS TO THE TWO WAR efforts, it is easy to find positive experiences. From serving in the military to finding higher-paying, meaningful work, the world wars gave women opportunities they would not have had otherwise. Women have also been more likely to discuss, publicly, the positive aspects of their wars, while keeping their darker moments hidden and private. But over-emphasizing the positive risks glossing over the fact that wars are overwhelmingly negative. While the physical toll of war is relatively easy to measure—over 100,000 Canadians lost their lives and more than 220,000 were wounded as a result of the world wars—it is more difficult to quantify the emotional toll of these conflicts. Every Canadian with loved ones in uniform experienced varying levels of worry and dread, and when the worst did occur, grief. Even for women whose family and friends returned to Canada safely after wars' end, the years of anxiety, physical distance, and sometimes trauma, left their mark. This chapter looks at the stress and anguish that was women's persistent and most commonly shared experience of the world wars.

The objects and archival material related to wartime grief are as varied as the women who lived it. Here, we consider objects that suggest women's losses, emotions, and the ways they coped. These stories highlight the personal cost of war, as well as how society recognized and shaped women's grief. Some objects, such as scrapbooks, photo albums, and letters, women created themselves and therefore offer a multidimensional glimpse into what women experienced during, and after, the wars. Other stories are more two-dimensional, as we have read women's lives through collections usually interpreted as part of a man's story. During and after the wars, women's personal losses were often framed as noble sacrifices, as contributions to the war effort. In some cases, this may have helped ease the pain, but it never erased the grief. While women's wartime experiences were as individual as the women themselves, loss, or the fear of loss, was the emotion that united almost everyone.

JEANNIE CASSELS BOUCHER

The small mass-produced brown cardboard box in figure 4.1 is pre-stamped with lines to indicate where twine should go, and bears little relation to a mother's experience of her living, breathing child.[1] And yet, along with a small collection of documents and ephemera, it was all that was left for Jeannie Cassels Boucher following her son's death on the battlefields of Europe. The box, labelled "EFFECTS," "Lieut. W. R. Boucher, 46th Can. Inf. Battn," is 20 cm tall, 27 cm wide, and 8 cm deep. A label, long gone, has been torn from the front. The remains of sealing wax appear on one side. According to the family, the parcel contained his wallet and chequebook, greeting cards, a flashlight, several battlefield souvenirs, a few small military-issue buttons, and a good-luck charm. The box and its contents were a poor substitute for Jeannie Boucher's son, but it was not possible to repatriate bodies for the comfort of grieving families. This was all that could be returned.

The parcel followed on the heels of a blunt, impersonal telegram that brought news no one wanted to receive. "Deeply regret inform you," it read, "Lieutenant

OPPOSITE: FIGURE 4.2. Jeannie Cassels Boucher, ca. 1930.
Source: Courtesy of Susan Harvie.

---

[1]   Personal Effects Box, Lt. William Robert Boucher, CWM 20050205-011.

William Robert Boucher infantry officially reported killed in action March twenty sixth nineteen seventeen."[2] Jeannie Boucher, pictured in figure 4.2, received the telegram two days after her son was killed by a shell near Vimy Ridge. Known to friends and family as Bob, he had enlisted a year before, at age 24.[3] The routine nature of death on the Western Front meant that much official correspondence related to loved ones killed seems, over a hundred years later, particularly bureaucratic and brutal. A letter Boucher had mailed to her son was also returned undelivered, unread, and stamped "Killed in Action."[4] The Minister of Militia and Defence's condolences arrived as a form letter, with "Madam" and "Lieut. William Robert Boucher" typed into an existing template. The number of deaths made impersonal form letters and mass-produced personal effects boxes a necessity.

More personal condolences of various kinds duly arrived at the family's home in Sudbury, Ontario. Countering the coldness of the bureaucratic form letters, battlefield comrades and friends of those killed spent considerable time writing to the families in Canada, describing how their loved ones lived and died overseas. Jeannie Boucher received sympathetic notes from H. J. Dawson, Lieutenant-Colonel of the 46th Battalion, as well as the regimental chaplain. A letter from Bob's close friend and fellow officer Fred McCulloch discussed the circumstances of his death. McCulloch explained that "Bob's body has been well looked after and will be buried at Villers aux Bois cemetery which is a few miles behind the lines."[5]

Friends and family on the home front also sent letters when they heard the news. One woman wrote to Jeannie Boucher that "Somehow I had never thought that anything would happen to Bob. He was so big and brave and strong."[6] A Mrs. Wallace sent her sentiments: "I think that only a mother knows how to sympathize with a mother. My own dear boy is in England, waiting orders to go to France, and God only knows if we shall see him again, but I just leave him in the Lord's hands."[7] Flora Bruce exhibited anger alongside sympathy: "When will this accursed war ever end. There are thousands of aching hearts in Canada & the end

2   Jeannie Cassels Boucher, telegram, March 28, 1917, CWM 20050205-033.
3   William Robert Boucher, CEF Personnel Record.
4   Jeannie Cassells Boucher to William Robert Boucher, March 15, 1917, CWM 20050205-033.
5   Fred McCulloch to the Boucher family, March 27, 1917, CWM 20050205-033.
6   M. G. Davison to Jeannie Cassells Boucher, March 29, 1917, CWM 20050205-033.
7   Mrs. Wallace to Jeannie Cassells Boucher, April 2, 1917, CWM 20050205-033.

is not yet in sight."[8] Another letter, from "Cousin Mary," also expressed weariness with the war and the ceaseless sorrow:

My thoughts flew to you and I said poor Jean, you are his Mother and I know loved him dearly, but you are not the only mother lost a dear son in this cruel war and there will be many more but I know when one of my boys put on the Khaki I will mourn him as dead. Death I am sure would be preferable to some than be like some of the fellows that are returning home here, and I am sure half of them never killed a German.[9]

Many of the women who wrote had family overseas themselves. Their letters, written out of shared experiences of worry and grief, likely still make sense to a twenty-first-century reader. In contrast, the language contained in a telegram from the Regina Victoria hockey club might seem remarkably out of place today. Sent to her, under her husband's name, it reads:

Mrs W. A. Boucher.
You are a sad but proud mother today. Your heroic son Robert died the noblest death of all that of giving his life for his country. He died as he had lived one of Natures noblemen and we extend to you our heartfelt sympathy with the firm belief that his death was not in vain.[10]

While the sentiments in this telegram may seem exaggerated to today's reader, Jeannie Boucher would have been very familiar with the language of sacrifice common at the time. Employed frequently during the world wars by the government, the press, and, as can be seen in this telegram, by private citizens, words that glorified battlefield death provided comfort and meaning. The emphasis on patriotic sacrifice shaped how women mourned. It reinforced the notion that the biggest contribution a woman could make was sacrificing her son or husband and dealing privately with the consequences. Keeping grief private (which

8   Flora N. Bruce to Jeannie Cassells Boucher, April 9, 1917, CWM 20050205-033.
9   "Cousin Mary" to Jeannie Cassells Boucher, April 10, 1917, CWM 20050205-033.
10   Regina Victoria Hockey Club to Mrs. W. A. (Jeannie) Boucher, telegram, March 29, 1917, CWM 20050205-033.

many may have done anyway) while valorizing loss minimized negative impacts on civilian morale.

Historians Carol Acton and Jay Winter have described grief as "the crucial experience through which individuals lived the 'meaning' of the First World War."[11] Accordingly, wartime literature, poetry, and newspaper headlines elevated mourning mothers like Jeannie Boucher to near-mythic status. Mothers' sacrifice of their beloved sons was glorified to encourage new recruits and maintain social order. Suzanne Evans, who has written about Canadian wartime mourning culture in *Mothers of Heroes, Mothers of Martyrs: World War I and the Politics of Grief*, notes that "the image of the war-supportive mother had a powerful influence over public opinion and was able to draw supporters to the cause."[12] Women were called upon to send their second son to the front to fill the gaps in the Canadian ranks left by their wounded or dead first sons. Jeannie Boucher's second son, Clarence did in fact serve in the CEF, having enlisted just two months after his elder brother. Thankfully, he survived the war. Like many Canadian families, the loss of a son in war was felt for generations. The Bouchers kept Jeannie's collection of material related to Bob's death intact for decades, and descendants donated it to the Canadian War Museum (CWM) almost 100 years after his death.

MEMORIAL CROSSES

The small object in figure 4.3—a silver medal measuring 3.5 cm × 3 cm—carries immense meaning.[13] It takes the shape of cross and laurel wreath, and has a royal cipher—in this case that of George V—in the centre. Maple leaves, symbolizing Canada, adorn the foot and arms of the cross, while the upright bears a crown. This is a Memorial Cross, and it stands as material evidence that women's losses were valorized as perhaps the highest contribution they could make to the war effort. The Canadian government authorized the creation of this honour, popularly known as the Silver Cross, in 1919. While the awards were inscribed with the name, rank, and service number of the deceased, they were given to women, namely

11   Acton, *Grief in Wartime*, 1, citing Winter, *Sites of Memory*, 224.
12   Evans, *Mothers of Heroes*, x. See also Evans, "Raising 'Human Ammunition.'"
13   Memorial Cross for Mason Francis Scott, received by Edna Scott, CWM 19890211-014.

the widows and mothers of the dead, who were encouraged to wear them. The honours were initially issued with a purple ribbon, similar to the one included in figure 4.3. Someone—possibly the recipient—has personalized this one by removing the ribbon and replacing it with a chain, perhaps a more secure way of wearing it. This particular Memorial Cross belonged to Edna Scott of Ottawa, who received it in honour of her son, Mason Francis Scott, who died from war-related causes in 1919.

FIGURE 4.3. A Memorial Cross.
Source: Tilston Memorial Collection of Canadian Military Medals, Canadian War Museum 19890211-014.

In the century since its inception, the Memorial Cross has become an iconic symbol. During the interwar years (and after), rituals such as Remembrance Day ceremonies and the 1936 Vimy pilgrimage put Memorial Cross women front and centre. They became, in a certain respect, Canada's vanguard of grief, a living connection to the dead who would never "break faith," as John McCrae wrote in "In Flanders Fields."[14] After the Second World War, some women who had lost loved ones banded together to form groups, such as the Remembrance Association Silver Cross Women of Canada. These organizations offered mutual support and the opportunity to help others affected by conflict. While these women hoped they would be the last of their kind, this was not to be.[15] Although the scale of the losses are smaller, Canadian participation in wars and other military missions have ensured that more women (and

14   McCrae, *In Flanders Fields.*
15   "They Seek No New Recruits," 41.

men, who can now receive the honour) have been added to the Memorial Cross rolls. And each year, the Royal Canadian Legion still selects a Silver Cross Mother to place a wreath at Canada's National War Memorial on November 11.

MARY HALL

On this bronze medal (figure 4.5), a lion stands atop the Royal crown, with "FOR VALOUR" inscribed below. It was not awarded to a woman, but a woman received it nevertheless. This is a Victoria Cross (VC), the British Empire's highest award

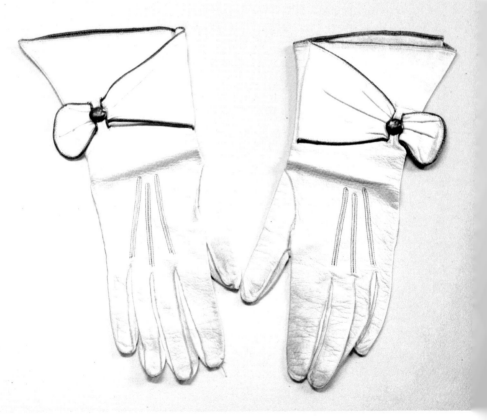

FIGURE 4.4. The gloves Mary Hall wore to receive Sergeant Major Frederick William Hall's Victoria Cross.
Source: Canadian War Museum 20130123-013.

for gallantry.[16] It can be—and all too often is—awarded posthumously, as in the case of Frederick William Hall, who earned this VC through an extraordinary act of self-sacrifice, a fatal attempt to save a wounded comrade from the battlefield. His mother, Mary Hall, received her late son's award in August 1915.[17] While Frederick Hall is well known as one of the three VC recipients who lived on Winnipeg's Pine Street, now known as Valour Road, what about his mother? Who thinks of her and how she felt? Who tells of her part in the wider story of war? The pair of cream-coloured, black-trimmed leather gloves pictured in figure 4.4 belonged to Mary Hall, and she was wearing them when she received her son's medal.[18] These gloves moved us to consider her experience of losing a son and the complicated feelings that this loss must have engendered.

The loss of Frederick may have been the worst moment of Mary Hall's war, but she bore other burdens as well. She had two more sons in service overseas, and their absence resulted in financial woes for Mary and her daughters, who gave music lessons to help

FIGURE 4.5. Sergeant Major Frederick William Hall's Victoria Cross.
Source: Tilston Memorial Collection of Canadian Military Medals, Canadian War Museum 20110146-001.

16   Sergeant Major Frederick William Hall's Victoria Cross, CWM 20110146-001.
17   Frederick William Hall, CSM, RG 150, CEF Personnel Record.
18   Mary Hall's Gloves, CWM 20130123-013.

MRS. HALL wearing the Victoria Cross won by her son, Company Sergeant Major Frederick Hall, of the Canadian Battalion, near Ypres in 19

FIGURE 4.6. Mary Hall, 1936.
Source: Courtesy of Gail Cargo and Joan Hall Paulseth.

make ends meet. She had been in Canada for just over a year when the First World War began.[19] A widow with seven adult children, Hall left England in April 1913, bound for Winnipeg. Several of her offspring joined her, including her eldest son, Frederick, "Fred," who had just finished a 12-year term of service in the British army. Once in Winnipeg, he assisted his family financially, giving his mother "$40 or $50 a month" out of his clerk's pay.[20] But when war broke out in August 1914, Fred Hall enlisted with the Canadian Expeditionary Force, along with his younger brother Harry. Another brother, Edmund, known as "Ted," had been serving with the Second Scottish Rifles for over a decade, and would also fight in the war. Like many other women at the time, she found it difficult to manage financially with male relations off at war, and the downturn in their fortunes forced Mary Hall and her daughters into more affordable accommodations after Fred's death.

A year after Fred had left Winnipeg, Mary Hall held his VC in her hands. After receiving it, she spoke with the *Manitoba Free Press*. "He never thought of himself," she said. "He did not fear anything." [21] The article suggests Hall's mixed emotions about the death of her son and her ongoing anxiety for those that remained.

---

19   Nadler, *Valour Road*, chap: "The Pine Street Boys," Kindle.
20   "Mother Receives Victoria Cross," 8.
21   *Manitoba Free Press*, August 26, 1915, 8.

Harry had been wounded and was in hospital. Edmund, the article noted, had won the Distinguished Service Medal for rescuing comrades at the battle of Neuve Chapelle. As proud as she was of all of them, Fred's VC, the paper noted, "could not heal a mother's broken heart." Through tears, she struggled to speak of her son, his actions, and her sorrow. Her pride in her son's actions, no matter how considerable, could never erase the grief that resulted. Even 20 years later, Mary Hall, photographed in 1936 at Vimy, France (figure 4.6), displayed both that pride (wearing her son's VC and other medals as was customary at the time) as well as sorrow (in her pained expression) at a memorial service in honour of Canada's First World War dead.[22]

MADELINE JONES

In this photograph (figure 4.7), widow Madeline Jones stands outside in a garden with her three-year-old daughter Anne. The image provides a window into the nature of wartime grief.[23] Her expression is downcast, and she is carefully attired in dark clothing—dark blouse, skirt, shirt, scarf, gloves—and mourning veil. These clothes demonstrate one of the ways the discourse of sacrifice and loss permeated women's behaviour during the First World War. Madeline Jones and her sister-in-law Gwen had travelled from Canada to England to be closer to their husbands, who were fighting at the front. They were not alone in this move, as many Canadians still had strong family ties to Britain during the First World War, and thousands of women went overseas to be near loved ones in service or to live with family while their husbands were away at war.[24] After Madeline's husband, Trafford Jones, was killed in May 1916, Madeline, Anne, and Gwen were left in London to navigate their grief. As is visible in this image, Madeline followed accepted social conventions by wearing mourning dress. In the early years of the war, many middle- and upper-class women still followed Victorian mourning traditions. This etiquette dictated strict guidelines for appropriate behaviours and

---

22   *The Times*, July 7, 1936, RG 25, Department of External Affairs, Vimy Ridge Celebrations, Newspapers Clippings, vol. 694.

23   The authors would like to thank Suzanne Evans and other descendants of Madeline Jones for lending us a copy of this photograph for the purposes of the exhibition and this book.

24   Hanna, *Anxious Days*, 118, 138, Kindle.

clothing. After being widowed, women often entered a period of "deep mourning," wearing only black clothing and refusing all invitations for at least a year. Deep mourning could be followed by years of "second mourning," during which women wore modest greys or pale purples.[25] Jones's clothing marks her as being in this state of deep mourning, for example, wearing a black-trimmed mourning veil. These long rectangular veils, one of which survives in the Canadian Museum of History (CMH) textile collection, were made of a see-through black netting, and trimmed with a wide black ribbon for greater visual impact.[26]

Women could recut or repurpose black clothing of sober fabrics (lightly trimmed, plain cuts, matte rather than shiny textures) as mourning clothing. For women of the era, whose clothing was more often tailor-made than commercially purchased, the repurposing of old clothing items was a familiar practice. Following the mourning period, women could reincorporate utilitarian black mourning clothing (sometimes called widow's weeds) into their everyday wardrobes. Because most pieces could be worn again (dark skirts, blouses, or jackets could be matched with other items when the mourning period was over) until they were discarded, little First World War-era mourning clothing survives in museum collections.[27] Small items such as handkerchiefs, veils, and gloves were often trimmed with black and sold commercially as mourning accessories for women. These accessories have survived in museum collections (for example, a handkerchief at the Glenbow Museum, a veil at CMH, and Mary Hall's black-trimmed leather gloves [figure 4.5]) with greater frequency than clothing as they were less likely to be worn through.[28]

During both world wars, women's grief was both politicized and commercialized. Governments used images of mourning mothers to rally new recruits. Patriotic organizations raised funds for the war efforts by selling "sons in service"

OPPOSITE: FIGURE 4.7. Madeline Jones and her daughter Anne, 1916.
Source: Private Collection, care of Suzanne Evans.

---

25   Meyer, *Little Black Dress*, 13.
26   Mourning Veil, CMH D-9309.
27   Meyer, *Little Black Dress*, 8.
28   Several museums have First World War era mourning accessories in their collections: veil CMH D-9309; hankies CMH 2012.54.57; mourning pins CMH C-511b-c.; hankie Glenbow C-21934.

flags or mourning armbands, while private companies sold a range of mourning products, particularly during the First World War. One 1917 Victory Bond advertisement shows a grieving mother and child dramatically slumped at a table across an opened letter with the caption reading, "She's Given All! You Are Only Asked to Lend."[29] Using sacrifice and grief as a lever to increase sales was a widespread phenomenon. As a purveyor of mourning goods, Eaton's department store in Toronto encouraged women's adherence to socially accepted mourning customs through one of their advertisements, stating, "The making of mourning wear is an art all in itself... Not a shiny weave or exaggerated line can be permitted. Dull fabrics of best quality and dye, developed in some modish but conservative style— this is the ideal."[30] Madeline Jones's clothing (blouse, jacket, skirt, and gloves) was appropriately sombre, unadorned with splashes of colour or shiny beadwork. Her hat, in a style that probably predated the war (had it been bought specially for mourning it would have been darker in colour), was embellished only with a mourning veil and black band.

With so many women mourning, conventions changed over the course of the First World War. Suzanne Evans, a descendant of Madeline Jones, has written movingly of the Canadian women who mourned lost loved ones during the First World War.[31] Women in mourning were needed for valuable home front labour and could not isolate themselves socially, and perhaps more importantly, public mourning could be damaging to military recruitment. Mothers and wives of those killed at the front were expected to carry on, much as men in a previous era had been expected to remove their black armbands and return to their public duties immediately after the funeral of a loved one. Later in the war, magazines and newspapers that had encouraged women to purchase mourning accoutrements began to suggest that less emphasis be placed on mourning wear. "Sons in service" flags and pins began to be marketed as a more appropriate means for families to mark patriotic pride along with their grief. In 1915, following the massive casualties at the Second Battle of Ypres, the National Council of Women suggested that Canadian women should "refrain from wearing the conventional mourning, and to wear, instead, a band of royal purple on the arm, to signify that the soldier they

---

29 *Saturday Night*, Toronto, 1917.
30 "For Those Who Are Wearing Black," 14.
31 See Evans, *Mothers of Heroes*.

mourn died gloriously for his King and Country."[32] This practice was similar to those encouraged in Britain and, several years later, in the United States, emphasizing heroic sacrifice rather than personal grief.[33] By the time the Second World War dawned, the public saw Victorian mourning practices as old-fashioned and had almost completely replaced them with the use of patriotic service flags and service pins. While respecting women in mourning for their personal losses, public discourse reframed mourning women as having valiantly sacrificed sons and husbands as an essential part of the war effort, which reduced the emphasis on grief. Individual women, however, no doubt harboured mixed emotions about the loss of their loved ones, in spite of the wartime rhetoric of patriotic sacrifice.

SERVICE FLAGS

Ada Lake hung this red and white flag (figure 4.8) with a blue maple leaf in the centre of the window of her North Bay, Ontario, home, bringing attention to her son's First World War service, his continued good health, and her own role as a patriotic war mother.[34] The flag measures 43 cm by 28 cm, roughly 1/3 of the size of a standard-sized flag. These service flags could be purchased with multiple leaves (or stars, in the United States) for every family member in service. If the son or husband was killed, women

FIGURE 4.8. A service flag.
Source: Canadian War Museum 20120160-001.

---

32   Miller, *Our Glory and Our Grief*, 110.

33   Whitmore, "A Matter of Individual Opinion," 582–585.

34   Service Flag, 1917, CWM 20120160-001.

changed the maple leaf's colour by painting or embroidering over it. At a time when massive casualty lists and home front anxiety threatened to engulf Canada in a wave of grief, worry, and black mourning garb, service flags instead combined pride and patriotism with commemoration and loss. An October 1917 letter to the editor encouraged more Canadians to purchase service flags, writing, "when you pass a house with a flag out, you feel like saluting."[35]

Service flags were a highly gendered product, as was First World War military service. Advertisers of the flags and authors who wrote about them often assumed the maple leaves could only symbolize men serving their country. Producers and advertisers perceived women as the primary consumers of service flags, targeting them as the person responsible for home decoration. The flags were advertised in women's magazines, promoted through popular culture imagery like song sheets and posters, and sewn or distributed through women's war work groups. Women who hung a service flag in their window became part of a national movement, what historians Sarah Glassford and Amy Shaw have termed "a sisterhood of suffering," for the anxious women waiting at home for their loved ones.[36] The *Toronto Star* claimed that service flags "will make the residential streets of this city more compatible places for the mothers and wives of the absent ones to walk along... These little flags will be mute but eloquent evidence that far more homes in Toronto are sharing the hopes and anxieties of the war than anyone had supposed."[37]

In addition to being targeted by advertisers as a ready market for patriotic goods and services, women had traditionally assumed the role of keepers of family memory. Keeping alive the memory of dead loved ones was "part of women's purposeful efforts to act as myth-makers and memory banks in a world in which their lives and identities were largely defined by the nexus of home and family."[38] Along with compil-

---

35 Letter to the Editor, "Military Service Flag," 6.
36 Glassford and Shaw, *A Sisterhood of Suffering.*
37 *Toronto Star*, April 17, 1918, 10.
38 Zielke, "Forget-Me-Nots," 53.

ing scrapbooks, maintaining family correspondence, and quilting with scraps of cherished family fabrics, women took on the responsibility of chief mourner at a family level. Service flags, embraced by Canadian women during the First World War, continued to be a popular way of showing wartime support in the Second World War.

HENRIETTE POPE

Among this collection of wartime correspondence (figure 4.9) are letters revealing a mother greatly distressed by her son's intent to go to war. Handwritten in elegant cursive, these letters are interspersed among other documents in the Maurice Pope collection at the CWM.[39] In them, Henriette Pope repeatedly begs her son Maurice to stay home rather than sign up. Writing just days after the outbreak of war in August 1914, she pleads with him, in French, to wait: "Wait to enroll until they really need more recruits. Don't go with the first contingent. I think it would be the death of your father if you went."[40] A few months later she urges Maurice to stay on the home front for, as she argues, Canada needs a strong home guard to defend against possible German aggression. "According to the secret communications received by your father, we need an efficient Home Guard in all of Canada's cities. The Germans in the United States are trying to organize a raid against Canada." In the same letter, she also urges him to think of his career, and to not give up his promising position with the Canadian Pacific Railway, writing, "Think again my dear Maurice, before you abandon a promising future with the CPR."[41] Maurice did in fact wait almost a year to enlist, joining up in August of 1915.[42]

It is likely that many mothers felt the same sentiments as Pope and refrained from expressing them publicly. The pressure on women to support the war by "giving" their sons willingly is particularly evident if we contrast Pope's public persona with the worries she shared privately in correspondence. Henriette Pope was Lady

---

39 Fonds of Lt. Gen. Maurice A. Pope, CWM 20030022-001.

40 Lady Henriette Pope to Maurice Pope, August 7, 1914, CWM 20030022-001. Translation by authors.

41 Lady Henriette Pope to Maurice Pope, November 8, 1914, CWM 20030022-001. Translation by authors.

42 Lt. Maurice Pope, CEF Personnel Record.

ABOVE: FIGURE 4.9. Letters to Maurice Pope.
Source: George Metcalf Archival Collection, Canadian War
Museum 20030022/Textual Records 58A 1 177-58A 1 179.
OPPOSITE: FIGURE 4.10. "They Know the Meaning of Sacrifice," *Everywoman's World* article featuring Lady Henriette Pope (*bottom centre*).
Source: Everywoman's World, August 1917. Library and Archives Canada/OCLC 317944269.

Henriette Pope, wife of Sir Joseph Pope, Canada's Under-Secretary of State for External Affairs. In this role, he was essentially Canada's chief diplomat (at a time when the country's foreign affairs were still under the ultimate control of Great Britain). In addition, Lady Pope's sister-in-law was Georgina Fane Pope, famed Canadian military nurse who served in the South African War and the First World War, and who had been chief matron of Canada's army nursing service from 1908 to 1914. To the public, then, Lady Pope projected very different feelings about her family's involvement in the war. A 1917 article in *Everywoman's World* featured her as one of "Nine Canadian Mothers Who Have Sent Forty-Seven Sons to Fight." The article noted that Pope (figure 4.10, *bottom left*) was the proud mother of four khaki-clad sons and that "Lady Pope's gift to the Empire represents her entire family."[43] Lady Pope was Francophone (born Marie Louise Josephine Henriette

---

43   "Nine Canadian Mothers," 5.

THEY KNOW
THE MEANING OF SACRIFICE

Nine Canadian Mothers Who Have Sent Forty-Seven Sons to Fight

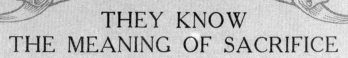

Husband Greatest Recruiter

MRS. GORDON WRIGHT, London, Ont., President Dominion W.C.T.U., Vice-President London Red Cross, has sent three sons: Major Wright; Corporal Wright; Captain Wright, who is the younger Divisional Quartermaster in the Service. Her husband, Chief Recruiting Officer, R.N.C.V.R., has secured more recruits than any man in Canada.

Seven Sons for King and Country

MRS. SCOBIE, Kars, Ont., has given seven sons: Private J. B. Scobie; Lieutenant S. M. Scobie; Corporal Sandy Scobie; Lieutenant A. A. Scobie; Private Russell Scobie; Sapper Sterling Scobie; and Dr. T. J. Scobie. One son remains at home as he is too young.

The Fighting Spirit Lives

MRS. LORNE McDOUGALL has four sons fighting for the Empire; Brigadier-General Alex. McDougall, Captain Kenneth McDougall; Captain Morris McDougall; and Lieutenant Archie McDougall. This young soldier was in the trenches for eleven consecutive months, but was wounded quite lately and invalided to the north of Scotland.

A Gifted Mother Sends Three Sons

MRS. ADAM INCH, President, The Woman's Institute, Mount Hamilton, Ont., has greatly in demand as a platform speaker; but now work for the soldiers has crowded everything else out of her life.

Six Sons Answered the Call

MRS. BILLINGS, Hamilton, Ont., has six sons on Active Service; two in France, one in England; three in training. Mrs. Billings has one other son, a lad of thirteen, whose chief desire is that the War may be prolonged until he is of military age—he wants to strike a blow for the Empire.

Ten Men From One Family

THE Desormeau family is an example of Northern Ontario patriotism. Mr. Joseph Desormeau enlisted, but did not survive the sea voyage. Frank, Albert, James, and Joseph, Jr., have all been wounded. A brother and five sons are also in khaki.

No Need of Conscription Here

"I PRAY God to spare my boys to fight to the finish" said Mrs. Adolphe La France, a little French Canadian mother who has sent six sons: Private Joseph La France enlisted in 1914; Private Fred went a year later; Private Noe, and, in turn, the three younger brothers answered the call. Conscription makes no difference to this family.

Her All—Four Khaki-Clad Sons

LADY POPE, the charming wife of Sir Joseph Pope, K.C.M.G., Under-Secretary of State for External Affairs, is the proud mother of four khaki-clad sons: Major C. W. Pope, with the Royal Canadian Regiment; Lieutenant Maurice Pope, with the Canadian Engineers; Lieutenant Harold Pope, with the Canadian Army Service Corps; and Lieutenant Alfred Pope, with the Royal Canadian Regiment. Lady Pope's gift to the Empire represents her entire family.

Seven Sons Serve

MRS. LANGSFORD has given her husband, seven sons, and two sons-in-law. Her husband was invalided from the service and is now at a Military Hospital; one fine lad has paid the supreme price; the others are scattered from France to Egypt, and figure in every kind of battalion from the Bantams to the Army Medical Corps.

Taschereau), and her home province of Quebec was lukewarm about Canada's participation in a European war. If only for the sake of her husband's career, it would have been particularly important for her to never publicly express anything that could be construed as unpatriotic.

War gave rise to complicated, at times contradictory feelings for many women. Famed author and women's rights activist Nellie McClung spoke out against the First World War as a pacifist but shifted her position once her own son Jack departed for the front.[44] Other stories of women's dissent come to light in letters, revealing small, private acts of resistance and despair. Often these letters came from mothers, writing angrily to the Canadian government railing against conscription, describing their family's need for a son's labour on the farm or a husband's financial support through a steady job. Their dissent was deeply personal and tied to their circumstances. Later in the war, Lady Pope joined her husband in lobbying to improve Maurice's position in the army, fearing for his safety and hoping to safeguard him from harm with less dangerous postings. He survived the war and made the military his career, rising to the rank of Lieutenant General. While Lady Pope did not lose her sons in the war, like many other Canadian mothers, her war was marked by complex, shifting, and at times conflicting sentiments towards the conflict.

EDNA SCOTT

When seen from the back, this simple silver locket bearing the engraved monogram EGS does not immediately suggest the emotional turmoil associated with war.[45] But flip the locket over (figure 4.11b) and its military links become more apparent. On the front is the regimental insignia for the 28th Battalion of the Canadian Expeditionary Force. Open the locket (figure 4.11a) and two small photographs appear. In one, a young man smiles towards the camera. He is wearing what appear to be hospital (or convalescent) blues, essentially a loose, almost

OPPOSITE: FIGURE 4.11a. and 4.11b. Edna Scott's locket.
Source: Canadian War Museum 19890211-007.

---

44   Oosterom, "Nellie McClung."
45   Scott Family Locket, CWM 19890211-007.

pyjama-like uniform worn by ill or injured soldiers during the First World War. In the centre of his tie, he wears a pin very much like the cap badge on the locket. The same young man appears in the second photo, but here he is joined by a woman, possibly his mother. Through other photos, we have been able to identify the soldier as Mason Francis Scott, son of Edna Genevieve Scott. This piece of jewelry, which we believe belonged to Edna Scott because of the monogram, would have been a way for her to preserve memories of her son and to keep him close to her heart. Mason Scott died as a result of the First World War.

Like many women, Edna Scott had much cause for worry during the First World War. Mason, her eldest son, was only 19 when he enlisted in March 1916, abandoning his job as a schoolteacher. A few months later, her 44-year-old husband Francis also joined the Canadian Expeditionary Force.[46] With both her husband and eldest son overseas, she was left in sole charge of her remaining children. She moved from Fort William, where the Scotts had been living, to her parents' home in Ottawa. This detail of Edna Scott's story reflects another aspect of the worry and stress women experienced during the war. With the main family breadwinners gone, and with children to care for, she may have had limited options. Like many soldiers, both her husband and son assigned part of their pay to her ($20 and $18 per month, respectively).[47] While helpful, this money would not have covered all their needs, which perhaps necessitated the move to Ottawa. Many women suffered increased financial worries as a result of wartime absences. Desmond Morton's *Fight or Pay: Soldiers' Families in the Great War* included the desperate words of Agnes Georgeson, who wrote, "I ain't getting my money from the army the way I ought to... I wonder how they expect me and my 3 children to exist. [...] I have got to have money soon or I must have my husband home to see if he can't get a job, as we are practically starving."[48]

Francis and Mason Scott served in different units. Mason arrived in England in July 1916 and was attached to the 28th Infantry Battalion. Francis joined the Canadian Field Artillery as a gunner. Mason served in France and fought at the Battle of Hill 70 in August 1917. Then, in the spring of 1918 while stationed near

---

46   Francis Mason Scott, CEF Personnel Record.

47   Mason Francis Scott, CEF Personnel Record; Francis Mason Scott, CEF Personnel Record.

48   Morton, *Fight or Pay*, 105.

Lens, he contracted lymphangitis, an infection of the lymphatic system. He ended up in a military hospital for an extended stay.[49]

Both Edna Scott's husband and son returned home from the war, but Mason was not well. He spent time convalescing in a Kingston hospital, then finally made it back to his family in Ottawa. Edna's reunion with her son was brief. The effects of the war, the gas, and the infections, all caught up to him and he died at home on September 23, 1919. Edna Scott too became a Memorial Cross recipient. Along with this medal, the locket—with its photos of Mason carefully tucked inside—became a talisman carrying the memory of a lost son.

DOROTHY (EFFEMY) CANNON

This treasured album (figure 4.12) of carefully annotated photographs is an important memento of a life shaped by the First World War. Its owner, Dorothy Cannon (née Effemy), was born a decade after it ended, and yet it profoundly influenced her world. The photographs in the album, along with the memoirs Cannon wrote in her later years, document her journey overseas with her veteran father (who assembled the album) to attend the Vimy pilgrimage.[50] In 1936, more than 6,200 Canadians (mainly veterans) sailed to France in "a great ocean armada" to remember Canada's war dead and to attend the unveiling of the Vimy memorial by King Edward VIII.[51] Hundreds of Silver Cross wives and mothers, including Mary Hall (pictured in figure 4.6 wearing her Vimy beret), travelled to France to see the land that had irrevocably shaped the lives of their veteran fathers, husbands, sons, and daughters.

Children were a part of the trip as well, including seven-year-old Dorothy Effemy. Her father, George Douglas Effemy, had been wounded in the Battle of Ypres and suffered terribly throughout his life as a result. After the war, George Effemy returned to Canada, married, raised children, and worked as a civil servant in Ottawa, but he continued to have health problems due to his war service. As

---

49 Francis Mason Scott and Mason Francis Scott, CEF Personnel Records; Mason Francis Scott, War Graves Registers (Circumstances of Casualty), 1914–1918, Ancestry.ca.

50 The authors are grateful to Dorothy Cannon (née Effemy) for sharing the album, her written memoirs, and many other stories and allowing their use in this book.

51 "Great Ocean Armada," 15; Cook and Brown, "The 1936 Vimy Pilgrimage," 37–39.

a child, Dorothy Cannon bore witness to his suffering. She later described the "festering wounds to his leg" and his trips to "the nearest hospital to have pieces of shrapnel removed."[52] As he aged, he frequently suffered from blood clots, debilitating swelling from the shrapnel in his damaged leg, and lumbago.[53] In addition to the continuing physical pain caused by his wounds, Effemy was also marked by psychological trauma. While recuperating in hospital in France and England, he had volunteered to help nurse other wounded soldiers. His daughter later wrote that "war had been horrible for my Dad. He had seen death, seen young men bleed profusely, had assisted them to stop the bleeding by pressure, but eventually saw them weaken and die."[54] George Effemy carried painful memories, walked with a limp, and died young "in bed with that damaged leg" at the age of 55. His ill health and, in later years, his self-medication with alcohol caused difficulties for his family. Dorothy Cannon recalled how her mother "became a woman who never smiled or laughed" as her father's health declined. As was the case with so many veterans' families, George Effemy's war service marked the lives of his wife and children for decades after the end of the war.

Veterans commemorated their service and grieved their war dead through ritualistic actions such as the Vimy pilgrimage. For men like George Effemy, who attended with his daughter Dorothy, the pilgrimage also helped their families understand the enormity of their sacrifice. Young Dorothy only came to understand the trauma her father suffered much later in her life, but the Vimy pilgrimage remained a significant moment in their relationship. One book described the Vimy event as "the supreme gesture of the Great War generation. They had gone back and connected to the fallen and touched the souls beyond... All that remains are their mementoes, and a beautiful monument that crowns Hill 145 on Vimy Ridge."[55] This photo album was one such memento for Dorothy (Effemy)

OPPOSITE TOP: FIGURE 4.12. Dorothy (Effemy) Cannon's scrapbook showing the Vimy Pilgrimage.
Source: Private collection of Dorothy Cannon.
OPPOSITE BOTTOM: FIGURE 4.13. Dorothy (Effemy) Cannon, 1936.
Source: Courtesy of Dorothy Cannon.

52   Cannon, "Mom and Dad."
53   Cannon, interview.
54   Cannon, "Mom and Dad."
55   Christie and Roncetti, *For Our Old Comrades*, 104.

Cannon. Photographs show young Dorothy on the journey to Europe, amid the crowds of other pilgrims, and exploring the broken landscape near Vimy Ridge. In the images, Dorothy wears the beret that marked her as a pilgrim (green for veterans, blue for family members). She stands in a recreated sandbagged trench and beside signs that denote the 1917 Canadian and German front lines. In figure 4.13, she sits on a picnic blanket, proudly holding open a box of food. The lid on a closed second box reads "Hotel de Flandre," which presumably supplied the lunch. The photos, when contrasted with wartime imagery of blasted trenches and exhausted soldiers, are almost surreal. What must it have been like for the veterans to see their wives and children strolling through and picnicking in this formerly hellish, blood-soaked landscape?

Dorothy Cannon later set down her memories of the pilgrimage in the form of letters written from the perspective of her younger self, on the Vimy trip, to her mother back home. Eva Effemy had remained in Canada with a new baby, unable to make the trip to Europe.[56] In the letters, Dorothy tries to capture the feelings of exhilaration and solemnity that she remembers feeling as a child at Vimy. Through stories of picnicking on boxed lunches, sighting the King, and being freed from a tangle of barbed wire by her father, Cannon's letters reflect her memories of childish excitement at her great adventure. They also include impressions of sadness, with descriptions of the vast and quiet crowds, with many people weeping, and awe at the scale of the giant memorial. The fictionalized letters add to the captions that George Effemy included in the photo album, which he assembled after their journey, and succeed in capturing his personality in a way the captions do not. Dorothy Cannon's memories of her father as written in the letters reveal a caring man and loving father. His decision to travel alone with his daughter necessitated special arrangements, as most children were accompanied by their mothers and slept in the women's quarters.[57] Throughout the voyage, he looked out for his daughter's well-being while gently teaching her about his wartime experiences. In one letter, she recalled how after climbing into a crater and becoming tangled in barbed wire she "stayed perfectly still and waited for Daddy to lift me out" and in another, "Daddy showed me where he was wounded in

---

56   Cannon, interview.
57   Cannon, interview.

Ypres."[58] Upon seeing the sandbagged trenches, cemented in place for the commemoration, she recalled him saying, "I wish they had been solid like this when I was in them."[59] Without diary entries or the actual letters written by a young Dorothy Effemy to her mother (now lost), these fictionalized letters are a way of capturing the experiences of a child on the Vimy pilgrimage. They cannot, however, begin to explain how Dorothy Effemy understood her father's war experiences at the time.

An epilogue to the letters captures Dorothy Cannon's adult perspective. Here, she reflects that during the pilgrimage she had "wandered among the trenches and the detritus of war but did not understand that men had died and were buried. My father was a victim who was wounded. He went to an early grave because of his service."[60] The soldiers of the First World War, even those lucky enough to return to Canada without serious wounds, were marked by their experience. Many veterans were weakened by gas, bullets, and trauma, and some struggled with alcohol or mental illness. They passed their grief on to their families and to their children, some of whom would later serve in the Second World War, which erupted just three years after the Vimy pilgrimage. Cannon felt compelled to travel to Vimy Ridge again in 1986 as a grown woman to pay her respects. Both her family and that of her husband had been touched by the First World War, and visiting France held an important place in their imagination. As she later wrote: "I made a promise to my father-in-law that I would visit his brother's grave in France. He had been there [in the war] with his father and brother. However, he was never able to return during his lifetime."[61] By travelling for a second time to France and the Vimy memorial, Cannon was able to process her father's pain and her own grief, writing, "I began to understand how that war affected him... [and it] becomes a grief I cannot share. It is singular and, as with all people, belongs to me alone."[62] Dorothy Cannon's story, like so many others, is that of the intergenerational trauma of war.

58   Cannon, "A Prospect of Heroes."
59   Cannon, "A Prospect of Heroes."
60   Cannon, "A Prospect of Heroes."
61   Cannon, "A Prospect of Heroes."
62   Cannon, "A Prospect of Heroes."

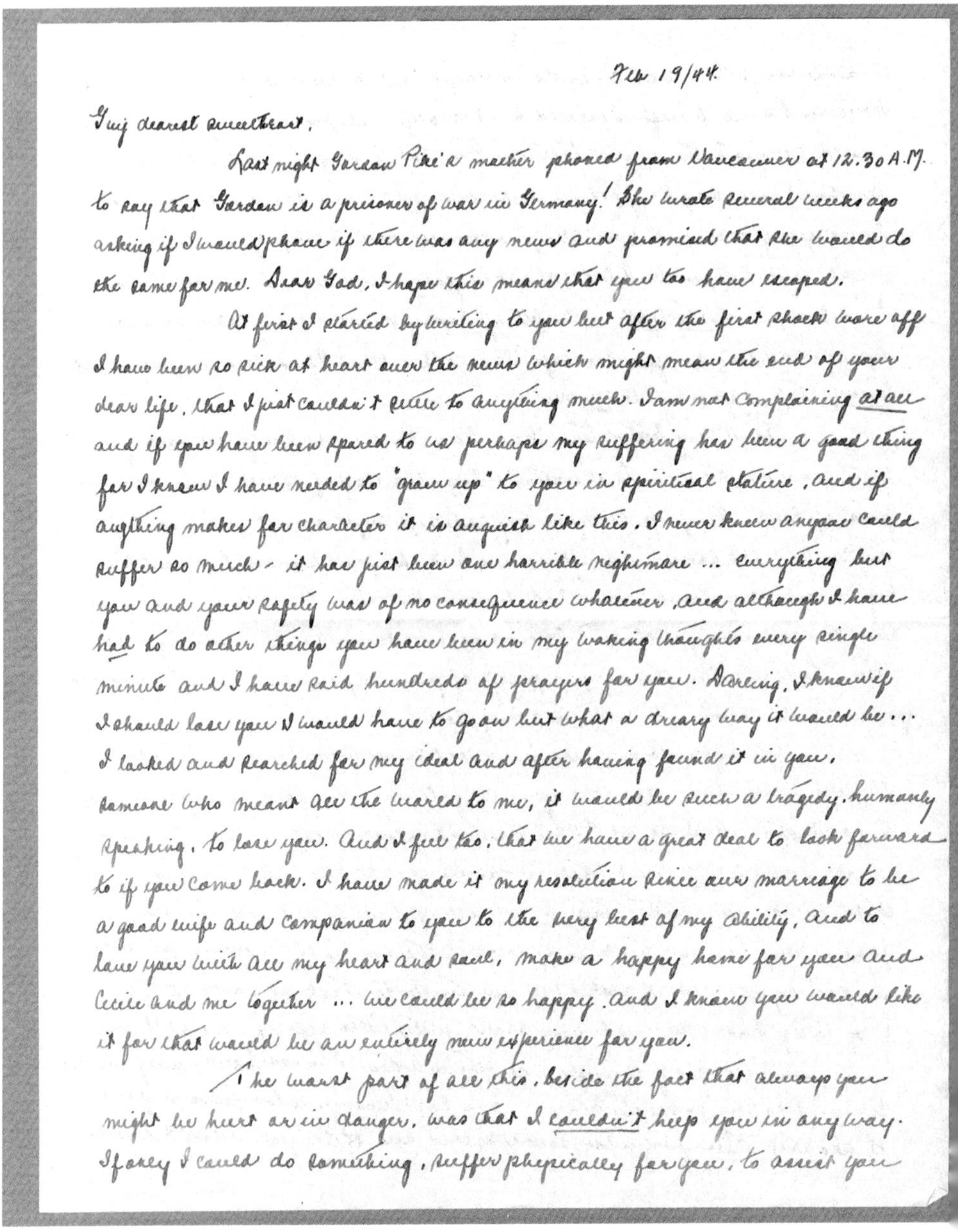

Feb 19/44.

My dearest sweetheart,

Last night Gordon Pike's mother phoned from Vancouver at 12.30 A.M. to say that Gordon is a prisoner of war in Germany! She wrote several weeks ago asking if I would phone if there was any news and promised that she would do the same for me. Dear God, I hope this means that you too have escaped.

At first I started by writing to you but after the first shock wore off I have been so sick at heart over the news which might mean the end of your dear life, that I just couldn't settle to anything much. I am not complaining _at all_ and if you have been spared to us perhaps my suffering has been a good thing for I know I have needed to "grow up" to you in spiritual stature, and if anything makes for character it is anguish like this. I never knew anyone could suffer so much - it has just been one horrible nightmare ... everything but you and your safety was of no consequence whatever, and although I have _had_ to do other things you have been in my waking thoughts every single minute and I have said hundreds of prayers for you. Darling, I know if I should lose you I would have to go on but what a dreary way it would be... I looked and searched for my ideal and after having found it in you, someone who meant all the world to me, it would be such a tragedy, humanly speaking, to lose you. And I feel too, that we have a great deal to look forward to if you come back. I have made it my resolution since our marriage to be a good wife and companion to you to the very best of my ability, and to love you with all my heart and soul, make a happy home for you and Cecile and me together ... we could be so happy. And I know you would like it for that would be an entirely new experience for you.

The worst part of all this, beside the fact that always you might be hurt or in danger, was that I _couldn't_ help you in any way. If only I could do something, suffer physically for you, to assist you

FIGURE 4.14. Peggy (Hayes) Rainville's letter to her husband, written while he was missing in action.
Source: Letter, February 19, 1944, George Metcalf Archival Collection, Canadian War Museum 20030359-028 #28.

PEGGY (HAYES) RAINVILLE

Letters were the bedrock of Peggy Hayes and Guy Rainville's wartime romance. They also offer first-person testimony to Peggy's deep anxiety over Guy's service and the emotional roller coaster she experienced while he was fighting overseas. Wars give rise to extremes in human behaviour and emotion, and it can be difficult for museums to preserve this element of conflict. Thankfully, we can look to this correspondence for evidence of what women thought and felt during these times of upheaval. War-fractured families relied heavily on mail to stay connected, sending vast numbers of letters, packages, and postcards across the country and the world. The correspondence of the Rainville family eloquently expresses the pain its members felt while Guy Rainville was away at war. His wife Peggy in Port Perry, Ontario, his mother Emma and father Paul in Québec City, and his aunt Rachel in Montréal frequently wrote to him and to each other for support throughout their ordeal. Their letters and documents are now held at the CWM, and this collection of correspondence is one of hundreds that open a window onto the lives of Canadian families touched by war. Letters that capture the woman's point of view are unusual but extremely rich sources in helping to understand the home front experience.[63] In the case of the Rainville material, researchers benefit from having a full collection of correspondence at once capturing the experience of anxiously waiting for news of a husband, son, and nephew from different points of view.

Peggy Hayes and Guy Rainville met in Toronto in 1940, before he left for service in Europe. He was in training with the air force, and she was working at a local bank while studying to be an opera singer. Despite the language barrier, the couple fell in love. According to their son, Guy could barely speak English and Peggy had no French, but they "found a common language in music, particularly opera."[64] After Guy went overseas, their romance continued and developed through correspondence. They married in 1942 in Toronto while Guy was at home on a Victory Bond speaking tour. In this candid photograph (figure 4.15), taken around the time of their marriage, Guy, in his uniform, holds Peggy; they are laughing and appear very much in love.

---

63   Mélanie Morin-Pelletier, "The Anxious Ones Waiting at Home," 357.
64   Details about his parents were generously shared by their son, Paul Rainville.

Shortly after their marriage in November 1942, Guy returned to England for a second tour of duty, leaving a pregnant Peggy behind. Guy had reassured his family that he would no longer be flying, but even with this reassurance, Peggy worried. In March 1943, she wrote, "To my brown-eyed lover... My dear, my thoughts are constantly with you. Every night I pray for your safety for even if you aren't flying there is a certain danger in England. I hope you won't have to go back up again, although I know you like it. That is being very selfish, but somehow I feel better when you are on the ground."[65]

Their baby Cecile was less than a year old when Guy was reported missing in action. Though Guy had told his family he was no longer flying, he in fact flew 13 more missions before his aircraft went down in January 1944. Peggy received a telegram that read: "Regret to advise that your husband Flight Lieutenant Guy Henri Rainville [...] is reported missing after air operations overseas January fifteenth."[66] The news spread quickly among the family. Guy's aunt Rachel in Montréal wrote to his parents that she was mystified at Guy's disappearance: "Our dear Guy, reported missing! I'm devastated—I can only hope that he is only a prisoner. How did he come to be flying over Germany? I had thought he wasn't supposed to be flying."[67] In a letter to Guy's parents a few days later, Peggy confirmed that Guy had made no mention of flying: "I had no idea Guy had even considered flying again. [...] the last letter I had from Guy was dated Dec. 28th, and in it he made no mention of flying."[68]

The family's letters following Guy's disappearance show the extent of their worry and pain. Peggy admits her desperation, writing that, "If he were dead, the light would be gone in my life and I shouldn't want to live even for Cecile."[69] The family were each other's support network; the letters offering a measure of comfort in a time of great despair. Peggy wrote of six-month-old Cecile and the need

OPPOSITE: FIGURE 4.15. Peggy and Guy Rainville, ca. 1942.
Source: George Metcalf Archival Collection, Canadian War Museum 20030359-096.

65   Peggy Rainville to Guy Rainville, March 1, 1943, CWM 20030359-028.
66   Royal Canadian Air Force Casualties Officer to Peggy Rainville, telegram, January 18, 1944, CWM 20030359-025.
67   Aunt Rachel to Paul Rainville, January 19, 1944, CWM 20030359-27.
68   Peggy Rainville to Paul and Emma Rainville, January 21, 1944, CWM 20030359-27.
69   Peggy Rainville to Paul and Emma Rainville, January 21, 1944, CWM 20030359-27.

to keep calm for the baby's sake, "I am trying to follow your advice and be very brave... After all the baby depends on me a great deal as I am still nursing her, and I know it is how Guy would want me to act. I eat, though I haven't any appetite, and I sleep a bit by praying myself to sleep... but one cannot control the imagination."[70] Weeks went by without news of Guy's whereabouts and Peggy wrote openly to Guy and to Guy's family about her ongoing anxiety.

A month after Guy's disappearance, the family rejoiced to learn that other members of Guy's crew had been found alive in a prisoner of war camp. Although it was not proof that Guy was also alive, the family was cautiously optimistic about his chances for survival. Peggy wrote to Guy, "I realize that this news about Gordon Pike's safety does not necessarily mean that you are safe but it gives me much more hope."[71] The Rainvilles were not alone in their worry about missing loved ones. Some families were relatively lucky: over 9,000 Canadians were taken by the Germans as prisoners of war (POW) during the Second World War.[72] However, many airmen initially listed as missing were eventually confirmed to have been killed in action.

Almost six weeks after Guy was reported missing, his family received word that he was safe in a prisoner of war camp in Germany. His first postcard to Peggy brought brief but welcome news. He describes himself as being "In good health. Not a scratch."[73] Other letters soon followed between Guy and Peggy, Peggy and the Rainvilles in Quebec, Aunt Rachel in Montréal, and from Peggy back to Guy. Guy's first letter to his parents, held with the rest of his collection at the CWM is typed, in English. Because Peggy spoke no French, we believe that Guy's father Paul translated and transcribed the letter to share with Peggy.

Hearing from Guy in Germany did not put an end to the family's worries. Guy spent from January 1944 to May 1945 in various POW camps, but the family at home in Canada did not always know his condition and where he was. In January 1945, the circumstances in Germany became unstable and their letters and packages to Guy were returned. Officials wrote that "the situation within Germany is obscure and in a state of confusion as far as the prison camps are concerned. We

70   Peggy Rainville to Paul and Emma Rainville, January 21, 1944, CWM 20030359-027.
71   Peggy Rainville to Guy Rainville, February 19, 1944, CWM 20030359-028.
72   Vance, *Objects of Concern*, 253.
73   Guy Rainville to Peggy Rainville, January 31, 1944, CWM 20030359-026.

have recently been informed that the above camp is now closed and the prisoners have been transferred. We regret, however, we have received no official information regarding the prisoner's present address."[74]

For months Peggy wrote to Guy in hopes that her letters would find him eventually, saying, "I have found it so hard to write... I try again and again and end up in despair and tears for it is so dreadful not knowing where you are or what you are having to suffer."[75] Finally, on May 12, she received an official telegram from the Canadian military informing her that Guy was safe and sound in the United Kingdom. She notified her in-laws of the good news that very morning. Their ordeal, and the grinding anxiety that had gnawed at them for years, was finally over.

ELIZABETH "BETTY" BUTCHER

This scrapbook (figure 4.16) is stuffed with clippings and photos, collected fragments that provide insight into a young life shaped by war.[76] It belonged to Elizabeth "Betty" Butcher, who was a 13-year-old Grade eight student in the small prairie town of Carman, Manitoba, when war erupted in September 1939.[77] Although she herself did not leave home to fight, the involvement of those around her marked her formative years. The scrapbook is shown open to pages of particular significance, displaying Missing in Action notices, an obituary, and letters of condolence written to Betty following the death of her fiancé in 1944. Like many women, Butcher documented her experiences by keeping a scrapbook of the goings-on in her small town. The newspaper clippings, programs from special events, postcards, and photographs begin in 1937 and span the duration of the war. It is a chronicle of the Second World War from the perspective of a teenage girl.

The first pages of Butcher's scrapbook cover 1937–1941 and contain high school report cards, dance programs, and records of parties she attended and hosted. During that time, she later recalled, the boys slowly trickled away until there were

---

74   George D. Allen to Peggy Rainville, March 23, 1945, CWM 20030359-025.
75   Peggy Rainville to Guy Rainville, March 28, 1945, CWM 20030359-026.
76   Elizabeth Butcher's Scrapbook, Evans Family Fonds, CMH2008-H0025.
77   Elizabeth (Butcher) Evans was author Krista Cooke's grandmother.

FIGURE 4.16. Betty Butcher's scrapbook, showing her fiancé Lyle's obituary.
Source: Canadian Museum of History 2008-H0025.

hardly any young men left in her small town.[78] There were none at all in her graduating class. They had all gone off to war, signing up for military service or moving to Canadian cities to find war jobs. The community's increasing involvement in the Canadian war effort is mirrored in the pages of the scrapbook, which swings from gaiety to grief and back again over the course of the war. Betty Butcher's story offers an unusual perspective into wartime Canada, a vantage point that is often missed in histories of war, which tend to focus on male teens working to enlist, adult women, or younger children. Combined with Butcher's family photo albums, autograph books, knitting notebooks, and a series of late in life interviews, the scrapbook provides insights into the experiences of a "Girl in a Sloppy Joe Sweater," as author Mary Peate titled her Second World War memoir, one of the few published reminiscences of the Canadian home front featuring a teenaged girl protagonist.[79]

In the scrapbook, we learn of war-related fundraisers and of young men in Butcher's circle of friends who were leaving to join the services, including her brothers Joe and Reg. Joe joined the air force and Reg the navy. We know from the family that Joe was an aspiring pilot who had tried to sign up with the Royal Canadian Air Force on the first day that war broke out but was not immediately accepted. Of her four siblings, Betty was closest to Joe, whom she looked up to and who, unlike her other siblings, was still living at home at the beginning of the war.[80] Joe's correspondence, which is glued into the scrapbook, is cheerful, full of details about his training with the RCAF and his love of flying. In one letter, he thanks her for a scarf she had knit, and described the thrill of night flying over Ottawa: "Seeing a city all lit up is like being in Fairyland."[81]

Shortly after this letter was written, Joe (Sergeant J. G. Butcher) was killed in a flying accident at Oak Lake, Manitoba, while in training.[82] Betty was in Grade 10. The Butcher family gathered for the funeral, which took place at the United Church in Carman on February 28, 1941. A photograph taken on the day of the funeral (figure 4.17) shows three siblings seated in the family living room beneath the map on which Betty's father kept track of the war's progress. Reg is absent,

---

78   Evans, interviews.
79   Peate, *Girl in a Sloppy Joe Sweater*.
80   Evans, interviews.
81   Evans, interviews.
82   Joseph Goodwin Butcher, Service Files of the Second World War – War Dead, 1939–1947.

FIGURE 4.17. Lorraine, Kathleen, and Betty Butcher (*left to right*), 1941.
Source: Canadian Museum of History IMB2014-0028-0414Dm.

possibly because war service kept him away. The sisters are wearing rings, which Betty believed to have been made from the propeller of Joe's downed plane. Betty Butcher's ring is now in the collections of the CMH.[83]

After Joe's death, the scrapbook shows that Betty left Carman for Winnipeg. Her father had hoped that Joe would take over the family law firm. As a result, Betty was needed at home more than ever and decided to further her schooling so that she could be of assistance in her father's office. Following her high school graduation in 1942, Butcher began training as a secretary at the Angus School of Commerce in Winnipeg. Clippings related to her coursework in Winnipeg, life boarding with a family friend, and social engagements fill the pages. At the time, she was dating a boy named Russell "Lyle" Porter. They were high school sweethearts and his name appears in her autograph book and frequently in her scrapbook. Shortly after she arrived home from stenography school in Winnipeg, Betty saw Lyle off to Europe. He had enlisted with the air force, another young pilot with dreams of overseas adventure. The young couple were engaged in April, shortly before Lyle left for overseas duty in Europe. Butcher turned 18 the following month. Her story of a quick engagement at a young age is similar to that of so many other young women across Canada. Faced with years of uncertainty and

83   CMH Acquisition File 2016.12.2.

anxiety, engagements and marriages skyrocketed throughout the war years, with marriage rates reaching highs in 1940, 1941, and 1942.[84] Betty Butcher and Lyle Porter's shared story came to an abrupt end. In June, only months after his arrival in Europe, Lyle Porter and his aircrew were reported missing.

A small service flag is tucked carefully into Betty Butcher's scrapbook. The three maple leaves on this service flag represent Reg, Joe, and Lyle. Maple leaves on service flags like this one were overpainted or embroidered in a different colour if the person they symbolized was killed. The centre leaf is overpainted with gold, while the two others are red. Betty Butcher and Lyle Porter's family waited for a full year before he was confirmed to have been killed in action in the skies over France.[85] She may not have been able to bring herself to overpaint a second leaf on her service flag.

In her scrapbook, alongside the cherished miniature pilot's wings that Lyle had given to her before his departure, Butcher kept mementoes of events they had attended together, photographs, the florist's card that went with the roses he had sent to her for her 18th birthday, and condolence cards. In one such card, a family friend wrote, "Your love was young and very sweet, Betty, and now it can never change."[86] By this period, Betty's scrapbook was focused almost entirely on keeping track of Carman friends and acquaintances off at war through newspaper clippings and correspondence. Looking for a change, in the fall of 1944, Betty applied to go overseas. However, the Canadian Red Cross had a surplus of applicants; the rejection letter is filed alongside the newspaper clippings in her scrapbook. Butcher spent the remainder of the war in Carman. She was well supported by friends and family throughout her period of grief; however, this was not the case for all Canadian teens who came of age during the turmoil of the Second World War. Youth organizations of the period reported that young people were preoccupied with anxiety about their uncertain futures and that some girls had "problems—some of which were the result of the long years of depression and the growing complexity of family life and which were further complicated in many cases by conditions arising from the war."[87]

84   Statistics Canada, "Crude Marriage Rate."
85   Evans Family Fonds; Russell Lyle Porter, Service Files of the Second World War – War Dead, 1939–1947.
86   Evans Family Fonds.
87   Comacchio, The Dominion of Youth, 40.

While the war brought grief and pain to Betty Butcher's young life, it also brought love. A year after Lyle's disappearance, she got to know a serviceman from Carman. Jack Evans, also with the RCAF, was home on leave in the summer of 1944 when he was re-introduced to Butcher. Invited by her friend Verna to join a golf outing, Butcher did not hit it off as intended with Evans's cousin. Instead, she and Evans became friends and correspondents. He had also experienced recent sadness: a failed long-distance relationship that resulted in a broken engagement. Hundreds of letters cemented Evans's and Butcher's connection while he was overseas. Both sides of the correspondence survive in the collections at the CMH, and through the letters we can trace the evolution of their budding relationship.[88] The last pages of the scrapbook contain telegrams, cards, and other mementoes related to Butcher's new romance. Like so many women who had lost a loved one to the war, Betty Butcher eventually rebuilt her life. She found new love and put the tragic losses of the war behind her. The couple married in 1946, raised four children in Thunder Bay, Ontario, and were together for 58 years.

MICHIKO ISHII

This photograph album (figure 4.18) tells a very different story of loss than the other artifacts in this chapter. Many of the photographs show smiling young people living seemingly normal teenaged lives, but there are a number of clues that the album depicts something out of the ordinary. First, the images almost exclusively show Japanese Canadians. Second, there are three major geographical changes over the course of the photograph collection. The earliest photos are taken in and around Vancouver, British Columbia. The ones from the second half of the Second World War are taken in Lemon Creek, deep in the British Columbia interior. After the war, the photographs are set in Ontario. This photo album, which Michiko Ishii owned and assembled, documents the forced relocation and dispossession of Japanese Canadians during the Second World War. Through it we see loss of home and possessions, friends, routines, work, education, and freedom. Over the course of her life, Ishii often spoke and wrote about her experiences, and

---

88   Evans Family Fonds.

FIGURE 4.18. Michiko Ishii's photo album.
Source: George Metcalf Archival Collection, Canadian War Museum 20150279-001_p12.

this album, now a part of the CWM's collection, offers visual testimony to a very difficult, unjust period for Japanese Canadians.[89]

The first pages show a family with young children growing into adolescence. The handwritten labels identify the locations (Abbotsford and Vancouver), the years (1920s through to the early 1940s), and the people pictured (most often Michiko and her brothers Hideo, Yoshio, and Kazuo). Page 12 (figure 4.18) is the first page that shows something amiss. Two photos, taken in the same year, show Michiko Ishii's parents hundreds of kilometres apart, in dramatically different settings. The photo in the top left corner shows a group of Japanese Canadian men, a few holding tools, on a log bridge. Behind them is a cabin at the edge of a forest. Written beside the image is "Dad at Road camp" and "Thunder River, Blue River, B.C. 1942." On the right-hand side of the page, a woman walks down a busy city street, pulling a child behind her. He looks shyly at the camera. Written underneath the photo, "Evacuation year, 1942. Vancouver, B.C. Kazuo (6 yrs) + mom."[90]

---

89   The authors would like to thank Carla Ayukawa for sharing stories of her mother and family.
90   Michiko (Ishii) Ayukawa, Lemon Creek Japanese Canadian Internment Camp, Photo Album, CWM 20150279-001.

Michiko Ishii's family was one of thousands that the Canadian government forcibly removed from the Pacific Coast after Japan's entry into the Second World War. Nearly 21,000 individuals, the vast majority of whom were born in Canada or were naturalized Canadian citizens, were expelled from their homes and moved to remote areas in the interior, isolated detention camps, road construction camps, and prairie sugar beet farms.[91] Like many families, the Ishiis were separated months before their move, with Michiko Ishii's father and eldest brother being taken to a road camp, in March and May 1942, respectively. They were among the workers who prepared the landscape and built houses for thousands of women, children, and elderly who would arrive imminently.[92] In September of that year, the government moved the rest of Michiko's family to remote Lemon Creek. With these forced relocations, thousands of people lost their homes, their businesses, and their possessions. When Michiko (Ishii) Ayukawa was interviewed in the 1990s, she remembered snippets of the day when her 12-year-old self, Yoshio, Kazuo, and her mother Misayo hurriedly packed their belongings and left their Georgia Street home in Vancouver with less than 24-hours' notice.[93] Included in her memories are decisions about what would fit into hastily packed suitcases and trunks. Blankets and mattresses, yes. Her younger brother's heirloom ornaments from relatives in Japan, no. A hard-earned, brand new wood-burning kitchen stove that her mother had scrimped and saved to buy, yes. The family piano and Ishii's favourite doll, no. Even before the relocation, the family had lost possessions. Cameras, along with cars, radios, and fishing boats were among the first items seized—and later sold without consent—by the Canadian government.[94] Ishii's father had smashed his camera in anger with a hammer when he was ordered to turn it in to authorities. Having treasured objects confiscated by strangers or sold at bargain basement prices was too painful to endure without protest.[95]

The photographs from the evacuation year do not depict the terrible chaos of separation and constant uncertainty that these families faced between the

91 Kitagawa and Miki, *This Is My Own*, 2.
92 Ayukawa, interview.
93 Hawthorne, "Sting of Dispossession," A7.
94 Adams and Stanger-Ross, "Promises of Law," 690.
95 Ayukawa, interview.

bombing of Pearl Harbor in December 1941 and the completion of the forced relocation a year later. Muriel Kitagawa, a journalist and mother of four children whose personal letters to her brother Wes were published many years later, wrote of the crisis in British Columbia in March 1942, saying, "Perhaps we can move together, I don't know. This uncertainty is more nerve-wracking than anything that can happen. I don't know whether to pack all my stuff or sell it. I can only take the irreplaceables... I am worried about Eiko and Fumi and Uncle and Aunt Toyofuko, Nobi and the rest of them. When shall we ever meet again if we scatter?"[96] Fathers and husbands working in faraway road camps dealt with harsh living and working conditions and worried about their families left behind in a constantly worsening political situation. Mothers tried to shield their children from stress, keeping daily routines while negotiating confiscations, rapidly disappearing family members and friends, an evening curfew, and the fear of losing homes and family treasures. Even the physical journey east was fraught with uncertainty and fear. One woman recalled how she, "put name tags on all the children, in case we got separated [...] died or something, well then, they'd know who we were."[97] Ayukawa later reflected that as a child she "was very curious. I was young enough to think that everything was an adventure. I often shudder when I think of how my mother must have reacted. But she never showed it."[98]

Another thing that is not pictured in the album is the family's bittersweet reunion with Michiko's father, Kenji, and eldest brother, Hideo, in Slocan City.[99] Some 12,000 exiled Japanese Canadians ended up in the Slocan Valley, with one of the largest camps being Lemon Creek, located around five kilometres from Slocan City.[100] From Slocan City, the family spent weeks in a tent at Popoff, then moved to sturdier housing at Lemon Creek. Many others were not so lucky and spent cold months in tents waiting for housing to be completed.[101] The Ishii's rough, uninsulated, wooden shack was cold, and the family nearly suffered tragedy after Michiko, six-year-old Kazuo, and their mother could not get out of bed after

96 Kitagawa and Miki, *This Is My Own*, 93.

97 Itter and Marlatt, *Opening Doors*, 121.

98 Ayukawa, interview.

99 Ayukawa, interview; Ayukawa, "Lemon Creek Memories," 11–16; Ayukawa, "Lemon Creek Memories: September 1942," 22–23; Hawthorne, "Sting of Dispossession," A7.

100 Ayukawa, "Japanese After All"; Hawthorne, "Sting of Dispossession."

101 Adachi, *The Enemy That Never Was*, 253.

using a makeshift recycled nail keg stove. They were suffering from carbon mon-oxide poisoning. "It was a wonder we didn't die," Ayukawa recalled, noting that her mother had to call out the door for help from a passing neighbour as the two teenaged boys and her father had already left for work that morning.[102] Water had to be trucked to each family from a nearby creek, heaters were in scarce supply, and families coped with communal outhouses, mess halls, and long journeys to the nearest bath house. Young Michiko Ishii was responsible for learning to bake bread when rice shortages made bread more of a staple and caused the price of a loaf to spike. She used her old Grade seven home economics book to try to figure it out, but "it didn't work out very well," until a neighbour who had been a profes-sional baker helped her to master the art. The bread was baked in pans made from repurposed stove pipes.[103]

It is notable that Ishii's album is so full of photographs after the family's cam-era was confiscated. Some Vancouver photographs are from street photographers. The work camp image might be an official photograph, taken by one of the few photographers given special dispensation by the RCMP to take photographs inside the camps between 1942 and 1944.[104] There are few in the album from 1943, after the family left Vancouver. Photographs start again in May 1944, shortly after the camera ban was lifted.[105] When the ban was lifted, the Ishii household did not have money to buy another camera. Once the camp housing was completed, there was little call for Michiko's father's carpentry skills and the family suffered financial-ly.[106] The Ishiis, like many relocated families, had to rely on government relief.[107] Friends sent some of the images in the album as a way of keeping friendships alive. For instance, Ishii's friend Mitsuko Matsuoka (who is also pictured in a street photograph with Ishii in Vancouver) sent a photograph of herself from the deten-tion camp at Tashme, British Columbia. The photograph is labelled "Mitsuko Matsuoka: a friend of old." Other images come from a camera Michiko Ishii and her friends borrowed. They helped pay for developing costs, or they would pur-chase film in Slocan City and share the film with the photographer. Ishii played the

102   Ayukawa, interview.
103   Ayukawa, interview.
104   Ayukawa, interview.
105   Ken Adachi, *The Enemy That Never Was,* 268.
106   Ayukawa, interview.
107   Adachi, *The Enemy That Never Was,* 260.

organ at special events and weddings and, after helping her mother make ends meet, was able to put a few coins aside for herself, which went towards photographs.[108]

By the time the camera ban was lifted in April 1944, and photos appear regularly in Ishii's album, life seems to have settled in at Lemon Creek. The album photographs depict fairly typical teen activities. Almost all the photographs feature people. One picture shows a group of students gathered for a formal photograph in front of a newly built school building. The image is labelled, "L.C.S. '44 Graduating Class."[109] Another group photo presents a gathering of boys, some with their fists raised in a fighting stance. It is described as the Lemon Creek High "L.C.H. boxing club" with the caption, "Bet I could beat you, one & all!"[110] On another page, seven majorettes in matching hats and short skirts hold batons on a stage, playfully captioned, "What gams!"[111] We see photos of girls reading books in school, enjoying sunshiny picnics, sports days, and youth group gatherings.[112] In the photograph captions, Ishii's tone is often light and playful. Though we do not know when the album was assembled and the photographs labelled, we can easily hear the voice of a teenage girl in the captions. Her 1944 school photo is labelled "Those Were the Days!," male acquaintances are often tagged with a "Hubba Hubba!," and a winter image of Ishii with her two closest friends standing in front of a barbed-wire fence is labelled only "Brrr—Isn't It Cold?"[113] Perhaps with the adjustment period over, the harsh living conditions were viewed as normal, or maybe for teenaged Ishii, friendships, picnics, and special events were the most pressing concerns. After a first unsettled fall and winter without schooling, the newly constructed Lemon Creek school house had opened in April 1943, putting an end to the chaos parents and students felt without regular routines. Parents had built a school for their children, and residents roughly insulated their houses with tarpaper and installed water pipes as some creature comforts were restored to the community.[114] By 1944, life had taken a regular, if abnormal, shape for the children of Lemon Creek.

---

108 Ayukawa, interview.
109 Ayukawa (Ishii), Photo Album, CWM, 18.
110 Ayukawa (Ishii), Photo Album, CWM, 21.
111 Ayukawa (Ishii), Photo Album, CWM, 32.
112 Ayukawa (Ishii), Photo Album, CWM, 16, 24, 33, 36.
113 Ayukawa (Ishii), Photo Album, CWM, 18, 25, 49.
114 Ayukawa, "Lemon Creek Memories: September 1942."

Many of the photographs are autographed portraits of Ishii's friends. As another young woman, given the pseudonym "Haru" in Mona Oikawa's *Cartographies of Violence: Japanese Canadian Women, Memory, and the Subjects of Internment*, recalled, "We were scattered all over. I used to write to a lot of boys and girls that went to work somewhere else... [I]f they were going to leave for road camps or other places, they gave you snaps and signed in our autograph books."[115] The government relaxed censorship for mail coming in and out of the camps as the war ground on and teens exchanged photos for sentimental reasons and as a way of keeping in touch. Sending photographs and letters between camps was a favourite pastime for Ishii and her friends. She recalled that "we knew we were all going to be separated," so the autographed photographs became a life line not just between camps but also within the confines of Lemon Creek camp in preparation for the next uprooting. Ayukawa explained, "Always at the back of our minds was the fact that this was temporary. And that we wanted to remember it."[116]

Ishii's photo album's focus on schoolgirl concerns is similar to scrapbooks and photo albums belonging to any other Canadian schoolgirl. Notably absent from this scrapbook, however, is any discussion of the war effort that seems to have been ever-present in the lives of many Canadian children at the time. Scrap drives, military recruitment parades, Canadian Red Cross fundraisers, and letters to soldiers overseas are absent. The children in Lemon Creek, in contrast, lived in a bubble, isolated from the rest of Canadian society through no fault of their own. One Slocan teacher, after realizing how few of her middle school students were even aware of the name of the country's prime minister, remarked that "these are the children shut up inside a huge stone wall, utterly oblivious of the gigantic change outside."[117] Occasional images of friends and family at labour camps broke up the teenaged gaiety of the album. Young men weighted heavily with fruit picking bags, working with pick axes on a section of the CPR railway line near Field, British Columbia, and using heavy machinery to process logs are reminders that the harsh realities of forced labour and work camps lurked not far from the edges of Michiko Ishii's Lemon Creek existence.[118]

115 Oikawa, *Cartographies of Violence*, 160.
116 Ayukawa, interview.
117 Roy, *Mutual Hostages*, 128.
118 Ayukawa, Photo Album, CWM, 20, 43, 52, 61.

The experience of forced relocation depended greatly on age, gender, social class, occupation, and geography. As Ayukawa later said, it "varied according to your age. If it *had* to happen to me, I think that was the best time that it could have happened. I made a lot of good friends."[119] The suffering of men and women also differed greatly. As Muriel Kitagawa wrote to her brother, "the men are luckier than the women. They are fed, they work, they have no children to look after. Of course the fathers are awfully worried about their families. But it is the women who are burdened with all the responsibility of keeping what's left of the family together."[120] Published letters between husband and wife Koichiro and Yoshiko Miyazaki document Yoshiko's attempts to shield her seven-year-old daughter Reika from the harsh realities of Vancouver's racial tensions, her failed struggle to leave Canada for Japan on a POW exchange, the couple's year-long separation while interned in separate provinces, and her anger, depression, and eventual decision to move to Montréal to work as a housemaid in spite of her husband's wishes.[121] Life for most Japanese Canadian women, particularly mothers, was exceptionally difficult, in sharp contrast to the teen gaiety depicted in Michiko Ishii's photographs.

Photographs of life at Lemon Creek continue after the war, and when the family does leave, the album does not picture them returning to Vancouver, but instead moving to Ontario. The government disbanded the Lemon Creek camp in 1946, but rather than allowing camp residents to return to their homes and businesses, the government presented them with a stark ultimatum: relocate further east, away from British Columbia or be deported to Japan, a land most had never seen. The Ishii family decided to head east, to Hamilton, Ontario. Ayukawa later wrote, "The day the first 'returnees' left [for Japan] was one of the saddest days of my life. A friend from Strathcona School days, and one of our trio ('the long, the short and the tall') was the first to go. I wept. Our days in Lemon Creek had been an idyllic time. I was afraid of what the future would be like."[122] Figure 4.19 shows this trio, "Peg, Terrie & Mich," as they were known.[123] Ishii's photo album

119   Ayukawa, interview.
120   Kitagawa and Miki, *This Is My Own*, 117.
121   Ōiwa, *Stone Voices*, 29–89.
122   Ayukawa, "Lemon Creek Memories," 16.
123   Ayukawa (Ishii), Photo Album, CWM, 44.

documents the difficulties in saying goodbye to her Lemon Creek friends and familiar places as the community experienced its second large dispersal. The captions read, "Farewell, June 1946. We'll Meet Again! (Let's Hope)."[124]

The first pictures away from Lemon Creek show remote Neys, located on the shores of Lake Superior in northern Ontario. One photo is titled "Wow—you made it!!" while a second, formal portrait of a friend, is poignantly captioned "Where are you now?"[125] Michiko, her parents, and younger brother spent eight weeks in an isolated camp that had previously been occupied by German POWs. The living conditions there were even more primitive than they had been at Lemon Creek, with communal dormitories and meal halls.[126] Michiko, ever upbeat, subtitled her Neys photos "Life's a Beach!" and "Wonderful scenery, in't."[127] The Neys images show the Lemon Creek residents sticking together, clinging to the familiar during another uprooting. The photographs are labelled, "All ex-LC [Lemon Creek]."[128]

Michiko's album ends with the family in Hamilton in the late 1940s. The photos document the Ishii's new home, a brick duplex with a front lawn, a first winter skate on a frozen pond, as well as photographs sent by Lemon Creek friends, including Terrie, who was by then living in Japan ("I miss your smile, Terrie!!"), and her 1945 Christmas dinner dance date, Mas Yamamoto.[129] Many Japanese Canadians, including the Ishiis, made Ontario their new, permanent home. Community bonds that had seemed temporarily disrupted by the forced relocation during the war years were now understood to have been interrupted forever. Some close friends successfully kept their friendships alive by sending each other letters and photographs, like Terrie, Peggy, and Michiko, who remained friends into their old age, but for many Japanese Canadians, the postwar years were primarily spent looking forward rather than back. Families buckled down to rebuild financially and tried to establish new connections in unfamiliar surroundings.

OPPOSITE: FIGURE 4.19. Michiko Ishii (*front*) with friends at Lemon Creek, 1946.
Source: George Metcalf Archival Collection, Canadian War Museum 20150279-001_p49.

---

124   Ayukawa (Ishii), Photo Album, CWM, 75.
125   Ayukawa (Ishii), Photo Album, CWM, 80.
126   Adachi, *The Enemy That Never Was*, 339.
127   Ayukawa (Ishii), Photo Album, CWM, 83.
128   Ayukawa (Ishii), Photo Album, CWM, 83.
129   Ayukawa (Ishii), Photo Album, CWM, 88.

With the promise of employment, McMaster University accepting Japanese Canadians (which was not the case at many other Canadian universities), and a growing community of Japanese Canadians relocating from British Columbia, the Ishii family likely saw Hamilton as a good place to start over.[130]

ALTA WILKINSON

Women coped with wartime loss in deeply personal ways. For Alta Wilkinson, the death of her son Arthur compelled her to work both publicly and privately to keep his memory alive. Privately, she kept scrapbooks (figure 4.20) in which she carefully documented Arthur's life, his war service, and his death. For many women of her generation, books like these provided a tactile means to arrange and display cuttings, photos, and other small items. Pasting them onto a page imbued these artifacts with order and permanence. Within these pages, Wilkinson sought

FIGURE 4.20. Alta Wilkinson's scrapbooks.
Source: George Metcalf Archival Collection, Canadian War Museum 19830600-002, 006, 007.

130 Taylor, *A Black Mark*, 107.

to hold on to Arthur's memory even if, physically, he was lost to her forever. She also projected her grief outward by publishing a selection of his correspondence in a book and by helping to found the Remembrance Association Silver Cross Women of Canada.[131]

Like Betty Butcher, Alta Wilkinson's early life had been marked by war. Born Alta Rockefeller Campbell in 1898, as a teenager she watched as two of her older brothers went off to fight in the First World War; only one returned home. Her eventual husband, Curt Lorne Wilkinson, was also a veteran of that war. With two sons (born in 1920 and 1924) who would also serve in a world war, she was a member of a generation that twice felt the painful, personal impact of conflict.

Arthur Campbell Wilkinson, her eldest child, shared a name with Alta Wilkinson's late brother, killed in the First World War.[132] When war again broke out in September 1939, Arthur had finished school and was working in Ottawa for the Dominion government as a post-office clerk. After he enlisted in November 1939, he was shipped overseas as a member of the Canadian Postal Corps. The first few pages in Alta's scrapbook follow his trajectory, with a map of England and the words "World War II Sept. 3, 1939" printed underneath.[133] Snapshots of Arthur in his uniform follow, all taken in the days and moments before he departed. Like many other Canadian troops, he would spend the next several years in England, working, training, and waiting for action. Back on the home front, his mother also waited. Alta and Arthur regularly exchanged letters, and he was greatly appreciative of the care parcels and money she often sent. Soon, she had an additional cause for worry as her second son, Richard, joined the Royal Canadian Navy.[134]

Wilkinson filled the scrapbook with newspaper clippings pertaining to the war, to Canadian troops overseas, and the Postal Corps. Some things Arthur clearly sent home, such as a souvenir guide from Madame Tussaud's in London. Wilkinson also pasted in envelopes, on YMCA or Salvation Army stationery, addressed to "Mrs. C. L. Wilkinson." Photos of Arthur overseas, on a motorcycle, with friends, or in uniform with fellow soldiers, begin to appear in greater numbers.

131 Wilkinson, *Ottawa to Caen*.

132 Arthur Prentiss Campbell, CEF Personnel Record.

133 Scrapbook Pertaining to Private Arthur Campbell Wilkinson, 1937–1945, CWM 19830600-002.

134 "Pte. A. C. Wilkinson Killed," 13.

By the beginning of 1944, tired of postal work, Arthur transferred to the Royal Highland Regiment of Canada (The Black Watch) and began infantry training.[135] His father served in this regiment during the First World War. Wilkinson's second scrapbook devoted to her son documents this change. Less coherent than the first scrapbook, here items are inserted in an almost random fashion, with little concern for chronology. This album has a darker tone as well, including pages of "Killed in Action" clippings, mostly young men from the Ottawa area. Then, on one page, we see Arthur, looking a bit older, smiling in a snapshot. The annotation next to it includes the words "Last leave... before joining Black Watch."[136]

Arthur, like many others at home and in uniform, was anticipating the long-rumoured Allied invasion of Northwest Europe. Finally, on June 6, 1944, the wait was over, and news of the D-Day landings in France filtered out. Arthur was not in the first wave; he landed in France with the rest of his battalion in early July, as part of the 5th Infantry Brigade, 2nd Canadian Infantry Division.[137] Meanwhile, Alta anxiously followed the news from overseas, writing to Arthur that "We listen & read every scrap of news about the Canadians & think of you and pray that God will keep you safe & that it will be over soon. Good night my darling boy. XXXX Mother."[138] But by the time Alta sat down to write these words, the Black Watch had already gone into action as part of combat operations to wrest the city of Caen from the Germans. Arthur Wilkinson was killed as his unit crossed the River Orne.[139] The letter was eventually returned to Alta, unread.

Not surprisingly, some of the most poignant entries in the scrapbooks are those associated with Arthur's death. One page contains a newspaper clipping of a list of soldiers killed in action with Arthur's name circled, news about the Battle of Caen, a church service program, and a dried rose. Beside the preserved rose, Alta wrote: "The rose is one of a beautiful bouquet I received from Arthur on July 28, 1944. The day I received the telegram saying he was killed in action 18 July 1944."[140] Arthur had arranged to have it sent to Alta before he left

135   Arthur Wilkinson to Curt Lorne Wilkinson, January 17, 1944, CWM 19830600-008.
136   Scrapbook, Pertaining to Private Arthur Campbell Wilkinson and the Second World War, CWM 19830600-006.
137   Stacey, *Official History of the Canadian Army,* 152.
138   Alta Wilkinson to Arthur Wilkinson, July 19, 1944, CWM 19830600-008.
139   Arthur Campbell Wilkinson, Service Files of the Second World War – War Dead, 1939–1947.
140   Scrapbook, CWM 19830600-006.

for France and by coincidence both flowers and telegram arrived the same day. The telegram appears on the left-hand side of the open scrap book in figure 4.20. Alta pasted the condolence card from the Minister of National Defence sent to casualties' next-of-kin below. A note from King George VI, also sent to all bereaved next of kin, offering sympathies, appears on the facing page beside a photograph of Arthur in battle dress, his helmet and gun on the ground in front of him. There are more photographs on this page: Arthur's wooden grave marker, an image of the cemetery in which he was first interred, and a photo of Caen in ruins. Alta labelled the little package taped between the photographs "Earth from Arthur's Grave."[141]

The cemetery photos and earth from the grave tell an interesting story of their own. As in the First World War, Canadian dead were not repatriated—they were interred near where they were killed. Alta wrote on the grave photo, "Bretteville-sur-Laize Cdn Cemetery France," which is where her son was buried, just south of Caen.[142] In the years following the war, the Commonwealth War Graves Commission cared for the cemeteries and the plots, eventually replacing the wooden crosses with headstones. Residents of northwest France volunteered to act as grave attendants for Canadian families whose loved ones were now buried in French soil. These attendants added personal touches to the gravesites. The Raoult family from Calvados, near Caen, adopted Arthur's grave. They visited the plot on behalf of the Wilkinsons, laying flowers, taking and sending photos, and also collecting small packets of earth and dried wildflowers from the grave. Alta preserved some of these wildflowers in her scrapbooks. For the people of Normandy, these actions were a way of expressing gratitude to the Allied soldiers who gave their lives to liberate them from Nazi tyranny and of paying respect to their families. In a letter sent with the grave earth, Jean Raoult described it as "a little of the soil of Normandy, sprinkled with his blood."[143] For women like Alta Wilkinson, these gestures not only gave them reassurance that their sons' final resting places were being respected and cared for but also that their own unbearable grief was not in vain. It reinforced the belief that their sons had achieved something significant in helping to rescue a people from fascist occupation. This

141   Scrapbook, CWM 19830600-006.
142   Scrapbook, CWM 19830600-006.
143   Raoult Family to Alta Wilkinson, April 18, 1947, CWM 19830600-017.

FIGURE 4.21. Alta and Curt Wilkinson at their son Arthur's grave in France, 1953.
Source: George Metcalf Archival Collection, Canadian War Museum 19830600-007_p135f.

alone could never heal their emotional wounds, but it must have at least given them a sense of pride and purpose.

Wilkinson corresponded with the Raoult family for years, creating a bond that spanned the physical distance between them. The Raoults sent the Wilkinsons photographs, a book about Caen's wartime history, and news about the cemetery where Arthur was buried. In return, Wilkinson sent precious foodstuffs and even, in 1949, a set of Meccano building toys as a Christmas present for six-year-old Daniel Raoult.[144] In 1953, Alta and her husband Curt made the journey overseas to see their son's grave in person and to meet the Raoult family. In a photograph (figure 4.21), they pose behind Arthur's grave. This was a pilgrimage many Canadians made in the postwar years, if they had the means to afford it. Visiting the gravesites of sons, husbands, brothers, and friends killed in the war offered solace and, in some cases, much needed closure.

In addition to the scrapbooks, which were entirely personal reflections of her lost son, Alta sought more public ways of memorialization. Just as the Raoults aided her through her sorrow, she too supported other grieving women. She helped to found the Remembrance Association Silver Cross Women of Canada, thereby mobilizing thousands of other Canadian women mourning loved ones, giving them a purpose for their grief as well. This group—made up of Memorial Cross recipients—offered mutual support and the opportunity to help others affected by conflict.[145] Alta served as President of the Ottawa chapter, and in 1975, she accepted the honour of being named Canada's National Silver Cross Mother. In this role, she laid a wreath at the National War Memorial in Ottawa on Remembrance Day, a solemn and symbolic act of commemoration.[146]

---

144 Raoult Family to Alta Wilkinson, December 29, 1949, CWM 19830600-017.
145 "Silver Cross Women," 2.
146 "Lest We Forget," 1.

CONCLUSION

"DOESN'T SEEM POSSIBLE," WROTE HELEN WALTER TO HER mother on May 7, 1945. It was the day before Victory in Europe (VE) Day, and the realization that the war in Europe was about to end was dawning in the minds of many. What would happen next? After years of dislocation, a return to peace was on the horizon. Walter was somewhat dazed by the prospect, adding that she and her fellow CWACs "just don't know how to act, nor does anyone else."[1] Like Walter, many Canadian women emerged from both world wars facing similar uncertainties. The end of the fighting was greeted with jubilation. It meant the return of loved ones, no more anxious days and nights waiting and hoping for peacetime. It meant an end to shortages and "making do." It meant—in other words—a return to normalcy. But what would "normal" look like for postwar women? Women had made considerable gains in wartime. They had pushed for active wartime roles, created some of their own, and took advantage of new opportunities. For her part, Helen Walter had been an ambitious

---

1   Helen Walter to Vera Walter, May 7, 1945, CWM 20030265-002.

soldier, taking every occasion to improve her standing in the army. She had not been alone. Seizing the moment, many women had entered into new fields of endeavour in the workplace, the military, and the public sphere in general. In so doing, they stretched the boundaries of social norms and proved they had a place in areas previously shut to them. One major question facing women in both 1918 and 1945 was clear: after helping to win a war, to what extent would they share in the dividends of peace?

The world wars had brought immense stress and grief to many, emotional burdens had left scars that would mark their lives forever. Thousands of women went into the postwar years having lost sons (and sometimes daughters), husbands, brothers, and friends. Families had dispersed, young people taking war jobs far from their home communities, never to return. Others had male relations returning home broken in body or spirit, or both, casualties of combat and the psychological degradation of war. People on the home front were ill-equipped to handle the shock of seeing what they believed were insurmountable injuries. In the wake of her son's death, a correspondent wrote to a mourning Jeannie Cassels Boucher: "If you could see some of those poor boys at the hospital here, there are three in particular all tied to wheel chairs, for the rest of their lives. I often wonder if they, young big athletic boys, would not just as soon be left in France."[2] For both women and men, on the home front and the battle front, the world wars extracted an enormous price.

For the women in this book, the return to normalcy was a mixed bag. Some, like Molly Lamb Bobak, had been able to use their wartime opportunities to the fullest. Entering the army after graduating from art school and successfully lobbying for an appointment as an official war artist, Bobak arguably had a "good" war. Both her career and personal life (she married fellow official war artist Bruno Bobak in 1945) benefitted from her war service. "I don't believe in war," she later recalled, "but it was a wonderful experience. We were damn lucky."[3] Edith Anderson Monture took her expertise back to her home community, where she worked as a nurse and advocate for Indigenous health care.[4] Minnie Gray, who could only find work as a domestic servant before the war, parlayed the medical training she received in the army into a postwar career as a nursing assistant. Of the women in

2   Minnie Craig to Jeannie Cassels Boucher, May 17, 1917, CWM 20050205-037.
3   Amos, "Artist Broke New Ground," 46.
4   Moses, "Indigenous Nurse a Worthy Candidate," 8.

this book, nurses were most likely to continue in their field after the war, probably because the profession was an established, accepted one for women before the war. Mary Cooney married a fellow veteran after the war, had a child, and remained in nursing for several decades. Other women, in less traditional wartime occupations, had a much harder time translating these occupations into peacetime vocations.

Norma Etta Lee, who during the Second World War broke through to become a rare woman air traffic controller, found this career impossible to pursue outside the context of war. Lorna Stanger reported a similar story. Trained as a naval photographer, she found no opportunities to continue her work in civilian life. Like so many war plant employees, and the munitions workers of the First World War that had preceded them, the women of Can Car found themselves shunted out of the industry as the war ended and as male veterans returned home. For many women, marriage and family quickly followed on the heels of wartime adventure. At the end of the First World War, Mary Campbell Mays hung up her mob cap and married a former soldier. So too did Mary Robertson Gordon. Possibly because of the specificity of her skill set, ocularist Kathleen McGrath stayed in the workforce longer than most, but she too left it upon marriage in 1955. This is not to say that marriage and motherhood were unwelcome for these women, rather that even after the clear contribution wartime women made, society still encouraged them to return to their "proper" place in the home. But by the 1960s, women were once more entering the workforce in large numbers. Whether this had to do with liberalizing attitudes or a need for larger family incomes in the postwar consumer society, or both, the precedent set by wartime women had an undeniable impact.

None of the women in this book enjoyed lengthy peacetime military careers, nor did most women who served in the wars. After a concerted fight to get into the military, and after proving themselves to skeptics who scoffed at "girl soldiers," in the immediate aftermath of war, women were effectively shut out of military careers, save, once more, for nurses. At the end of the Second World War, the three women's service branches were quickly disbanded, leaving women who may have wished to continue bereft of options. Their effect had not been entirely lost, however. As the world settled into the Cold War era, the Canadian military once more saw a use for women recruits.[5] Some women who had served during the

5   Simpson, Toole, and Player, "Women in the Canadian Forces," 271; Dundas, *A History of Women*, 94–102.

Second World War, like Eva Roy, re-enlisted. While their numbers were limited for many years, women were now a permanent part of the Canadian military. Incremental changes over the next 50 years eventually led to equal opportunity in the Canadian Armed Forces for women, culminating in the 2001 decision to allow women to serve on submarines, the last remaining prohibition. While the road to get there was long, the servicewomen of the war years were significant catalysts in that process.

Has approaching the wartime experiences of women through the materials they left behind told us anything new? To start, it reveals that women's wartime history already exists within the collections of museums and archives but is not always obvious. When it can be uncovered, it offers a greater holistic understanding of the wars and their impact on Canadian society. It has also shown that traditional sources for finding and interpreting history (texts) are not the only way to get at those stories, and that artifacts, in conjunction with those other sources, can be very effective in bringing us closer to the actual lived experience of war. Additionally, it is clear that most of the stories that exist now in institutional collections are heavily weighted towards certain demographic groups. White, middle- and upper-class, heterosexual women with close connections to war-involved men predominate. As military historiography has broadened in recent decades to include women and other non-combat topics, so too have museum collections, and yet there is still work to be done. The subjects that we did not include in this book, anti-war protest and divorce, for example, are out there to be explored, but more research, more collecting, more digging is required to bring them to light. We hope that *Material Traces of War* will provide an impetus for future publications, collections development, and exhibitions.

REFERENCES

16-2 JCCA Revitalization-History Project, March 1, 1958. MG28 V7. Japanese Canadian Citizen's Association. Library and Archives Canada.

"7,319 Women Eager to Enlist Receive Application Forms." *Globe and Mail*, August 20, 1941, 8.

"48,000 Garments Re-Made in Canada." *Edmonton Journal*, April 21, 1944, 15.

"Active Committees Red Cross Societies." *Ottawa Citizen*, September 26, 1914, 17.

Acton, Carol. *Grief in Wartime: Private Pain, Public Discourse*. Basingstoke: Palgrave Macmillan, 2007.

Ada Sylvester's Can Car Mallet. 2007.86.3. Canadian Museum of History.

Adachi, Ken. *The Enemy That Never Was: A History of the Japanese Canadians*. Toronto: McClelland and Stewart, 1976.

Adams, Eric, and Jordan Stanger-Ross. "Promises of Law: The Unlawful Dispossession of Japanese Canadians." *Osgoode Hall Law Journal* 54, no. 3 (Spring 2017): 687–739.

"Address Given by Princess Alice." *Saskatoon Star-Phoenix*, December 1, 1941, 8.

"After a Storm Comes a Calm." *London Free Press*, April 6, 1918.

Agricultural Supplies Board. *Canada Urgently Needs More Wool: Special Pamphlet*. Ottawa: King's Printer, 1942.

"Airwoman Jeannett Touchette First Woman Instrument Maker – Women of Wentworth Hold Armistice Dance." *Hamilton Spectator*, November 13, 1942.

Allinson, Sidney. "A Petticoat Army." *Victoria Times-Colonist*, April 8, 2001, D12.

Alta R. Wilkinson fonds. CWM 19830600. George Metcalf Archival Collection. Canadian War Museum.

Amos, Robert. "Artist Broke New Ground in the War." *Victoria Times Colonist*, March 4, 2004, 46.

Anderson, Janice. "The Forgotten Artists Who Commemorated Canada's Women War Workers." *Concordia University News*, April 14, 2014. http://www.concordia.ca /cunews/main/stories/2014/04/14/how-2-sculptors-changedthewayweseewomen .html/.

Anderson, Margaret, and Kylie Winkworth. "Museums and Gender: An Australian Critique." *Museum International* 66 (2014): 127–131.

Andrews, Margaret W. "Epidemic and Public Health: Influenza in Vancouver, 1918-1919." *BC Studies* 34 (Summer, 1977): 21–44.

"Appearance – In Street Clothes – Personality and Talent Were Sought in Miss Canada Contest." *Ottawa Citizen*, August 15, 1951, 18.

Archer, Bernice. *The Internment of Western Civilians under the Japanese 1941–1945: A Patchwork of Internment*. Hong Kong: Hong Kong University Press, 2008.

Army Medical Services, Great Britain. *Instructions for Members of Canadian Army Medical Corps Nursing Service (When Mobilized)*. London: Vacher and Sons, 1917.

Arnold, Ken. "Museums and the Making of Medical History." In *Manifesting Medicine: Bodies and Machines*, edited by Robert Bud, Bernard Finn, and Helmuth Trischler, 145–170. Amsterdam: Harwood Academic Publishers, 1999.

Artificial Eyes, CWM 20110152-025. Canadian War Museum.

Ashley, Susan L. T. *A Museum in Public: Revisioning Canada's Royal Ontario Museum*. New York: Routledge, 2019.

Auger, Geneviève, and Raymonde Lamothe. *De la poêle à frire à la ligne de feu : la vie quotidienne des Québécoises pendant la guerre '39-'45*. Montréal: Boréal Express, 1981.

Auto Knitter Hosiery Company advertisement. *Ottawa Citizen*, October 4, 1919, 7.

Ayukawa, Michiko Midge. "Lemon Creek Memories: September 1942." *Japanese Canadian Citizens Association Bulletin* (April 1989): 22–23.

———. "Good Wives and Wise Mothers: Japanese Picture Brides in Early Twentieth-Century British Columbia." *BC Studies: The British Columbian Quarterly* (Spring/Summer 1995): 103–118.

———. "Lemon Creek Memories." Interview, Simon Fraser University, 1995.133.4.1.a. http://digital.lib.sfu.ca/johc-434/199513341a/.

———. "Japanese After All." In *Women's Changing Landscapes: Life Stories from Three Generations*, edited by Greta Nemiroff, 47–51. Toronto: Second Story Press, 1999.

———. *Hiroshima Immigrants in Canada 1891-1941*. Vancouver: UBC Press, 2008.

———. "Lemon Creek Memories." *Nikkei Images (Spring 2012)*.

"B.C. Woman Flees Red Secret Police." *Vancouver Sun*, December 2, 1950, 31.

Ball, Norman R. *Mind, Heart, and Vision: Professional Engineering in Canada, 1887 to 1987*. Ottawa: National Museum of Science and Technology, 1988.

Barbara McNutt's Miss Canada Apron. CWM 20070060-002. Canadian War Museum.

Bates, Christina, and Helen Knibb. "The Museum as a Teaching Resource for Women's History." In *Teaching Women's History: Challenges and Solutions*, edited by Bettina Bradbury et al., 245–254. Athabasca: Athabasca University, 1995.

Bates, Christina, Diane Dodd, and Nicole Rousseau. *On All Frontiers: Four Centuries of Canadian Nursing*. Ottawa: University of Ottawa Press, 2005.

"Beating the Regular Christmas Trade; Trench Box Sales Make New Record." *Canadian Grocer*, October 25, 1918, 79–81.

Beausaert, Rebecca. "Red Crosses and White Cotton: Memory and Meaning in First World War Quilts." *Active History*, July 4, 2017. http://activehistory.ca/2017/07 /red-crosses-and-white-cotton-memory-and-meaning-in-first-world-war-quilts/.

"Beauty Parlour Equipment Goes Into War Planes." *Hamilton Spectator*, May 5, 1941.

"Behind the Lines: Articles Knitted by Hamilton Women Have Brought Comfort to Soldiers Overseas." *Hamilton Spectator*, December 31, 1942.

Bellamy, Matthew J. *Profiting the Crown: Canada's Polymer Corporation, 1942-1990*. Montréal and Kingston: McGill-Queen's University Press, 2008.

Berger, Carl. *The Sense of Power: Studies in the Ideas of Canadian Imperialism, 1867–1914*. Toronto: University of Toronto Press, 1970.

Berger, Genie. "Three Balls of Yarn." *Sudbury Star*, October 24, 2015.

Berman, Shirley. "BILSKY, LILLIAN (Freiman)." In *Dictionary of Canadian Biography*. Vol. 16, University of Toronto/Université Laval, 2003–. Accessed October 22, 2020. http://www.biographi.ca/en/bio/bilsky_lillian_16E.html.

Bérubé, Allan. *Coming Out Under Fire: The History of Gay Men and Women in World War II*. Chapel Hill: University of North Carolina Press, 1990.

Blanchard, Jim. *Winnipeg's Great War: A City Comes of Age*. Winnipeg: University of Manitoba Press, 2010.

Bobak, Molly Lamb. *CMHQ Garage, Chelsea, London*, 1945. CWM 19710261-1566. Beaverbrook Collection of War Art. Canadian War Museum.

———. *Comedy Convoy Back Stage at the Tivoli Theater Apeldoorn*, 1945. CWM 19710261-1567. Beaverbrook Collection of War Art. Canadian War Museum.

———. *Number 1 Static Base Laundry*, 1945. CWM 19710261-1618. Beaverbrook Collection of War Art. Canadian War Museum.

———. *Private Roy, Canadian Women's Army Corps*, 1946. CWM 19710261-1626. Beaverbrook Collection of War Art. Canadian War Museum.

———. *Wildflowers of Canada: Impressions and Sketches of a Field Artist.* Toronto: Pagurian Corporation, 1983.

———. Interview by Laura Brandon, May 12, 2000. CWM 20020121-209. George Metcalf Archival Collection. Canadian War Museum.

———. "Molly Lamb Bobak: Canada's First Female Official War Artist (Part 3 of 3)." Video interview, March 20, 2012. Library and Archives Canada. https://www .youtube.com/watch?time_continue=18&v=4rn-7BM8LJo/.

Bodley's Overseas Cake advertisement. *Canadian Grocer*, October 4, 1918, 2.

Bogaert, Kandace L. "Military and Maritime Evidence of Pandemic Influenza in Canada during the Summer of 1918." *War & Society* 36, no. 1 (2017): 44–63.

Boyanoski, Christine. *Loring and Wyle: Sculptors' Legacy.* Toronto: Art Gallery of Ontario, 1987.

Braithwaite, Rella, and Tessa Benn-Ireland. *Some Black Women: Profiles of Black Women in Canada.* Toronto: Sister Vision, 1993.

Brand, Dionne. *No Burden to Carry: Narratives of Black Working Women in Ontario, 1920 to-1950s.* Toronto: Women's Press, 1991.

———. "'We Weren't Allowed to Go into Factory Work Until Hitler Started the War': The 1920s to the 1940s." In *We're Rooted Here and They Can't Pull Us up: Essays in African Canadian Women's History,* edited by Peggy Bristow, 171–192. Toronto: University of Toronto Press, 1994.

Brandon, Laura. "A Unique and Important Asset? The Transfer of the War Art Collections from the National Gallery of Canada to the CWM." *Material History Review* 42 (Fall 1995): 67–74.

———. *Art and War.* London: I. B. Tauris, 2007.

———. "Looking for the 'Total' Woman in Wartime: A Museological Work in Progress." In *Gender, Sexuality, and Museums: A Routledge Reader,* edited by Amy K. Levin, 105–114. London: Routledge, 2010.

Broad, Graham. *A Small Price to Pay: Consumer Culture on the Canadian Home Front, 1939-45.* Vancouver: UBC Press, 2013.

Brookbank Collection. 2009-H0016. Canadian Museum of History Archives.

Bruce, Jean. *Back the Attack! Canadian Women during the Second World War, at Home and Abroad.* Toronto: Macmillan, 1985.

Buck, Clair. "British Women's Writing of the Great War." In *The Cambridge Companion to the Literature of the First World War,* edited by Vincent Sherry, 85–112. Cambridge: Cambridge University Press, 2005.

Burkowski, Gordon. *Can-Car: A History, 1912-1992.* Thunder Bay: Bombardier, 1995.

Butlin, Susan. "Women Making Shells: Marking Women's Presence in the Munitions Work 1914–1918: The Art of Frances Loring, Florence Wyle, Mabel May, and Dorothy Stevens." *Canadian Military History Journal* 5, no. 1 (Spring 1996): 41–48.

Cameron, Elspeth. *And Beauty Answers: The Life of Frances Loring and Florence Wyle.* Toronto: Cormorant Books, 2007.

Canada at War: A Record of Heroism and Achievement 1914–1918. Toronto: Canadian Annual Review, 1919.

Canada Food Board. *Report of the Canada Food Board, February 11–December 31, 1918.* Ottawa: The Board, 1919.

Canada, Military Honours and Awards Citation Cards, 1900-1961. Ancestry.ca.

"Canada's Only Girl 'Bergen' Started Her Career at Age 4." *Globe and Mail,* June 18, 1948, 4.

"Canada's Registration: Its Purpose and Application." *Red Deer News,* June 5, 1918, 1.

Canada's War Effort, 1914–1918. Ottawa: Director of Public Information, 1918.

"The Canadian Bank of Commerce, Addresses of the President and General Manager at the Annual Meeting, Canada's Position in War Times Reviewed." *Industrial Canada,* February 1916, 1078.

Canadian Department Stores Ltd. advertisement. *Ottawa Journal,* May 20, 1938, 3.

Canadian Expeditionary Force (CEF), Personnel Files. RG 150. Accession 1992-93/166. Library and Archives Canada.

Canadian Museum of History Acquisition File 985.39.6.

Canadian Museum of History Acquisition File 2007.87.

Canadian Museum of History Acquisition File 2010.214.

Canadian Museum of History Acquisition File 2016.12.2.

Canadian Museum of History Acquisition File D-16997.

Canadian War Contingent Association. *Field Comforts for Fighting Canadians* (Summer 1917).

Canadian War Museum Acquisition File 19800471.

Canadian War Museum Acquisition File 20060047.

Canadian War Museum Acquisition File 20070060.

Canadian War Museum Acquisition File 20110152.

Canadian War Museum Acquisition File 20110057.

Canadian War Museum Acquisition File 20120014.

Canadian War Museum Acquisition File 20140301.

"Canadian Woman Made M.B.E.: Commanded Japanese." *Manchester Guardian,* October 3, 1946, 5.

Canadian Women's Army Corps. *Women in Khaki.* Toronto: Canadian Women's Army Corps, [1942].

"Canadian Wool Board Will Take Over Entire Wool Clip." *Ottawa Journal,* March 11, 1942, 3.

Cannon, Dorothy. "Mom and Dad." Unpublished manuscript, 2018.

———. "A Prospect of Heroes: The Great War Tour, From a Child's Eyes." Unpublished manuscript, 2018.

———. Interview by Krista Cooke and Stacey Barker, November 29, 2019.

"Can't Sell Tin Minus Permit, Ottawa Rules." *Globe and Mail*, December 20, 1941, 7.

Carnegie, David. *The History of Munitions Supply in Canada, 1914–1918*. London: Longmans, 1925.

Carry, Mary E. Diary, CWM 19850350-001. George Metcalf Archival Collection. Canadian War Museum.

Caton, Susan Turnbull. "Fashion and War in Canada." In *Fashion: A Canadian Perspective*, edited by Alexandra Palmer, 249–269. Toronto: University of Toronto, 2004.

Census of Canada, 1921. London, Ontario, Sub-District 4.

Chinese Canadian Military Museum. "Chinese Canadian Women in the War." Accessed April 19, 2021. http://www.ccmms.ca/veteran-stories/other/chinese-canadian -women-in-the-armed-forces/.

"Chorley Park Concert." *Globe and Mail*, August 19, 1941, 10.

Christie, Norm, and Gary Roncetti. *For Our Old Comrades: The Story and Ephemera of the Vimy Pilgrimage 1936*. Ottawa: CEF Books, 2011.

Clark, Gregory. "99." *Toronto Star*. n.d.

"Color Line is Drawn in Ontario." *Globe and Mail*, October 6, 1942, 15.

Comacchio, Cynthia. *The Dominion of Youth: Adolescence and the Making of Modern Canada, 1920 to 1950*. Waterloo: Wilfrid Laurier University Press, 2008.

Commemorative Plate, No. 14 Canadian General Hospital. CWM 19940080-001. Canadian War Museum.

"Connecting Link Between 'Tommy' and Canadian Socks." *Windsor Star*, October 15, 1915, 10.

"Connie and Charlotte." Press clipping, n.d. CWM 20130158.

Connie Laidlaw's Ventriloquist Figure. CWM 20130158-001. Canadian War Museum.

"Consumer Branch Launches Drive for Conservation of All Goods." *Montreal Gazette*, March 17, 1943, 4.

Converse, Cathy. *Against the Current: The Remarkable Life of Agnes Deans Cameron*. Victoria: Touchwood, 2018.

Cook, Norman. Notes from conversation with Krista Cooke, December 2016 and interview, February 2017.

Cook, Tim. *The Necessary War: Canadians Fighting the Second World War: 1939-1943*. Vol. 1. Toronto: Penguin, 2014.

———. *Fight to the Finish: Canadians in the Second World War*. Vol. 2. Toronto: Penguin, 2015.

———. *The Fight for History: 75 Years of Forgetting, Remembering, and Remaking Canada's Second World War*. Toronto: Penguin, 2020.

Cook, Tim, and Eric Brown. "The 1936 Vimy Pilgrimage." *Canadian Military History* 20, no. 2 (Spring 2011): 37–54.

Cooke, Krista. "Looking for the Helpers in a Time of Crisis." *Signatures: The Magazine of Library and Archives Canada*, Fall/Winter 2020, 3–4.

Cooney, Lorna. "Lorna Cooney – née Stanger." In *Equal to the Challenge: An Anthology of Women's Experiences During World War II*, 155–163. Ottawa: National Defence, 2001.

Cooper, Rowena. *The Ottawa Women's Canadian Club 1910–2010*. Ottawa: Ottawa Women's Canadian Club, 2018.

Coops, Lorraine. "Strength in Union: Patterns of Continuity and Change Within the Sir Robert Borden Chapter of the Imperial Order of the Daughters of the Empire 1915–1965." *Atlantis* 20, no. 1 (1995): 77–86.

Cott, Nancy F. *The Bonds of Womanhood: "Woman's Sphere" in New England, 1780–1835*. New Haven: Yale University Press, 1977.

Cowburn, Sergeant Eleanor (Barlow). Interview by A. E. Delamere, December 7, 2000. CWM 20020121-014. George Metcalf Archival Collection. Canadian War Museum.

Creelman Brothers. "Catalogue 101: The World's Best Family Knitting Machines," 1914.

Cumberland, Inge. "Knitting Our Country Together." *Globe and Mail*, May 27, 1993, A30.

Davis, Mary B., ed. *Native America in the Twentieth Century: An Encyclopedia*. New York: Routledge, 2014.

Davies, Adriana A., and Jeff Keshen, eds. *The Frontier of Patriotism: Alberta and the First World War*. Calgary: University of Calgary Press, 2016.

Davro, Mary. "Artificial Eyes: Their Early History and Modern Improvement." *Scientific American Supplement*, July 21, 1917.

Day, Frances Martin, Phyllis Spence, and Barbara Ladouceur, eds. *Women Overseas: Memoirs of the Canadian Red Cross Corps (Overseas Detachment)*. Vancouver: Ronsdale Press, 1998.

Department of External Affairs. RG 25. Vimy Ridge Celebrations. Newspapers Clippings, vol. 694. Library and Archives Canada.

Department of National Defence, Directorate of History and Heritage. Army Historical Section Report No. 15, "The Canadian Women's Army Corps, 1941–1946." Ottawa, 1947.

Department of National Defence, Directorate of History and Heritage. Report No. 120, "The Canadian Women's Army Corps Overseas, September 1939–June 1944." Historical Officer, Canadian Military Headquarters, July 31, 1944.

Department of National War Services. *Annual Report of National War Services for Fiscal Year Ended March 31, 1945*. Ottawa: King's Printer, 1945.

Department of National War Services. *Department of National War Services Act*. Ottawa: King's Printer, 1940.

"Des vacances qui hâteront la victoire." *Le Devoir*, July 12, 1944, 7.

Dickenson, Rachelle. "The Stories Told: Indigenous Art Collections, Museums, and National Identities." Master's thesis, McGill University, 2005.

Dickson, Barbara. *Bomb Girls: Trading Aprons for Ammo*. Toronto: Dundurn, 2015.

Dlholucky, Ada (Sylvester). Interview by Krista Cooke, February 24, 2007. CMH 2007.86. Canadian Museum of History Archives.

Doan, Laura. *Disturbing Practices: History, Sexuality and Women's Experience of Modern War*. Chicago: University of Chicago Press, 2013.

Doel, Marcus. *Geographies of Violence: Killing Space, Killing Time*. Thousand Oaks: SAGE, 2017.

Dominion Bridge Company. *Of Tasks Accomplished; The Story of the Accomplishments of Dominion Bridge Company, Limited and its Wholly Owned Subsidiaries in World War II*. Montréal: Dominion Bridge Company, 1945.

Dominion Bureau of Statistics. *Canada Yearbook 1918*. Ottawa: Minister of Trade and Commerce, 1919.

"Dominion Police May Be Replaced." *London Free Press*, April 4, 1918.

Dominion-Provincial Committee on Farm Labour advertisement, "We Can't Fight if We Don't Eat." *Ottawa Citizen*, April 7, 1943, 10.

Domm, Elizabeth. "From the Streets of Toronto to the Northwest Rebellion: Hannah Greer Coome's Call to Duty." In *Caregiving on the Periphery: Historical Perspectives on Nursing and Midwifery in Canada*, edited by Myra Rutherdale, 109–126. Montréal and Kingston: McGill-Queen's University Press, 2010.

Dornier, François. *Des bombardiers au-dessus du fleuve : historique de la 9e école de bombardement et de tir de Mont-Joli, 1941-1945*. Mont-Joli: F. Dornier, 1989.

Douglass, M. Ellen. "Winnipeg Women's Volunteer Reserve." *Imperial Order Daughters of the Empire Manitoba, Souvenir 1916*. IODE, 1916.

Doyle, Lucy Swanton. "Canadian Women Help the Empire: 'What Could Women Do in Time of War?'" Everywoman's World, November 1914, 32.

Dubrow, Gail Lee, and Jennifer B. Goodman, eds. *Restoring Women's History through Historic Preservation*. Baltimore: Johns Hopkins University Press, 2003.

Duder, Cameron. *Awfully Devoted Women: Lesbian Lives in Canada, 1900-65*. Vancouver: UBC Press, 2010.

Duguid, A. F. *Official History of the Canadian Forces in the Great War 1914-1919*. Vol. 1. Ottawa: King's Printer, 1938.

Duley, Margot I. "The Unquiet Knitters of Newfoundland: From Mothers of the Regiment to Mothers of the Nation." In *A Sisterhood of Suffering and Service: Women and Girls of Canada and Newfoundland During the First World War*, edited by Sarah Glassford and Amy Shaw, 51–74. Vancouver: UBC Press, 2012.

Dundas, Barbara. *A History of Women in the Canadian Military*. Montréal: Art Global, 2000.

Dundas, Barbara, and Serge Durflinger. "The Canadian Women's Army Corps, 1941-1946." *Dispatches: Backgrounders in Canadian Military History*. Canadian War

Museum. Accessed April 19, 2021. https://www.warmuseum.ca/learn/dispatches /the-canadian-womens-army-corps-1941-1946/#tabs.

Durflinger, Serge Marc. *Fighting from Home: The Second World War in Verdun, Quebec.* Vancouver: UBC Press, 2006.

———. *Veterans with a Vision: Canada's War Blinded in Peace and War.* Vancouver: UBC Press, 2010.

Dysievick, Frozina (Sportak). Interview with Krista Cooke, February 26, 2007. CMH 2007.93. Canadian Museum of History Archives.

Eaton's advertisement. *Winnipeg Tribune,* July 31, 1942, 20.

Ecker, Margaret. "Considers Service Training Fine Background for Matrimony." *Edmonton Journal,* May 1, 1943, 17.

Edmonton Bulletin. July 12, 1917, 4.

Ellanore Parker and Murney Pugh. Personal Papers. MS-1895. Royal British Columbia Museum and Archives.

Elrick, Nora and John (Jock). Interview with Krista Cooke, November 2008. CMH 2008.170. Canadian Museum of History Archives.

England, Kim, and Kate Boyer. "Women's Work: The Feminization and Shifting Meanings of Clerical Work." *Journal of Social History* 43, no. 2 (December 2009): 307–340.

Equal to the Challenge: An Anthology of Women's Experiences During World War II. Ottawa: National Defence, 2001.

Erpf, Stanley F., Victor H. Dietz, and Milton S. Wirtz. "Opthalmoprosthesis, U.S. Army, World War II." *The Military Surgeon* 101, no. 5 (November 1947).

Evans, Elizabeth (Butcher). Interviews with Krista Cooke, February, March, September 2007 and June 2009. CMH 2008.101. Canadian Museum of History Archives.

Evans Family fonds. 2008-H0025. Canadian Museum of History Archives.

Evans, Suzanne. *Mothers of Heroes, Mothers of Martyrs: World War I and the Politics of Grief.* Montréal and Kingston: McGill-Queen's University Press, 2007.

———. "Raising 'Human Ammunition': Motherhood, Propaganda, and the Great War." Active History.ca, August 18, 2015. http://activehistory.ca/2015/08/raising-human -ammunition-motherhood-propaganda-and-the-great-war/?utm_source= feedburner&utm_medium=email&utm_campaign=Feed%3A+Activehistoryca +%28ActiveHistory.ca%29.

L'Événement. April 26, 1918.

"Farmerettes Don Novel Costumes." *Windsor Star,* April 23, 1918, 6.

Feller, Carolyn M., and Debora R. Cox, eds. *Highlights in the History of the Army Nurse Corps.* Washington: U.S. Army Center of Military History, 2016.

Field Dressing. CWM 19800543-004. Canadian War Museum.

"First Peacetime CWAC Meeting Draws 1100 Veterans to Toronto." *Montreal Gazette,* June 13, 1949, 1.

Flascha, Carlo. "Prosthetics Under Trials of War." *Prospect: Journal of International Affairs at UCSD* (September 15, 2011). https://prospectjournal.org/2011/09/15/prosthetics-under-trials-of-war/.

Fleming, Margaret, Royal Canadian Air Force (Women's Division). Interview by Serge Durflinger, December 21, 1999. CWM 20020121-226. George Metcalf Archival Collection. Canadian War Museum.

"For Those Who Are Wearing Black." *Toronto Globe*, October 27, 1914, 14.

Fowler, T. Robert. "The Canadian Nursing Service and the British War Office: The Debate Over Awarding the Military Cross, 1918." *Canadian Military History* 14, no. 4 (2012): 31–42.

Fox, James. "Poppy Politics: Remembrance of Things Present." In *Cultural Heritage Ethics: Between Theory and Practice*, edited by Constantine Sandis. Open Book Publishers, 2014.

Frager, Ruth A. and Carmela Patrias. *Discounted Labour: Women Workers in Canada, 1870–1939*. Toronto: University of Toronto Press, 2005.

"Front Line Music-Halls." *Khaki Magazine*, February 19, 1945.

Gaffen, Fred. *Forgotten Soldiers*. Penticton: Theytus Books, 1985.

General Engineering Co., Ltd. *Scarboro Uniforms and Clothing*. Toronto: General Engineering Company, 1943.

General Engineering Company (Canada) fonds. F 2082. Archives of Ontario.

Gentile, Patrizia. *Queen of the Maple Leaf: Beauty Contests and Settler Femininity*. Vancouver: UBC Press, 2021.

Gewurtz, Michelle. *Molly Lamb Bobak: Life and Work*. Art Canada Institute. Accessed April 19, 2021. https://www.aci-iac.ca/art-books/molly-lamb-bobak/.

Gibson, Anita. "Plate – No. 14 Canadian General Hospital RCAMC." CWM 19810097-041.

"Girl Would Meet Boy – To Sell Him War Savings Stamps!" *Saskatoon Star-Phoenix*, July 21, 1942, 3.

Glassford, Sarah. "'The Greatest Mother in the World': Carework and the Discourse of Mothering in the Canadian Red Cross Society during the First World War." *Journal of the Association for Research on Mothering* 10, no. 1 (2008): 219–232.

———. *Mobilizing Mercy: A History of the Canadian Red Cross*. Montréal and Kingston: McGill-Queen's University Press, 2017.

———. "Volunteering in the First and Second World War." Wartime Canada. Accessed April 19, 2021. https://wartimecanada.ca/essay/volunteering/volunteering-first-and-second-world-war.

Glassford, Sarah, and Amy Shaw, eds. *A Sisterhood of Suffering and Service: Women and Girls of Canada and Newfoundland during the First World War*. Vancouver: UBC Press, 2012.

———. *Making the Best of It: Women and Girls of Canada and Newfoundland during the Second World War*. Vancouver: UBC Press, 2020.

Godin, Michelle. "The Brookbank Collection: Research on the Spencer, McTaggart and Ellis families." Canadian Museum of Civilization, unpublished research report, 2010.

"Goes to England." *Regina Leader-Post*, December 9, 1941, 7.

Gordon-Walker, Caitlin. *Exhibiting Nation: Multicultural Nationalism (and Its Limits) in Canada's Museums*. Vancouver: UBC Press, 2016.

Gossage, Carolyn. *Greatcoats and Glamour Boots: Canadian Women at War (1939–1945)*. Toronto: Dundurn Press, 1991.

Granatstein, J. L. "Conscription in the Great War." In *Canada and the First World War: Essays in Honour of Robert Craig Brown*, edited by David MacKenzie, 62–75. Toronto: University of Toronto Press, 2005.

Gray, Minnie. Birth Register. Register Year 1912. No. 55000808. Nova Scotia Births, Marriages, and Deaths. Nova Scotia Archives.

"Great Ocean Armada Speeding to France." *Windsor Star*, July 17, 1936, 15.

Greer, Rosamund. *The Girls of the King's Navy*. Victoria: Sono Nis Press, 1983.

Gaudio, Pam, and Bev Ellison. *Gone but Not Forgotten: A History of St. Luke's Churchyard*. Victoria, 2009.

"Gusty Gal." *Time,* November 11, 1946, 15.

Guy Henri Rainville fonds. CWM 20030359. George Metcalf Archival Collection. Canadian War Museum.

Halladay, Laurel. "'Ladies and Gentlemen, Soldiers and Artists': Canadian Military Entertainers, 1939-1946." Master's thesis, University of Calgary, 2000.

Hanna, Martha. *Anxious Days and Tearful Nights: Canadian War Wives during the Great War*. Montréal and Kingston: McGill-Queen's University Press, 2020.

Hargreaves, Eric L., and Margaret M. Gowing. *History of the Second World War, United Kingdom Civil Series: Civil Industry and Trade*. London: HMSO, 1952.

"Harvesting to Beat Hitler Fun for Farm Brigade Girls." *Ottawa Journal*, August 22, 1942, 23.

Hatch, F. J. *The Aerodrome of Democracy: Canada and the British Commonwealth Air Training Plan 1939-1945*. Ottawa: Department of National Defence, 1983.

Hawthorne, Tom. "Sting of Dispossession Has Not Faded." *Globe and Mail*, August 8, 2005, A7.

"Heard Around Town." *Ottawa Citizen*, October 11, 1921, 3.

"A Hearty Response to Queen Mary Movement." *Halifax Herald*, February 8, 1915, 2.

Hecht, Hermann. "Decalcomania: Some Preliminary Investigations into the History of Transfer Slides, A Lecture Given to the Society on October 1979." *New Magic Lantern Journal* 1, no. 3 (March 1980): 3–6.

Heinrich, Thomas, and Bob Batchelor. *Kotex, Kleenex, Huggies: Kimberly-Clark and the Consumer Revolution in American Business*. Columbus: Ohio State University Press, 2004.

Helen Walter fonds. CWM 20030265. George Metcalf Archival Collection. Canadian War Museum.

Heron, Craig. *The Canadian Labour Movement: A Short History*. Toronto: J. Lorimer, 2012.

Higonnet, Margaret. "Ventriloquizing Voices in World War I: Scribe, Poetess, Philosopher." In *Landscapes and Voices of the Great War*, edited by Angela K. Smith and Krista Cowman, 115–130. New York: Routledge, 2017.

Hill, Lawrence. *Women of Vision: The Story of the Canadian Negro Women's Association, 1951–1976*. Toronto: Umbrella Press, 1996.

Hogenbirk, Sarah. "Women Inside the Canadian Military, 1938-1966." PhD diss., Carleton University, 2017.

Holt, Richard. *Filling the Ranks: Manpower in the Canadian Expeditionary Force, 1914–1918*. Montréal and Kingston: McGill-Queen's University Press, 2017.

Humphries, Mark Osborne. "The Horror at Home: The Canadian Military and the 'Great' Influenza Pandemic of 1918." *Journal of the Canadian Historical Association* 16, no. 1 (2005): 235–260.

———. *The Last Plague: Spanish Influenza and the Politics of Public Health in Canada*. Toronto: University of Toronto Press, 2013.

Imperial Munitions Board. *Women in the Production of Munitions in Canada*. Canada: Imperial Munitions Board, 1916.

Imperial Order Daughters of the Empire and Children of the Empire. *Echoes*. No. 111 (March, 1928).

Inge (Oswald) Cumberland's Ontario Farm Service Force Sweatshirt. CWM 20120014-002. Canadian War Museum.

"Initial Drill is Enjoyed by Airwomen." *Globe and Mail*, October 25, 1941, 4.

"Is Home Life Breaking Up?" *Chatelaine*, June 1943, 8–9.

Itter, Carole, and Daphne Marlatt. *Opening Doors in Vancouver's East End: Strathcona*. Madeira Park, BC: Harbour Pub., 2011.

Ito, Roy. *We Went to War: The Story of the Japanese Canadians Who Served during the First and Second World Wars*. Stittsville: Canada's Wings, 1984.

Jackson, Paul. *One of the Boys: Homosexuality in the Military during World War II*. Montréal and Kingston: McGill-Queen's University Press, 2004.

"J**s Admire Canadian Woman Leader; But Think Her 'Too Tough' for Wife." *Vancouver Daily Province*, October 29, 1946, 8.

John King Gordon fonds. MG30 C24193. Library and Archives Canada.

Johnstone, Marjorie Winnifred. "Diverging and Contested Feminisms in Early Social Work History in Ontario (1900–1950)." PhD diss., University of Toronto, 2015.

Joseph, Nathan. *Uniforms and Nonuniforms: Communication Through Clothing*. New York: Greenwood Press, 1986.

Kalbfleisch, John. "War, Love and Women's Rights." *Montreal Gazette*, March 18, 2007, A18.

Kawano, Roland, ed. *A History of the Japanese Congregations of the United Church of Canada, 1892-1959*. Scarborough: The Japanese Canadian Christian Churches' Historical Project, 1998.

Kealey, Linda. *Enlisting Women for the Cause: Women, Labour, and the Left in Canada, 1890-1920*. Toronto: University of Toronto Press, 1998.

"Keeping Faith Fund Drive is Launched." *Ottawa Journal*, December 13, 1921, 3.

Kelm, Mary-Ellen. "British Columbia First Nations and the Influenza Pandemic of 1918-19." *BC Studies: The British Columbian Quarterly* (Summer 1999): 23–48.

Keshen, Jeff. "One for All or All for One: Government Controls, Black Marketing and the Limits of Patriotism, 1939-47." *Journal of Canadian Studies* (Winter 1994–95): 111–143.

———. *Saints, Sinners, and Soldiers: Canada's Second World War*. Vancouver: UBC Press, 2004.

Kinnear, Mary. *In Subordination: Professional Women, 1870–1970*. Montréal and Kingston: McGill-Queen's University Press, 1995.

Kinsman, Gary, and Patrizia Gentile. *The Canadian War on Queers: National Security as Sexual Regulation*. Vancouver: UBC Press, 2010.

Kishibe, Kaye. *Battlefield at Last: The Japanese Canadian Volunteers of the First World War, 1914-1918*. Toronto: K. Kishibe, 2007.

Kitagawa, Muriel, and Roy Miki. *This Is My Own: Letters to Wes & Other Writings on Japanese Canadians, 1941–1948*. Vancouver: Talonbooks, 1985.

Klausen, Susanne. "The Plywood Girls: Women and Gender Ideology at the Port Alberni Plywood Plant, 1942-1991." *Labour/Le Travail* 41 (1998): 199–235.

Knibb, Helen. "Present but Not Visible: Searching for Women's History in Museum Collections." *Gender & History* 6, no. 3 (November 1994): 352–369.

Knitting Machine. D-16997 a-y. Canadian Museum of History.

"Knitting Machines for the Women's Patriotic." *Toronto Globe*, February 20, 1917, 8.

Kovac, Claudine. Interview with Krista Cooke, February 28, 2007. CMH 2007.95. Canadian Museum of History Archives.

Kozar, Judy. *Canada's War Grooms and the Girls Who Stole Their Hearts*. Renfrew: General Store Publishing, 2007.

"Labour Leaders Support Women." *Victoria Times-Colonist*, May 7, 1942, 13.

Lackenbauer, P. Whitney, et al., eds. *Aboriginal Peoples and the Canadian Military: Historical Perspectives*. Winnipeg: Canadian Defence Academy Press, 2007.

Lambton, Gunda. *Sun in Winter: A Toronto Wartime Journal, 1942-1945*. Montréal and Kingston: McGill-Queen's University Press, 2003.

Lander, Jennifer Shaw. "Thanking the Jewish Ladies of Ottawa: Canadian Jewish Women's Work on the Home Front, 1939–1945." In *Behind the Lines: Canada's Home Front During the First and Second World Wars*, edited by Catherine Elliot Shaw, 198–209. London: McIntosh Gallery, 2017.

The Last Flight: A Pictorial History of the Operations and Personnel of the Royal Canadian Air Force and Quebec Airways (Observers) Ltd., 1941-1945. [1946].

Lebel, Faye. "Torpedoed!" *Victoria County Record*, April 2, 1981.

"Lest We Forget." *Ottawa Citizen*, November 11, 1975, 1.

Letter to the Editor, "Military Service Flag." *Toronto Globe*, October 11, 1917, 6.

"Lever Brothers Lifebuoy Follies." *Wetaskiwin Times*, May 2, 1945, 9.

Lévesque Andrée, and Yvonne M. Klein. *Making and Breaking the Rules: Women in Quebec, 1919-1939.* Toronto: University of Toronto Press, 2015.

"Life Behind Iron Curtain Described by Regina Woman." *Regina Leader-Post*, December 12, 1950, 3.

Light, Beth, and Ruth Roach Pierson, eds. *No Easy Road: Women in Canada 1920s to 1960s.* Toronto: New Hogtown Press, 1990.

Lipton, Saundra. "She Also Served: Bringing to Light the Contributions of the Canadian Jewish Servicewomen of the Second World War." *Canadian Jewish Studies/Études juives canadiennes* 25 (2017): 93–116.

Litalien, Michel. *Dans la tourmente : deux hôpitaux militaires canadiens-français dans la France en guerre, 1915-1919.* Outremont: Athéna, 2003.

_____. "MIGNAULT, ARTHUR (baptized Michel-Antoine-Arthur)." In *Dictionary of Canadian Biography.* Vol. 16, University of Toronto/Université Laval, 2003. Accessed April 19, 2021. http://www.biographi.ca/en/bio/mignault_arthur_16E.html.

Livingstone, Phaedra Janine. "Reading the Science Centre: An Interdisciplinary Feminist Analysis of Museum Communication." Ph.D. diss., University of Toronto, 2003.

Lloydlangston, Amber. "Molly Lamb Bobak Official War Artist (1920–2014)." *Canadian Military History* 23, no. 2 (Spring 2014): 119–127.

Lo, Laurelle. "The Path from Peddling: Jewish Economic Activity in Ottawa Prior to 1939." In *Ottawa: Making a Capital*, edited by Jeff Keshen and Nicole St-Onge, 239–250. Ottawa: University of Ottawa Press, 2001.

Lois Allan fonds. MG30-C173. Library and Archives Canada.

Lorida Landry's Brooch. 2010.214.5, Canadian Museum of History.

Loring, Frances. *The Shell Finisher*, 1918–1919. CWM 19710261-0414. Beaverbrook Collection of War Art. Canadian War Museum.

Lorna Stanger's WRCNS Service Dress Cap, Service Dress Jacket, and Service Dress Skirt. CWM 19790488-001, CWM 19790488-002, CWM 19790488-003. Canadian War Museum.

"Loss to Sculpture." *Windsor Star*, February 17, 1968, D5.

Lowe, Graham S. "Women, Work and the Office: The Feminization of Clerical Occupations in Canada, 1901–1931." *Canadian Journal of Sociology* 5, no. 4 (1980): 361–381.

Maines, Rachel P. "Socks at War: American Hand Knitters and Military Footwear Production for the World Wars." *Studia Historiae Oeconomicae* 37 (2009): 67–92.

Mann, Susan. *The War Diary of Clare Gass*. Montréal and Kingston: McGill-Queen's University Press, 2000.

——. "Where Have All the Bluebirds Gone? On the Trail of Canada's Military Nurses, 1914-1918." *Atlantis* 26, no. 1 (Fall/Winter 2001): 35–44.

"Many Pitiful Cases Appeal for Relief by Citizens of Capital." *Ottawa Citizen*, December 13, 1921, 9.

"Map Out Program to Sell More War Savings Certificates." *Ottawa Journal*, July 14, 1942, 13.

Maranda, Michael. "Hard Numbers: A Study on Diversity in Canada's Galleries.". *Canadian Art* (April 5, 2017). https://canadianart.ca/features/art-leadership -diversity.

Margaret Dobson fonds. 2009-H0025. Canadian Museum of History Archives.

Margaret McGrath fonds. CWM 20110152. George Metcalf Archival Collection. Canadian War Museum.

Marilyn Clark fonds. CWM 20130108. George Metcalf Archival Collection. Canadian War Museum.

Martin, Jean. "Francophone Enlistment in the Canadian Expeditionary Force, 1914–1918: The Evidence." *Canadian Military History* 25, no. 1 (2016): 1–16.

Mary Hall's Gloves. CWM 20130123-013. Canadian War Museum.

Mary Adelaide Cooney's Battle Dress Uniform. CWM 20130046-005, CWM 20130046-006, CWM 2013046-007. Canadian War Museum.

Mary Ann Sutton fonds. CWM 20140301. George Metcalf Archival Collection. Canadian War Museum.

Mary Campbell Mays' Imperial Munitions Board Woman War Worker Badge. CWM 19800471-001. Canadian War Museum.

Mary Robertson Gordon's Canadian Field Comforts Commission Service Dress Tunic and Service Dress Skirt. CWM 19760445-001, CWM 19760445-002. Canadian War Museum.

Mary Weaver's Wentworth Women's Auxiliary Corps Uniform. CWM 20110011-002. Canadian War Museum.

Mathews, Richard George. *Nursing Sister*, ca. 1916. CWM 19710261-6070. Beaverbrook Collection of War Art. Canadian War Museum.

"Mattawa Farmerettes Are Intrigued with New Life." *Ottawa Journal*, August 22, 1942, 31.

Maurice A. Pope fonds. CWM 20030022. George Metcalf Archival Collection. Canadian War Museum.

McCrae, John. *In Flanders Fields and Other Poems*. Toronto: Dundurn, 2015.

McCullough, Alan B. "Introduction" to "Part Six – Earning Their Bread." In *Framing Our Past: Canadian Women's History in the Twentieth Century*, edited by Sharon Anne Cook, Lorna R. McLean, and Kate O'Rourke, 312–332. Montréal and Kingston: McGill-Queen's University Press, 2001.

———. "Parks Canada and Women's History." In *Restoring Women's History through Historic Preservation*, edited by Gail Dubrow and Jennifer B. Goodman, 337–354. Baltimore: John Hopkins University Press, 2003.

McGowan and Co. advertisement. *Saskatoon Daily Star*, June 22, 1926, 2.

McKenzie, Andrea. "'Our Common Colonial Voices': Canadian Nurses, Patient Relations, and Nation on Lemnos." In *Other Fronts, Other Wars? First World War Studies on the Eve of the Centennial*, edited by Joachim Burgschwentner, Matthias Egger, and Gunda Barth-Scalmani, 92–123. Leiden: Brill, 2014.

———. *War-Torn Exchanges: The Lives and Letters of Nursing Sisters Laura Holland and Mildred Forbes*. Vancouver: UBC Press, 2016.

McKenzie, Andrea, and Jane Ledwell, eds. *L. M. Montgomery and War*. Montréal and Kingston: McGill-Queen's University Press, 2017.

McMaster University Archives. "Socks for the Boys: Marion Simpson and the Knitters of the First World War." Case Study: Digital Collections. Accessed April 19, 2021. http://pw2oc.mcmaster.ca/pw2oc/case-study/socks-boys-marion-simpson-and-knitters-first-world-war.

McPherson, Kathryn. *Bedside Matters: The Transformation of Canadian Nursing, 1900-1990*. Toronto: University of Toronto Press, 2012.

———. "The Nightingale Influence and the Rise of the Modern Hospital." In *On All Frontiers: Four Centuries of Canadian Nursing*, edited by Christina Bates et al., 73–88. Ottawa: University of Ottawa Press, 2012.

Meader, Joyce. *Knitskrieg! A Call to Yarns: A History of Military Knitting from the 1800s to the Present Day*. London: Uniform, 2016.

Memorial Cross for Mason Francis Scott, received by Edna Scott. CWM 19890211-014. Canadian War Museum.

Meyer, Shannon. *Little Black Dress: From Mourning to Night*. St. Louis: Missouri History Museum Press, 2016.

Michiko Ayukawa fonds. CWM 20150279. George Metcalf Archival Collection. Canadian War Museum.

Military Service Yarn, Second World War. CWM 20050085-002. Canadian War Museum.

Millar, Nancy. *The Unmentionable History of the West: Undressing Our History of Corsets and Crinolines, Bustles and Brassieres, Girdles and Garters, Secrets and Silences*. Calgary: Red Deer Press, 2006.

Miller, Ian Hugh Maclean. *Our Glory and Our Grief: Torontonians and the Great War*. Toronto: University of Toronto Press, 2002.

Minister of Overseas Military Services of Canada. RG9 III-A-I. Library and Archives Canada.

Minnie Eleanor Gray fonds. CWM 20110057. George Metcalf Archival Collection. Canadian War Museum.

"Miss Arnoldi Is Voted President." *Vancouver Daily Province*, May 31, 1920, 18.

"Miss Canadas Won't Take No for an Answer." *Ottawa Journal*, August 21, 1942, 10.

Monarch Book No. 87: Hand Knits for Men and Women in Service. Dunville: Monarch Yarns, 1941.

Montgomery, Lucy Maud. *Rilla of Ingleside*. New York: FA Stokes, 1921.

Monture, Charlotte Edith Anderson. *Diary of a War Nurse: Army Nurse Corps, American Expeditionary Force 1918*. Ohsweken, Ontario: Six Nations, 1996.

Monture, Don. "Foreword." In *Diary of a War Nurse: Army Nurse Corps, American Expeditionary Force 1918*, by Charlotte Edith Anderson Monture, 1. Ohsweken, ON: Six Nations, 1996.

Monture, Terry L. "Introduction: A Remarkable Life – The Story of Edith Anderson Monture." In *Diary of a War Nurse: Army Nurse Corps, American Expeditionary Force 1918*, by Charlotte Edith Anderson Monture, 2–4. Ohsweken, ON: Six Nations, 1996.

"Montreal Women Join Air Auxiliary." *Montreal Gazette*, October 24, 1941, 13.

Morin-Pelletier, Mélanie. "Des oiseaux bleus chez les Poilus: les infirmières des hôpitaux militaires canadien-français postés en France, 1915-1919." *Bulletin d'histoire politique* 17, no. 2 (Winter 2009): 57–74.

———. "'The Anxious Ones Waiting at Home': Deux familles canadiennes plongées dans le tourment de la Grande Guerre." *Histoire Sociale/Social History* 157, no. 94 (Juin/June 2014): 353–368.

Morton, Desmond. *Fight or Pay: Soldiers' Families in the Great War*. Vancouver: UBC Press, 2004.

Mosby, Ian. *Food Will Win the War: The Politics, Culture, and Science of Food on Canada's Home Front*. Vancouver: UBC Press, 2014.

Moses, John. "Indigenous Nurse a Worthy Candidate." *Ottawa Citizen*, March 14, 2016, 8.

"Mother Receives Victoria Cross / But Greatest Military Honour Does Not Console the Bereaved Parent for Son's Death." *Manitoba Free Press*, August 26, 1915, 8.

Mourning Veil. D-9309. Canadian Museum of History.

"Mrs. Aitken to Speak." *Montreal Gazette*, November 2, 1945, 4.

"Mrs. R.F. McWilliams to Open Re-Make Revue." *Winnipeg Tribune*, April 28, 1943, 10.

Muffin Tin. 985.39.6. Canadian Museum of History.

"Must Soon Lose Jobs." *Toronto Globe*, November 12, 1918, 3.

Nadler, John. *Valour Road.* Toronto: Viking, 2014.

Nakayama, Gordon G. *Issei, Stories of Japanese Canadian Pioneers.* Toronto: NC Press, 1984.

National War Finance Committee advertisement. *Windsor Star,* June 22, 1942, 6.

National Selective Service advertisement. *Toronto Star,* January 7, 1943, 32.

"National Y.W. Increases Camps to Care for Ontario Farmerettes." *Montreal Gazette,* June 23, 1942, 5.

Nelson, Charmaine. *Representing the Black Female Subject in Western Art.* New York: Routledge, 2010.

Newman, Vivien. *Tumult and Tears: The Story of the Great War through the Eyes and Lives of Its Women Poets.* Barnsley, South Yorkshire: Pen and Sword History, 2016.

Nicholson, G. W. L. *Official History of the Canadian Army in the Second World War.* Vol. 3, *The Canadians in Italy, 1943-1945.* Ottawa: Queen's Printer, 1956.

———. *Official History of the Canadian Army in the First World War: Canadian Expeditionary Force, 1914-1919.* Ottawa: Queen's Printer, 1962.

"Nine Canadian Mothers Who Have Sent Forty-Seven Sons to Fight." *Everywoman's World,* August 1917, 5.

Nixon, Laura E. "What Loving Hands Are Doing: The Spirit of Women Who Are Working for Our Heroes Overseas Through the Women's Institutes." *Everywoman's World,* October 1917, 12, 40.

Noakes, Lucy. *Women in the British Army: War and the Gentle Sex, 1907-1948.* London: Routledge, 2006.

Nora (Gibson) Elrick and John (Jock) Elrick's Can Car Lunch Boxes. 2007.94.2.1 and 2007.94.3. Canadian Museum of History.

Norma Etta Lee fonds. CWM 20060058. George Metcalf Archival Collection. Canadian War Museum.

Norman, Alison. "Race, Gender, and Colonialism: Public Life Among the Six Nations of Grand River, 1899-1939." PhD diss., University of Toronto, 2010.

———. "'In Defense of the Empire': The Six Nations of the Grand River and the Great War." In *Sisterhood of Suffering and Service: Canadian and Newfoundland Women and the First World War,* edited by Sarah Glassford and Amy Shaw, 29–50. Vancouver: UBC Press, 2012.

Nutty, Coleen Lou. "Cemetery Symbolism of Prairie Pioneers: Gravestone Art and Social Change in Story County, Iowa." Master's thesis, Iowa State University, 1978.

Obituary. Minnie Eleanor Gray. *Montreal Gazette,* October 29, 2005, B17.

Oikawa, Mona. *Cartographies of Violence: Japanese Canadian Women, Memory, and the Subjects of the Internment.* Toronto: University of Toronto Press, 2012.

Ōiwa, Keibō, ed. *Stone Voices: Wartime Writings of Japanese Canadian Issei.* Montréal: Véhicule Press, 1991.

Okawa, Eiji. "Nippon Fujinkai – Japanese Women's Associations." *Nikkei Images* 21, no. 3 (Fall 2016): 8–9.

O'Neill Patrick B. "The Halifax Concert Party in World War II." *Theatre Research in Canada* 20, no. 2 (1999). https://journals.lib.unb.ca/index.php/TRIC/article/view/7086.

"On Sale Today! War Savings Certificates." *Ottawa Journal*, May 27, 1940, 4.

Ontario Department of Public Works. *Women's Work on the Land: How You May Assist in Food Production this Summer*. Ontario Trades and Labour Branch, Department of Public Works, [1917].

Ontario Farm Service Force advertisement. *Ottawa Journal*, April 7, 1943, 18.

Oosterom, Nelle. "Nellie McClung and the Great War." Canada's History. Accessed April 19, 2021. https://www.canadashistory.ca/explore/military-war/nellie-mcclung-and-the-great-war.

"Order Poppies in Advance." *Saskatoon Star-Phoenix*, August 17, 1929, 5.

"Ottawa Decrees Sharp Decrease in Gay Raiment." *Saskatoon Star-Phoenix*, March 10, 1942, 5.

"Ottawa Girls Spend Summer in Helping Fruit Famers in Niagara Peninsula." *Ottawa Journal*, August 9, 1941, 7.

Pasolli, Lisa. "'I Ask You, Mr. Mitchell, Is the Emergency Over?': Debating Day Nurseries in the Second World War." *Canadian Historical Review* 96, no. 1 (March 2015): 1–31.

Patrias, Carmela. "More Menial than Housemaids? Racialized and Gendered Labour in the Fruit and Vegetable Industry of Canada's Niagara Region, 1880–1945." *Labour/ Le Travail* 78 (2016): 69–104.

Peate, Mary. *Girl in a Sloppy Joe Sweater: Life on the Canadian Home Front during World War Two*. Montréal: Optimum Pub. International, 1989.

Personal Effects Box. CWM 20050205-011. Canadian War Museum.

Peterson, Janice, and Margaret Lewis, eds. *The Elgar Companion to Feminist Economics*. Cheltenham: Edward Elgar, 1999.

Pierson, Ruth Roach. *They're Still Women After All: The Second World War and Canadian Womanhood*. Toronto: McClelland and Stewart, 1986.

"Plans Completed for Re-Make Revue Next Week." *Winnipeg Tribune*, April 22, 1943, 11.

"Plans to Make Armistice Day Big Poppy Day: Madame Guerin in Canada from France to Ask Co-operation of G.W.V.A." *Regina Leader-Post*, July 5, 1921, 7.

"Plant Regulations for Women Employees." CWM 20020045-1224. George Metcalf Archival Collection. Canadian War Museum.

"Plastic Jaw Souvenir of B.C. Girl's Heroism." *Toronto Star*, November 2, 1946, 1.

"Plight of Europe Described to Club." *Montreal Gazette*, November 8, 1945, 4.

Pope, Alexandra. "New Exhibit Features Women from First and Second World Wars." *Canadian Geographic*, November 11, 2015. https://www.canadiangeographic.ca/article/new-exhibit-features-women-first-and-second-world-wars/.

Popham, Hugh. *The FANY in Peace and War: The Story of the First Aid Nursing Yeomanry, 1907–2003*. Yorkshire: Pen and Sword, 2003.

"Poppies Made by Eastern Vetcraft Shops." *Chilliwack Progress*, October 30, 1946, 14.

Poppy Badge. CWM 19760167-008. Canadian War Museum.

Porter, Gaby. "Gender Bias: Representations of Work in History Museums." In *Bias in Museums*, edited by A. Carruthers. Museum Professionals Group Transactions 22 (1987).

———. "Seeing through Solidity: A Feminist Perspective on Museums." *The Sociological Review* 43, 1 suppl. (1995): 105–126.

Poulin, Grace. *Invisible Women: WWII Aboriginal Servicewomen in Canada*. Thunder Bay: D. G. Poulin, 2007.

"Prairie Girl Who Braved Sumatra Bandits First Heard of M.B.E. While in Saskatoon." *Saskatoon Star-Phoenix*, November 2, 1946, 18.

Pratt, William John. "Prostitutes and Prophylaxis: Venereal Disease, Surveillance, and Discipline in the Canadian Army in Europe, 1939-1945." *Journal of the Canadian Historical Association* 26, no. 2 (2015): 111–138.

Prentice, Alison L., ed. *Canadian Women: A History*. Toronto: Harcourt Brace Jovanovich, 1988.

Price, Leah. "Diary: The Death of Stenography." *London Review of Books* 30, no. 23 (December 2008).

"Princess Alice to Attend Air Women's Ceremony." *Globe and Mail*, November 22, 1941, 5.

Prud'homme, Guy. *Singer : histoire industrielle*. Saint-Jean-sur-Richelieu, Quebec: Éditions Archimède, 1994.

"Pte. A. C. Wilkinson Killed in Action." *Ottawa Journal*, July 31, 1944, 13.

"Public Gets Opportunity to Show Sympathy for Disabled Veterans; What This Poppy Business Means." *Ottawa Journal*, November 1, 1924, 19.

"The Purchase of Sugar is Now Regulated by Law." *Ottawa Citizen*, January 27, 1942, 19.

"Quebec Registrar Loses His Post." *London Free Press*, April 4, 1918.

"Quebec Registrar Ordered to Quit." *Edmonton Journal*, April 4, 1918, 3.

Quiney, Linda J. *This Small Army of Women: Canadian Volunteer Nurses and the First World War*. Vancouver: UBC Press, 2017.

Quinn, Edythe. *Greenwich Times 1760-1968: A History of Greenwich*. Greenwich, NS: The Women's Association of Greenwich United Church, 1968.

"R.C.A.F. (Women's Division) Now Name of the C.W.A.A.F." *Ottawa Citizen*, February 6, 1942, 12.

Raymond Tartre's Morse Code Practice Buzzer. CWM 20060047-001. Canadian War Museum.

"Récupération de l'aluminium commence." *Le Devoir*, July 22, 1941.

"Red Cross Organization Resembles Vast Factory." *Hamilton Spectator*, May 14, 1942.

Reich, Sue. *World War 1 Quilts*. Atglen, PA: Schiffer Publishing, 2014.

Reilly, Sharon. "Material History and the History of Women." In *First Days, Fighting Days: Women in Manitoba History*, edited by Mary Kinnear, 1–17. Regina: Canadian Plains Research Centre, 1987.

"Re-Make Centre Opens Tonight." *Ottawa Journal*, February 15, 1944, 8.

"Re-Make Revue Will Feature Fashions for 'Teen-Age Girls.'" *Winnipeg Tribune*, April 24, 1943, 11.

Render, Shirley. *No Place for a Lady: The Story of Canadian Women Pilots, 1928-1992*. Winnipeg: Portage and Main Press, 1992.

Richards, Anthony. *The Lusitania Sinking: Eyewitness Accounts from Survivors*. Toronto: Dundurn, 2019.

Riordon, Bernard, and the Beaverbrook Art Gallery, eds. *Bruno Bobak: The Full Palette*. Fredericton: Goose Lane Editions, 2006.

Ritter, Lacey. "Grave Exclamations: An Analysis of Tombstones and their Use as Narrative of Self." Master's thesis, Minnesota State University, 2012.

Roberts, David, and Gregory P. Marchildon. "PLUMMER, JAMES HENRY." In *Dictionary of Canadian Biography*. Vol. 16, University of Toronto/Université Laval, 2003–. Accessed October 22, 2020. http://www.biographi.ca/en/bio /plummer_james_henry_16E.html.

Roberts, Jennifer. "A Biography of the Trousered Munitions Women's Uniform of World War 1." *Apparence(s)* 7 (2017). http://journals.openedition.org/apparences/1355.

Rochon, Helen (Walter), Canadian Women's Army Corps. "Veteran's Stories: The Memory Project." Accessed April 19, 2021. http://www.thememoryproject.com /stories/149:helen-rochon-walter/.

Rogers, Lieutenant Lawrence Browning to May Rogers, October 10, 1917. CWM 20040015-005. George Metcalf Archival Collection. Canadian War Museum.

Rowell, Ethel, Canadian Women's Army Corps. "Veteran's Stories: The Memory Project." Accessed April 19, 2021. http://www.thememoryproject.com/stories/843:ethel -rowell/.

Roy, Patricia E. *Mutual Hostages: Canadians and Japanese During the Second World War*. Toronto: University of Toronto Press, 1992.

Ruck, Calvin W. *Canada's Black Battalion: No. 2 Construction, 1916-1920*. Halifax: Society for the Protection and Preservation of Black Culture in N.S., 1986.

Russell, Ruth Weber. *Proudly She Marched: Training Canada's World War II Women in Waterloo County*. Waterloo: Canadian Federation of University Women, Kitchener-Waterloo, 2006.

Ryell, Nora. "Natural-Born Leader Witnessed History with a Keen Social Conscience." *Globe and Mail*, August 31, 2010, S8.

"Salvage Drive to Be Started Across Nation." *Globe and Mail*, February 6, 1941, 13.

Samson, Hélène, and Suzanne Sauvage, eds. *Notman: A Visionary Photographer*. Montréal: McCord Museum, 2016.

Sangster, Joan. *Earning Respect: The Lives of Working Women in Small-Town Ontario, 1920-1960*. Toronto: University of Toronto Press, 1995.

Saturday Night, Toronto, 1917.

Saunders, Nicholas J. "Bodies of Metal, Shells of Memory: 'Trench Art' and the Great War Re-cycled." *Journal of Material Culture* 5, no. 1 (2000): 43–67.

———. *Trench Art: A Brief History & Guide, 1914-1939*. London: Leo Cooper, 2001.

Scott Family Locket. CWM 19890211-007. Canadian War Museum.

"Sell Souvenirs of Parliament Hill Fire." *Ottawa Journal*, February 23, 1916, 3.

Sergeant Major Frederick William Hall's Victoria Cross. CWM 20110146-001. Canadian War Museum.

Service Files of the Second World War – War Dead, 1939-1947. RG 24. Library and Archives Canada.

Service Flag, 1917. CWM 20120160-001. Canadian War Museum.

Service Yarn advertisements. *Regina Leader-Post*, September 15, 1941, 10, and October 9, 1942, 11.

"Sewing Clinic Opens – Setting Up of Rosemont Centre Makes 8 in City." *Montreal Gazette*, May 4, 1944, 5.

"She Gave Orders – the J**s Obeyed!" *Regina Leader-Post*, October 30, 1946, 6.

Shimotakahara, Ruth. "Biography of Kozo Shimotakahara, History Contest Entry, 16-31." MG28 V7. Japanese Canadian Citizen's Association. Library and Archives Canada.

"Short on Cloth, Long on Style, Is Rule for New Fall Clothes." *Montreal Gazette*, July 25, 1942, 5.

"Silver Cross Women Form Ottawa Chapter." *Ottawa Citizen*, April 19, 1955, 2.

Simpson, Suzanne, Doris Toole, and Cindy Player. "Women in the Canadian Forces: Past, Present and Future." *Atlantis* 4, no. 2 (1979): 267–283.

Sisler, Rebecca. *The Girls: A Biography of Frances Loring and Florence Wyle*. Toronto: Clarke, Irwin, 1972.

Sissons, Crystal. *Queen of the Hurricanes: The Fearless Elsie MacGill*. Toronto: Second Story Press, 2014.

"Slender Halifax Blonde Becomes 1948 Miss Canada." *Ottawa Journal*, August 21, 1948, 9.

Smith, Helen, and Pamela Wakewich. "'Beauty and the Helldivers': Representing Women's Work and Identities in a Warplant Newspaper." *Labour/Le Travail* 44 (1999): 71–107.

———. "'I Was Not Afraid of Work': Female War Plant Employees and Their Work Environment." In *Canadian Environments: Essays in Culture, Politics, and History*, edited by Robert C. Thomsen and Nanette Hale, 229–248. New York: P.I.E.-Peter Lang, 2006.

Smith, Julian A. "Potter, Charles – Optician and Instrument Maker." *Journal of the Royal Astronomical Society of Canada* 87, no. 1 (February 1993): 14–33.

Snider, Nick. *Sweetheart Jewelry and Collectibles.* Atglen, PA: Schiffer Pub., 1995.

"Some Novel Lines of Wagstaffe Products." *Canadian Grocer*, September 13, 1918, 41.

Souvenir, Parliament Hill Fire, 1916. 2011.161.1. Canadian Museum of History.

Speck, Catherine. *Beyond the Battlefield: Women Artists of the Two World Wars.* London: Reaktion Books, 2014.

Stacey, C. P. *Official History of the Canadian Army in the Second World War, Vol. III: The Victory Campaign – The Operations in North-West Europe, 1944-1945.* Ottawa: Queen's Printer, 1955–1960.

Statistics Canada. "Crude Marriage Rate and Crude Divorce Rate, Canada, 1926 to 2008." https://www150.statcan.gc.ca/n1/pub/89-503-x/2010001/article/11546/c-g/c-g006 -eng.htm.

Street, Kori. "Bankers and Bomb Makers: Gender Ideology and Women's Paid Work in Banking and Munitions during the First World War in Canada." PhD diss., University of Victoria, 2002.

———. "Patriotic, Not Permanent: Attitudes about Women's Making Bombs and Being Bankers." In *A Sisterhood of Suffering and Service: Women and Girls in Canada and Newfoundland During the First World War*, edited by Sarah Glassford and Amy J. Shaw, 148–170. Vancouver: UBC Press, 2012.

Strong-Boag, Veronica. *The New Day Recalled: Lives of Girls and Women in English Canada, 1919-1939.* Toronto: Copp Clark Pittman, 1988.

Sugiman, Pamela. *Labour's Dilemma: The Gender Politics of Auto Workers in Canada, 1937–1979.* Toronto: University of Toronto Press, 1994.

Summerby, Janice. *Native Soldiers, Foreign Battlefields.* Ottawa: Veterans Affairs Canada, 2005.

Summers, Julie. *Fashion on the Ration: Style in the Second World War.* London: Profile Books, 2015.

Sweetheart Jewelry. CWM 20110109-004, CWM 20110109-0005, CWM 20110109-006. Canadian War Museum.

Sword Given to Joan Bamford Fletcher in 1945. CWM 19800177-001. Canadian War Museum.

Talbot, Robert J. "'It Would Be Best to Leave Us Alone': First Nations Responses to the Canadian War Effort, 1914-18." *Journal of Canadian Studies* 45, no. 1 (Winter 2011): 90–120.

Taylor, Mary. *A Black Mark: The Japanese-Canadians in World War II.* Toronto: Oberon Press, 2004.

Tennyson, Brian Douglas. *Nova Scotia at War, 1914–1919.* Halifax: Nimbus Publishing, 2017.

"That the Government Intends Not to Relapse." *Quebec Telegraph*, April 4, 1918.

"...That Men May Fly." *Ottawa Citizen*, July 2, 1943, 6.

Theobald, Simon. "A False Sense of Equality: The Black Canadian Experience of the Second World War." Master's thesis, University of Ottawa, 2008.

"They Gave Her a Sword." *Soldier: The British Army Magazine*, February 16, 1946.

"They Seek No New Recruits." *Hamilton Spectator*, May 1965, 41.

"Thirty Young Women Ready for Air Traffic Control Work." *Winnipeg Tribune*, March 26, 1943, 8.

"This Scheme Should Get Everybody." *Calgary Herald*, April 22, 1918, 1.

Thomson, Alistair. "Memory and Remembering in Oral History." In *The Oxford Handbook of Oral History*, edited by Donald A. Ritchie, 77–95. New York: Oxford University Press, 2011.

Thomson, Colin A. *Born with a Call: A Biography of Dr. William Pearly Oliver, C.M.* Dartmouth, NS: Black Cultural Centre for Nova Scotia, 1986.

Thornton, Carole. "'And the Men Just Stood and Stared': Women's Recollections of their Work in Shipyards, Victoria, British Columbia, Canada, 1942–1945." *International Oral History Conference*, proceedings (1996).

Thorsheim, Peter. *Waste into Weapons: Recycling in Britain during the Second World War.* New York: Cambridge University Press, 2015.

Tippett, Maria. *Art at the Service of War: Canada, Art, and the Great War.* Toronto: University of Toronto Press, 2013.

Tobin's "Peerless" Soldier's Comfort Box. CWM 20030364-001. Canadian War Museum.

Tollefsen, Margaret. Interview, September 2007. CMH 2007.89. Canadian Museum of History Archives.

Toman, Cynthia. *An Officer and a Lady: Canadian Military Nursing and the Second World War.* Vancouver: UBC Press, 2007.

——. *Sister Soldiers of the Great War: The Nurses of the Canadian Army Medical Corps.* Vancouver: UBC Press, 2016.

"Top Graduate to Get Trophy." *Globe and Mail*, March 19, 1942, 4.

"Toronto Girls Receive Training at C.W.A.A.F. Depot." *Globe and Mail*, November 25, 1941, 4.

Toronto Star, April 17, 1918, 10.

"Toronto Woman is Appointed Supervisor of Conservation." *Vancouver Sun*, February 26, 1943, 10.

Tremblay, Mary. "Going Back to Main Street: The Development and Impact of Casualty Rehabilitation for Veterans with Disabilities, 1945–1948." In *The Veterans Charter and Post-World War II Canada*, edited by Peter Neary and J. L. Granatstein, 160–178. Montréal and Kingston: McGill-Queen's University Press, 1999.

"Union Accepts Women Welders." *Victoria Times-Colonist*, August 21, 1942, 14.

United States. Bureau of the Census. *Fourteenth Census of the United States, 1920.* San Gabriel, Los Angeles, California, Roll T65_118, Page 4B, Enumeration District 582. Accessed April 5, 2021. Ancestry.ca.

Vance, Jonathan F. *Objects of Concern: Canadian Prisoners of War through the Twentieth Century.* Vancouver: UBC Press, 1994.

———. *Death So Noble: Memory, Meaning, and the First World War.* Vancouver: UBC Press, 1997.

Van Vugt, Sarah. "Beauty on the Job: Visual Representation, Bodies, and Canada's Women War Workers, 1939-1945." PhD diss., University of Victoria, 2016.

Verda Sharp and Other Female Employees of Dominion Bridge Company, [1939–1941]. CWM 20190008-001. George Metcalf Archival Collection. Canadian War Museum.

"Veterans' Poppies for Armistice Day." *Ottawa Citizen,* August 20, 1923, 2.

Vickers, Emma. *Queen and Country: Same-Sex Desire in the British Armed Forces, 1939–1945.* Manchester: Manchester University Press, 2013.

Wadge, D. Collette, ed. *Women in Uniform.* London: Imperial War Museum, 2003.

Wakewich, Pamela, and Helen Smith. "The Politics of 'Selective' Memory: Re-Visioning Canadian Women's Wartime Work in the Public Record." *Oral History* 34, no. 2 (2006): 56–68.

Walker, Eric Keith. "Over the Top: Canadian Red Cross Fundraising during the Second World War." Master's thesis, University of Ottawa, 2011.

Wall Hanging. WDM-1996-MU-1. Western Development Museum.

"War Effort Racial Ban is Charged by Negroes." *Globe and Mail,* October 30, 1942, 4.

War Graves Registers (Circumstances of Casualty), 1914-1918. Ancestry.ca.

Wartime Prices and Trade Board. *The Miracle of Making Old Things New: A Re-make Revue.* Ottawa: Wartime Prices and Trade Board, 1943.

"What Happens Behind the Lines – Socks Are Needed Still – Soldiers Can Never Have Too Many." *Hamilton Spectator,* October 30, 1939.

"What Not to Send Overseas." *Toronto Globe,* July 4, 1918, 8.

White, G. C. Mary. "For Tommy in the Trenches: Where a Touch of Home Means Much." *Everywoman's World,* September 1917, 10.

Whitmore, Lucie. "'A Matter of Individual Opinion and Feeling': The Changing Culture of Mourning Dress in the First World War." *Women's History Review* 27, no. 4 (June 2018): 579–594.

Wilkinson, Alta R., ed. *Ottawa to Caen: Letters from Arthur Campbell Wilkinson.* Ottawa: Tower Books, 1947.

"Will Interview Women Monday for Air Force." *Globe and Mail,* September 11, 1941, 3.

"Will Organize Youth of Ontario for Farm Service." *Ottawa Journal,* April 10, 1941, 20.

Willa Walker fonds. MG30-E498. Vol. 1. Library and Archives Canada.

"Willa Walker is Promoted to O.C. of Manning Depot." *Ottawa Citizen,* June 4, 1942, 22.

"Willa Walker Promoted to Rank of Wing Officer." *Ottawa Journal*, May 12, 1943, 10.

Willa Walker's RCAF-WD Service Dress Jacket, Service Dress Skirt, and Service Dress Cap. CWM 19750344-012, CWM 19750344-250, CWM 19750344-014. Canadian War Museum.

William Robert Boucher fonds. CWM 20050205. George Metcalf Archival Collection. Canadian War Museum.

Wills, Kerry. *The Close-Knit Circle: American Knitters Today*. Westport: Praeger Publishers, 2007.

Winegard, Timothy C. *For King and Kanata: Canadian Indians and the First World War*. Winnipeg: University of Manitoba Press, 2012.

"Wing Officer is Top Rank in C.W.A. Air Force Corps; Ability to Bring Promotion." *Globe and Mail*, October 23, 1941, 11.

"Winnipeg Farewells First Detachment of Voluntary Aid Nurses." *Winnipeg Tribune*, January 22, 1918, 1.

Winter, Jay M. *Sites of Memory, Sites of Mourning: The Great War in European Cultural History*. Cambridge: Cambridge University Press, 1995.

Wodehouse, R. F. *A Checklist of the War Collections of World War I, 1914-1918 and World War II, 1939-1945*. National Gallery of Canada, 1968.

"Woman Describes Sumatra Service." *Edmonton Journal*, November 4, 1946, 12.

"Woman Physician to Take Nurses Abroad." *Winnipeg Tribune*, May 26, 1917, Women's Feature Section, 2.

"Woman Thrives on Knitting Problems." *Montreal Gazette*, February 5, 1940, 7.

"Woman Welder Meets Labour Opposition." *Victoria Times-Colonist*, May 6, 1942, 19.

"Women Given Service Medals." *Winnipeg Tribune*, November 29, 1923, 3.

"Women Reserves Sorry to Leave Camp at Gimli." *Winnipeg Tribune*, August 14, 1916, 5.

"Women Want to Help Win This War!" *Ottawa Journal*, November 20, 1940, 6.

Wong, Marjorie. *The Dragon and the Maple Leaf: Chinese Canadians in World War II*. London: Pirie Pub, 1994.

Wood Gundy advertisement. *Ottawa Journal*, May 28, 1940, 14.

Wood, Peter. Correspondence with Krista Cooke, November 2016–February 2017.

Woollacott, Angela. "Dressed to Kill: Clothes, Cultural Meaning and First World War Women Munitions Workers." In *Representations of Gender from Prehistory to the Present*, edited by M. Donald and L. Hurcombe, 198–217. London: Palgrave Macmillan, 2016.

Wyle, Florence. *On the Land, 1918–1919*. CWM 19710261-0421. Beaverbrook Collection of War Art. Canadian War Museum.

Yamazaki, Suno. "History Contest Entry, 16-7." MG28 V7. Japanese Canadian Citizen's Association. Library and Archives Canada.

Yatabe, Tsune. "History Contest Entry, 16-7." MG28 V7. Japanese Canadian Citizen's Association. Library and Archives Canada.

"Young Canadians! Starving Millions Count on You!," Ontario Farm Service Force advertisement. *Ottawa Journal*, June 4, 1946, 13.

Zankowicz, Kate. "'How to Keep a Husband on Packaged Foods' and Other Lessons: Gendered Education in the Canadian National Exhibition's Women's Division during the Kate Aitken Era, 1920s-1950s." *Cuizine* 6, no. 2 (2015). https://doi .org/10.7202/1033507ar.

Ziegler, Mary. *We Serve That Men May Fly*. Hamilton: RCAF (WD) Association, 1973.

Zielke, Melissa. "Forget-Me-Nots: Victorian Women, Mourning, and the Construction of a Feminine Historical Memory." *Material Culture Review* 58, no. 1 (2003): 52–66.

INDEX

Note: Page numbers in *italics* denote figures.

MERCURY SERIES / COLLECTION MERCURE

The best resource on the history, prehistory, and culture of Canada is proudly published by the University of Ottawa Press and the Canadian Museum of History.

Les Presses de l'Université d'Ottawa et le Musée canadien de l'histoire publient avec fierté la meilleure ressource en ce qui a trait à l'histoire, à la préhistoire et à la culture canadiennes.

Series Editor/Direction de la collection: Pierre M. Desrosiers
Editorial Committee/Comité éditorial: Laura Sanchini, Janet Young, John Willis
Managing Editor/Responsable de l'édition: Robyn Jeffrey
Coordination: Lee Wyndham

Strikingly Canadian and highly specialized, the *Mercury Series* presents works in the research domain of the Canadian Museum of History and benefits from the publishing expertise of the University of Ottawa Press. Created in 1972, the series is in line with the Canadian Museum of History's strategic directions. The *Mercury Series* consists of peer-reviewed academic research, and includes numerous landmark contributions in the disciplines of Canadian history, archaeology, culture, and ethnology. Books in the series are published in at least one of Canada's official languages, and may appear in other languages.

Remarquablement canadienne et hautement spécialisée, la *collection Mercure* réunit des ouvrages portant sur les domaines de recherches du Musée canadien de l'histoire et s'appuie sur le savoir-faire des Presses de l'Université d'Ottawa. Fondée en 1972, elle répond aux orientations stratégiques du Musée canadien de l'histoire. La *collection Mercure* propose des recherches scientifiques évaluées par les pairs et regroupe de nombreuses contributions majeures à l'histoire, à l'archéologie, à la culture et à l'ethnologie canadiennes. Les ouvrages sont publiés dans au moins une des langues officielles du Canada, avec possibilité de parution dans d'autres langues.

Recent Titles/Titres récents

Michael K. Hawes, Andrew C. Holman, and Christopher Kirkey, eds., *1968 in Canada: A Year and Its Legacies*, 2021.

Steven Schwinghamer and Jan Raska, *Pier 21: A History*, 2020.

Steven Schwinghamer et Jan Raska, *Quai 21 : une histoire*, 2020.

Robert Sweeny, ed., *Sharing Spaces: Essays in Honour of Sherry Olson*, 2020.

Matthew Betts, *Place-Making in the Pretty Harbour: The Archaeology of Port Joli, Nova Scotia*, 2019.

Lauriane Bourgeon, *Préhistoire béringienne : étude archéologique des Grottes du Poisson-Bleu (Yukon)*, 2018.

Jenny Ellison and Jennifer Anderson, eds., *Hockey: Challenging Canada's Game – Au-delà du sport national*, 2018.

Myron Momryk, *Mike Starr of Oshawa: A Political Biography*, 2018.

John Willis, ed., *Tu sais, mon vieux Jean-Pierre: Essays on the Archaeology and History of New France and Canadian Culture in Honour of Jean-Pierre Chrestien*, 2017.

Anna Kearney Guigné, *The Forgotten Songs of the Newfoundland Outports: As Taken from Kenneth Peacock's Newfoundland Field Collection, 1951–1961*, 2016.

For a complete list of the University of Ottawa Press titles, see:
Pour une liste complète des titres des Presses de l'Université d'Ottawa, voir :
press.uOttawa.ca

Printed in September 2021
by Gauvin, Gatineau (Quebec), Canada.